IMAGES
of America

NORTH DAKOTA

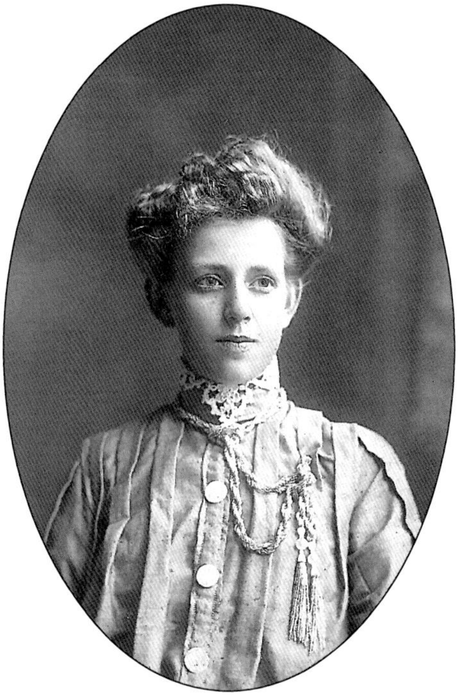

Two women, both named Clara, and both owning Eastman Kodak Box cameras, took many of the photos in this book. We thank my mother, Clara Aasen, and Clara Robinson, my old friend, for their work. We wish they were here to see their photos.

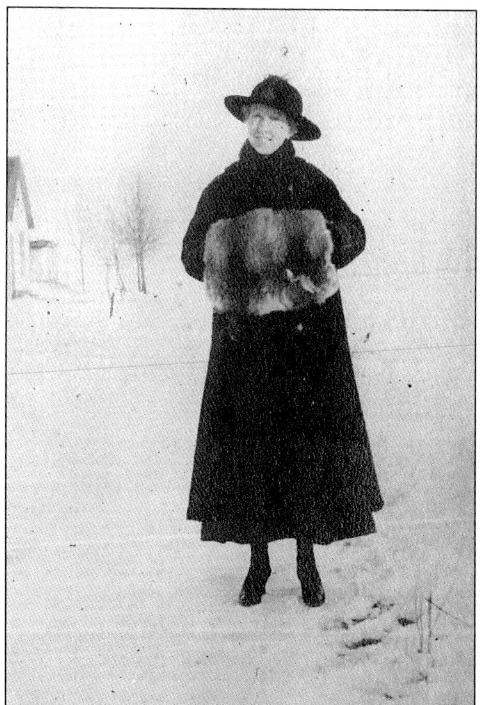

IMAGES
of America

NORTH DAKOTA

Larry Aasen

ARCADIA
PUBLISHING

ISBN 978-0-7385-0763-7

Published by Arcadia Publishing
Charleston, South Carolina

Printed in the United States of America

Library of Congress Catalog Card Number: 00105236

For all general information contact Arcadia Publishing at:
Telephone 843-853-2070
Fax 843-853-0044
E-mail sales@arcadiapublishing.com
For customer service and orders:
Toll-Free 1-888-313-2665

Visit us on the Internet at www.arcadiapublishing.com

Also by Larry Aasen:

North Dakota Tales (1990)
My Friend the Pig (1994)
More North Dakota Tales (1996)
Salute to North Dakota Writers (1998)
North Dakota Postcards 1900–1930 (Arcadia Publishing, 1999)

CONTENTS

ACKNOWLEDGMENTS

We hope these old photographs bring out the spirit and energy of North Dakotans. They have learned to turn adversity into opportunity and to go forward. The author would like to thank the following people for their help in putting this book together:

Martha Ann McMullan Aasen, Westport, CT
Tilford O.Aasen, Fridley, MN
Bill Shemorry, Williston, ND
Alan Ellenson, Gardner, ND
George Robinson, Marion, MA
Professor David Danbom, North Dakota State University, Fargo, ND
Jerry and Aagot Nysveen, Hillsboro, ND
Jim McAndrew, Solana Beach, CA

PHOTO CREDITS

Cover photo and photo on page 32 from Fred Hultstrand History in Pictures Collection
Clara Brenden Aasen, Hillsboro, ND (1885–1953)
Clara Myren Robinson, Hillsboro, ND (1870–1967)
North Dakota Blue Book 1995, 1999, Office of the Secretary of State, Alvin A. Jaeger.
University of North Dakota
North Dakota State University
North Dakota Institute for Regional Studies
Traill County Museum at Hillsboro
State Historical Society of North Dakota
Bill Shemorry, Williston, ND
Chuck Johnson, Whitefish Bay, WI
Valerie Coit, *Hillsboro Banner*, Hillsboro, ND

INTRODUCTION

In this book we take a glimpse at North Dakota from 1900 to about 1940, through the lens of the old box camera that Eastman Kodak sold for $1, and which most North Dakota families owned at that time. In fact, it was about the only cheap camera on the market, and it recorded the scene, perhaps not in color or well-focused, but as these photos will show, the end result was a fairly good picture. These photos allow us to obtain a rather clear idea of what life was like in North Dakota at that time.

The majority of these photos were taken by my father and mother, Theodore and Clara Aasen, between approximately 1920 and 1953. My mother's camera (see page 120) still works—not a bad deal for a buck! Other photographs have been added to illustrate a particular aspect of North Dakota during that time.

I am sure that almost every family in North Dakota has an old album around the house that contains photos very similar to these. Do not throw them away! So many of these old photos have been lost, discarded, or burned up, and much of that history is gone forever. Much has been written about this period in North Dakota, but these old photos from a box lens camera reveal a grim and real truth—a personal truth—that words cannot convey.

To say that 1900 to 1940 was a period of change would be a great understatement. Tractors, autos, and trucks began to replace the horse and wagon; electricity and running water were becoming common, and radios and other new gadgets appeared in farm homes. The population doubled—from 319,146 in 1900 to 641,935 in 1940. One thing that hasn't changed much is the weather—then and now, it varies widely. The images in this book will reveal many of these changes. The opinions expressed in this book are mine. I resided in North Dakota from 1922 to 1948, and return there every year.

I want to thank the many folks who helped me with this effort, (see page 6). In closing, I want to dedicate this book to those who had faith in North Dakota in the beginning, and to those who still have faith in the future of North Dakota. Listen to the gentle whisper of the cottonwood trees, and keep the faith.

Larry Aasen

O BEAUTIFUL
FOR SPACIOUS SKIES,
FOR AMBER WAVES OF GRAIN,
FOR PURPLE MOUNTAIN MAJESTIES,
ABOVE THE FRUITED PLAIN

One

SPORTS

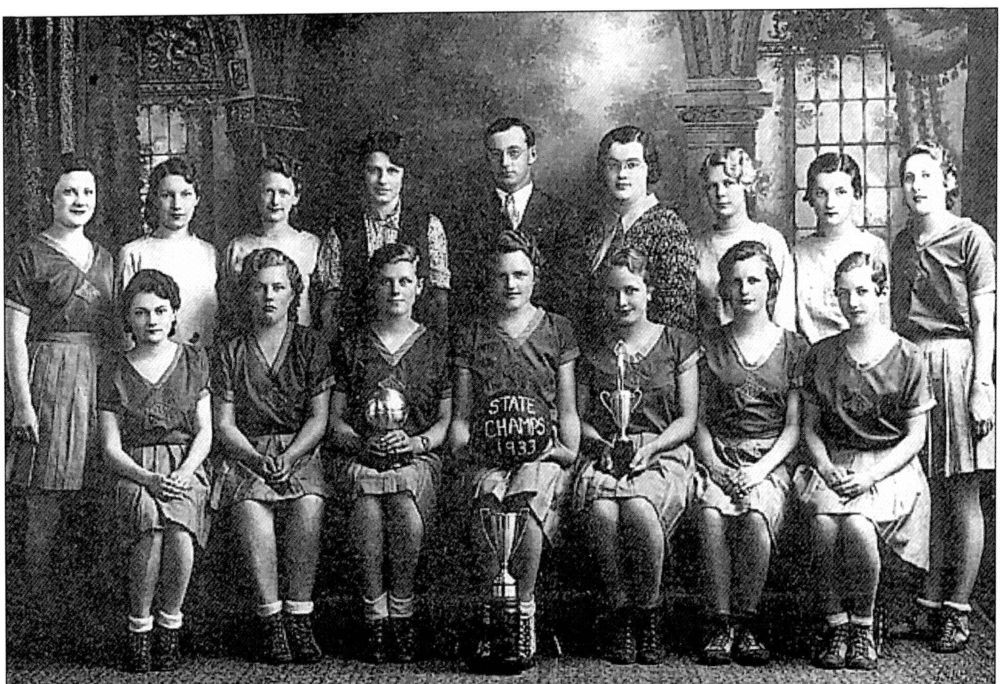

Pictured above is the 1932–33 Tioga, North Dakota, girls basketball team. Girls basketball has always been popular in North Dakota. In recent years, several North Dakota teams have won national championships.

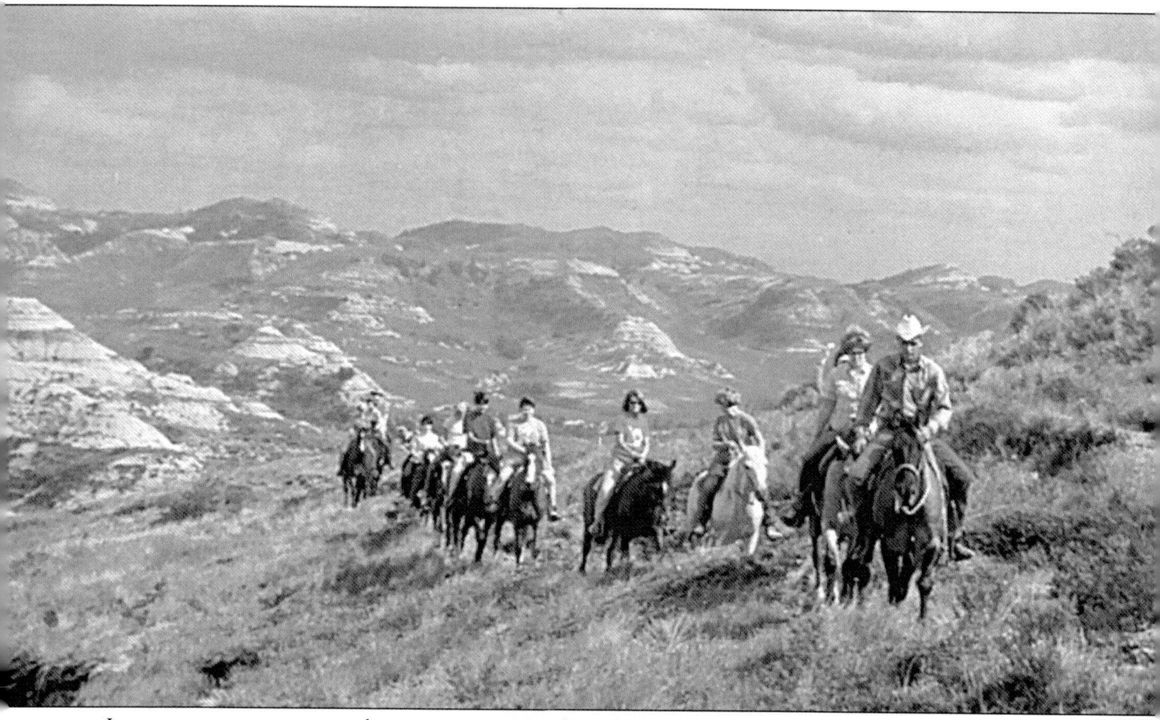

In recent years, tourism has grown in North Dakota, thanks to good promotional activity by the North Dakota Tourism Promotion Division. Tourists can ride the trails, like those pictured here, or fish and hunt. They can also stay in quality hotels or bed and breakfast establishments, visit buffalo-raising ranches, go riding on dude ranches, vacation on "working" farms, or just enjoy the quiet of the wide open spaces. Tourists often comment that their favorite attraction in North Dakota is the "Big Sky."

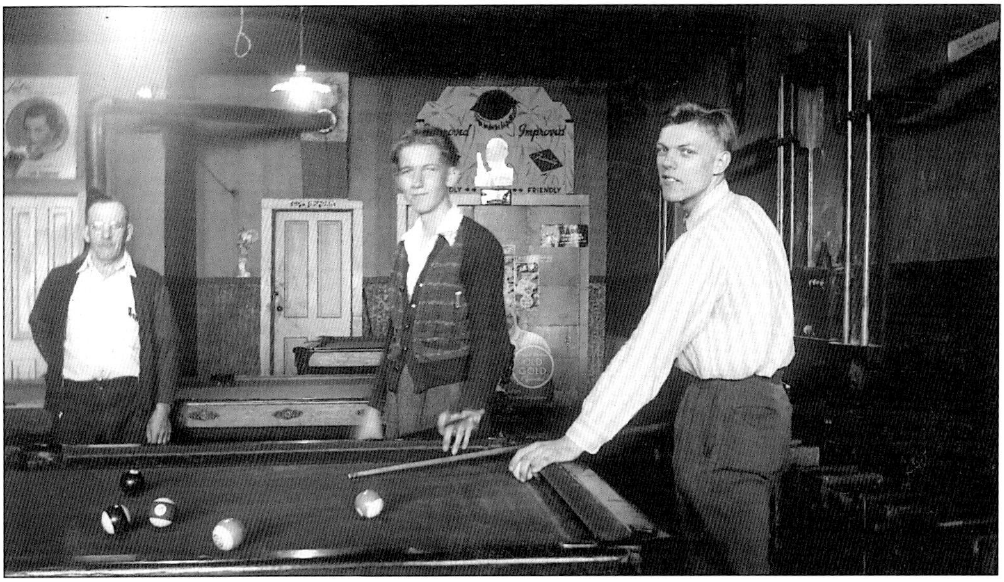

From 1900 to 1940, pool halls were very popular places in North Dakota towns for young men and boys. Some considered these pool halls sinful places, where idle youth wasted time and smoked cigarettes. A well-known church leader in the early 1940s used his radio program to urge North Dakota's fine young men to stay out of the smoky pool halls and stinking beer halls. Considering the popularity of the halls, it does not seem that his advice was followed.

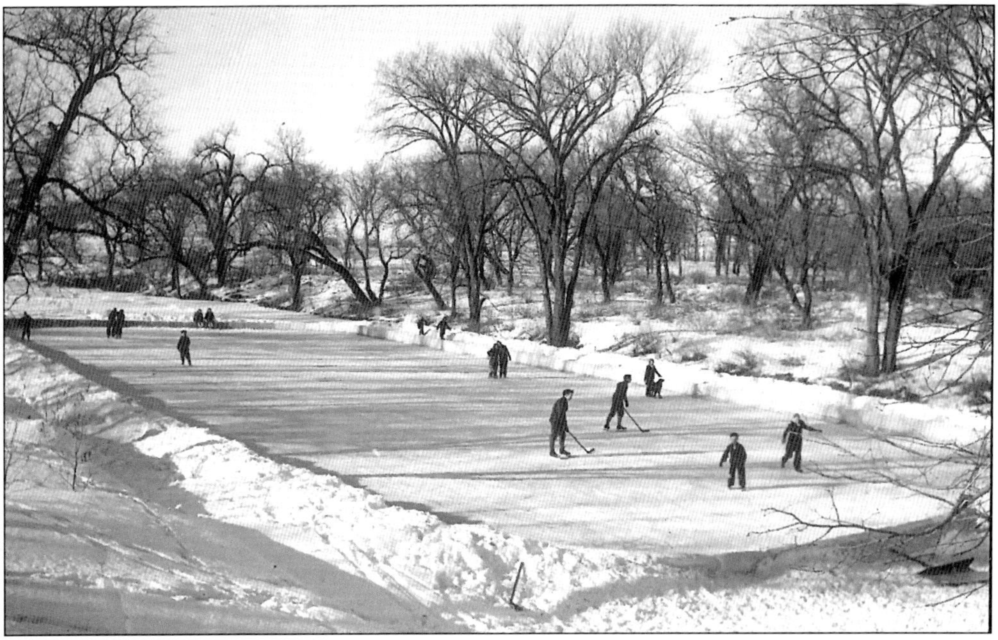

In early times, every town in North Dakota had an outdoor skating rink. The rink was located either on a river or a flooded lot. Because of the cold weather, it did not take long for the water to freeze. During this time period, none of the colleges or universities had hockey teams. However, today hockey is a very popular sport in the state. Clifford "Fido" Purpur of Grand Forks, North Dakota, is credited with boosting the popularity of hockey in the state. A college and professional player, he has received many awards.

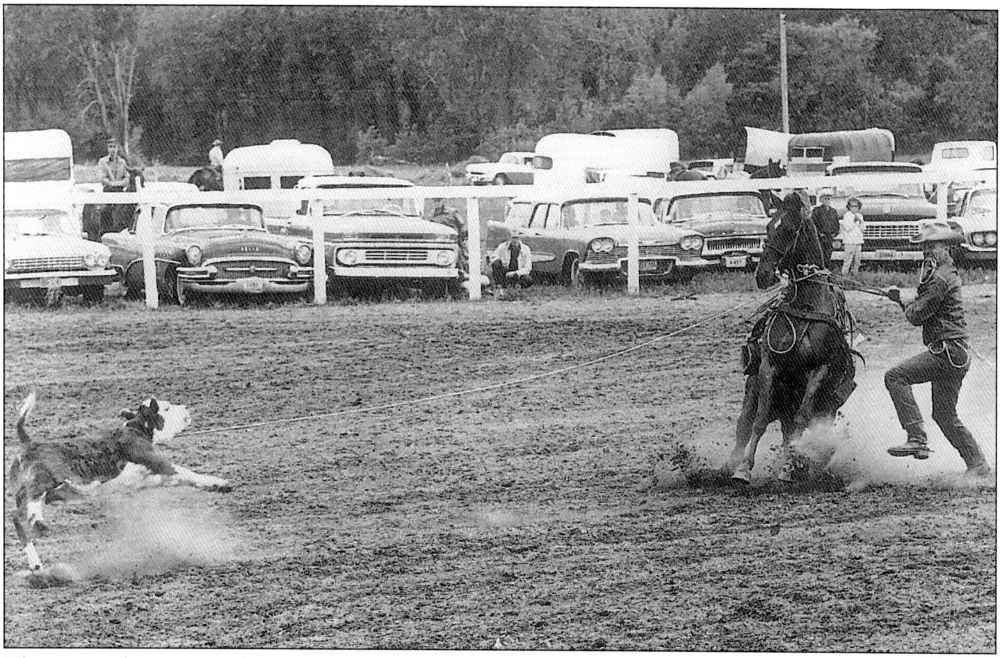

This is a rodeo in Mandan. Rodeos have been a major part of life in North Dakota from the very beginning. They are even more popular in the western part of the state because of the many ranchers and cowboys living there.

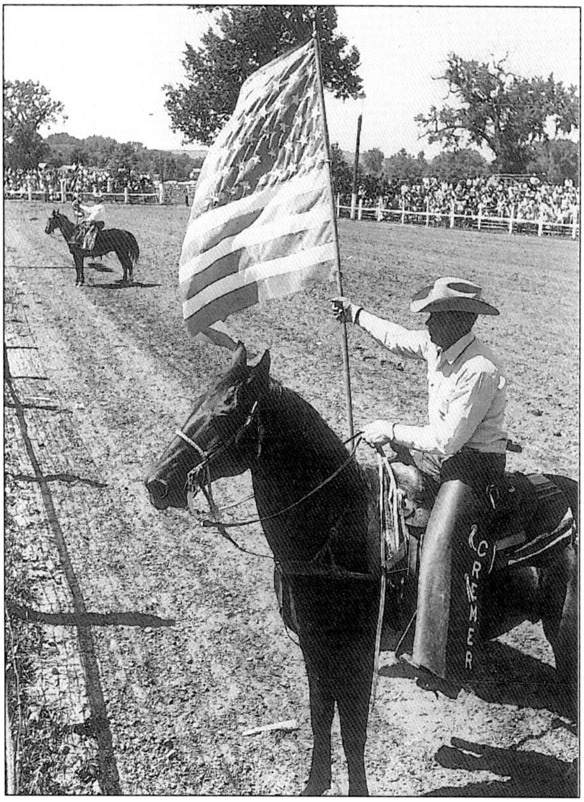

This rodeo photo was taken in Bismarck. North Dakota rodeo stars have performed all over the country, from the Cow Palace in San Francisco to Madison Square Garden in New York City.

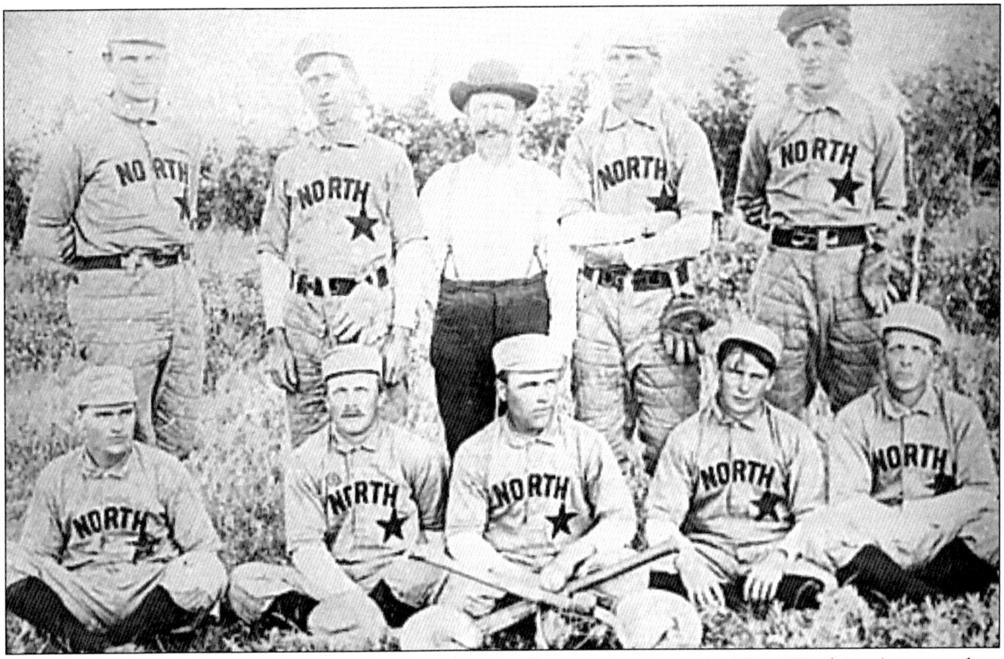

Pictured here is the Montrose North Stars baseball team in about 1910. J.Winkjer (pictured in the back row, far left) is the father of Williston lawyer, Dean Winkjer. The town of Montrose moved lock, stock, and barrel to Wildrose when the railroad bypassed Montrose to pass through Wildrose instead. All the town's buildings were hauled into Wildrose by steam engineer J. Winkjer.

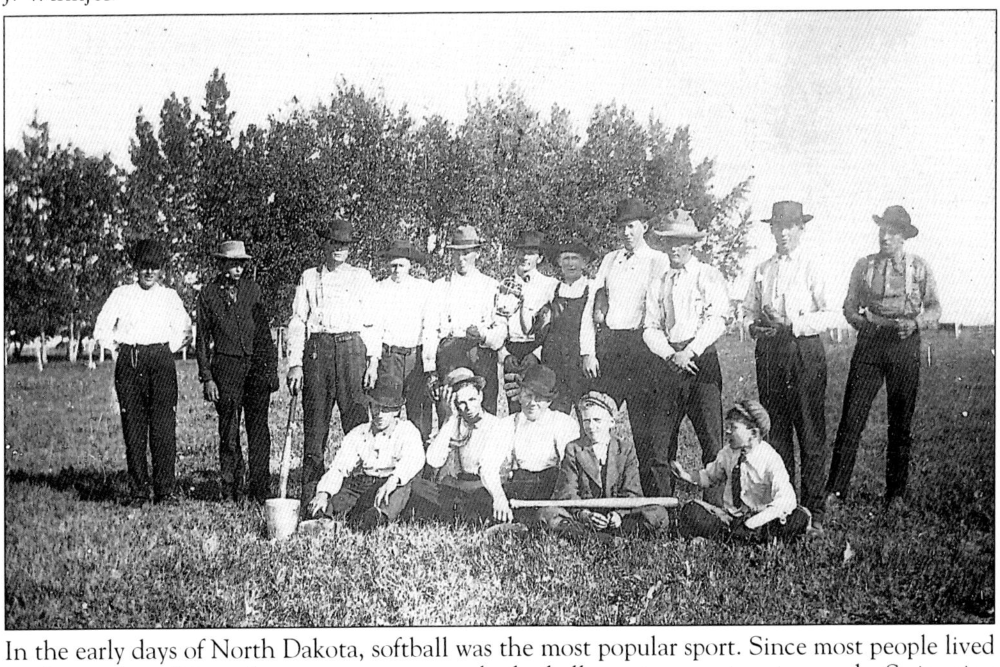

In the early days of North Dakota, softball was the most popular sport. Since most people lived on farms, they did not have access to gyms, basketball courts, or swimming pools. Swimming was done in rivers, which unfortunately also often carried the town's sewage. Some swimming was also done in gravel pits if water had collected in the bottoms.

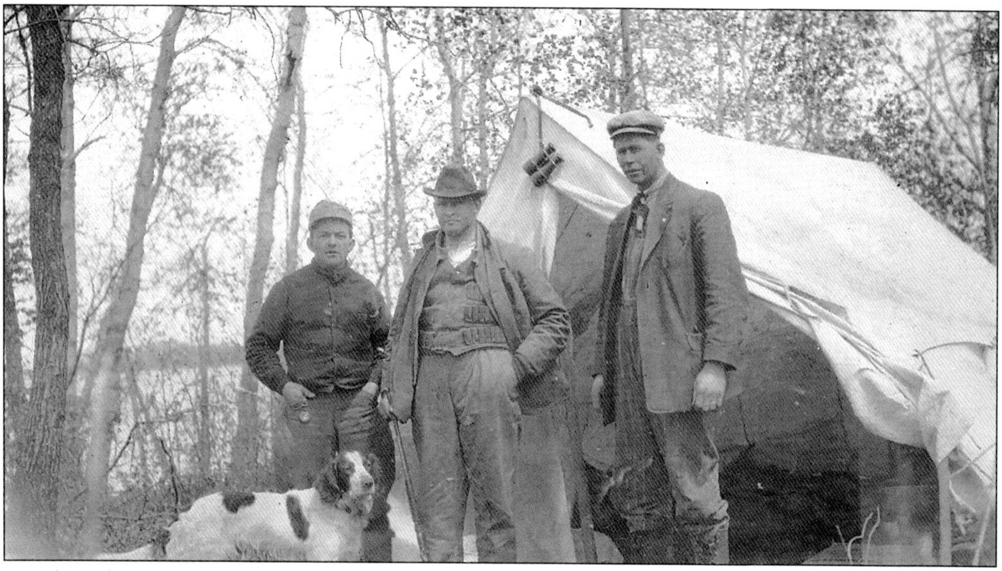

North Dakotans did a lot of hunting in those days. Luckily, there was a great deal to hunt—antelope, moose, elk, Hungarian partridges, grouse, prairie chickens, mourning doves, wild turkeys, ducks, coyotes, white-tailed and mule deer, and bighorn sheep. While hunting rabbits, hunters would form a straight line, walk through a section of land, and shoot all the rabbits they could find. However, North Dakota is probably most famous for its pheasant hunting, drawing hunters from all over the United States. The hunters pictured above camped out near Lake Park, Minnesota, to try their luck.

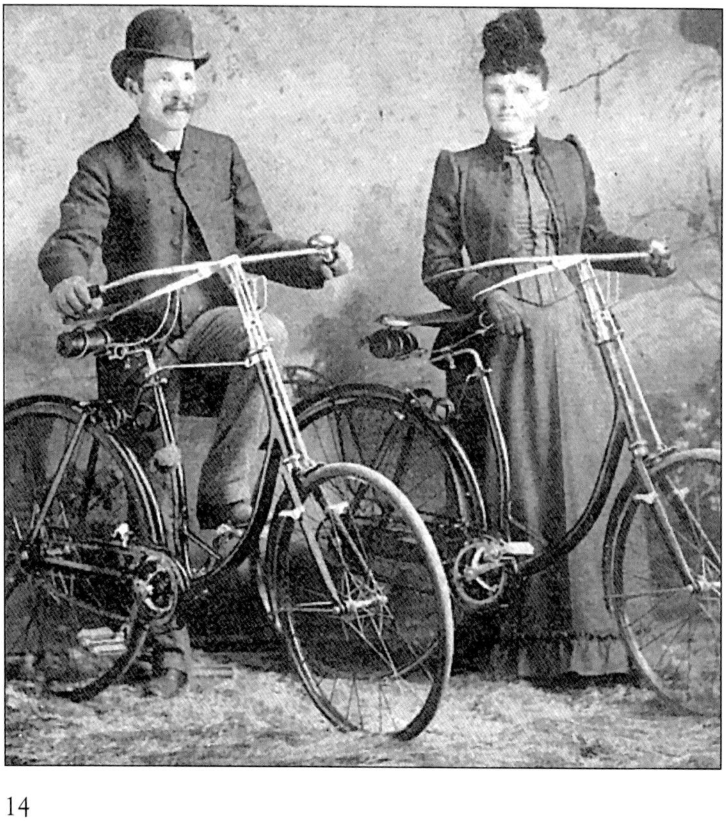

Bicycling was a good way to spend a Sunday afternoon as this couple did in 1924.

Two

FARMING

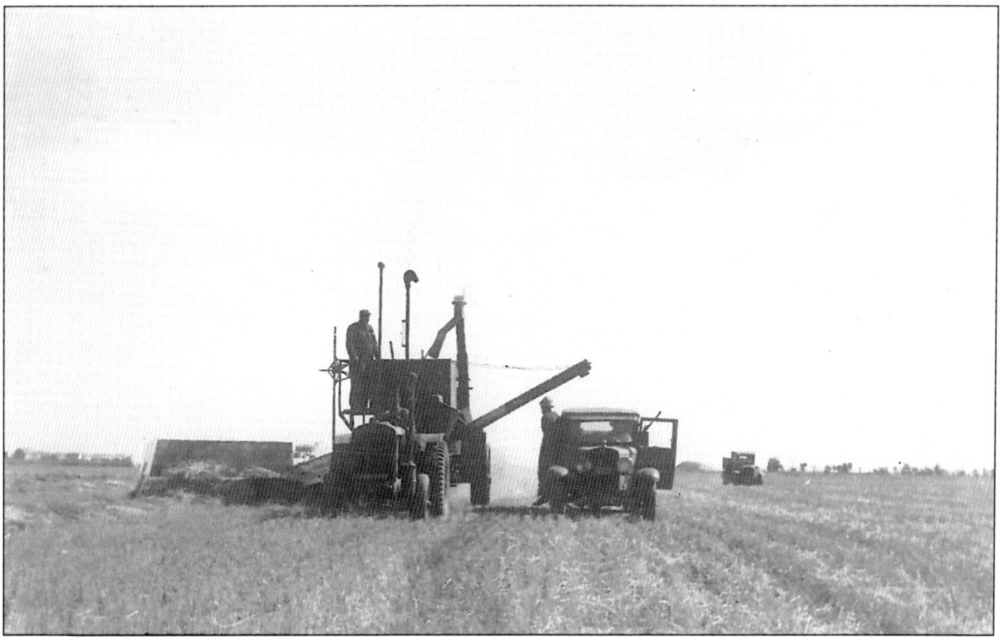

In the late 1930s, large, cumbersome combines made their appearance in North Dakota. It was a startling development, and one which meant that many farm hands would be out of work. Only a few people were necessary to run the combine, while it took 20 or 30 men to harvest and thresh grain. Many of the farm workers resented the combine, and there were rumors that some even threw rocks into the machinery.

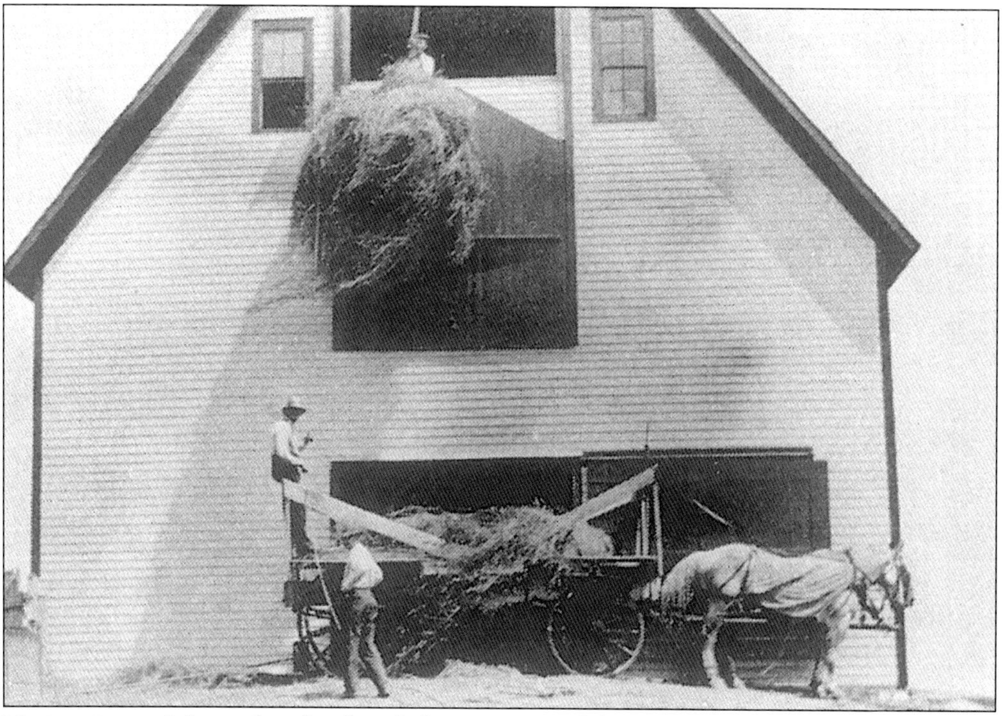

Haying time in July was hot, hard work, but necessary if the cows were going to eat that winter. The grass would be cut, raked into piles, picked up by men in a wagon (called a hayrack), and taken to the barn. Then a thick rope would pull the sling holding the hay up into the barn (while everyone yelled "There she goes!"). The hardest part about haying in July was watching the city folks drive by in their white shirts, on their way to the cool Minnesota lakes.

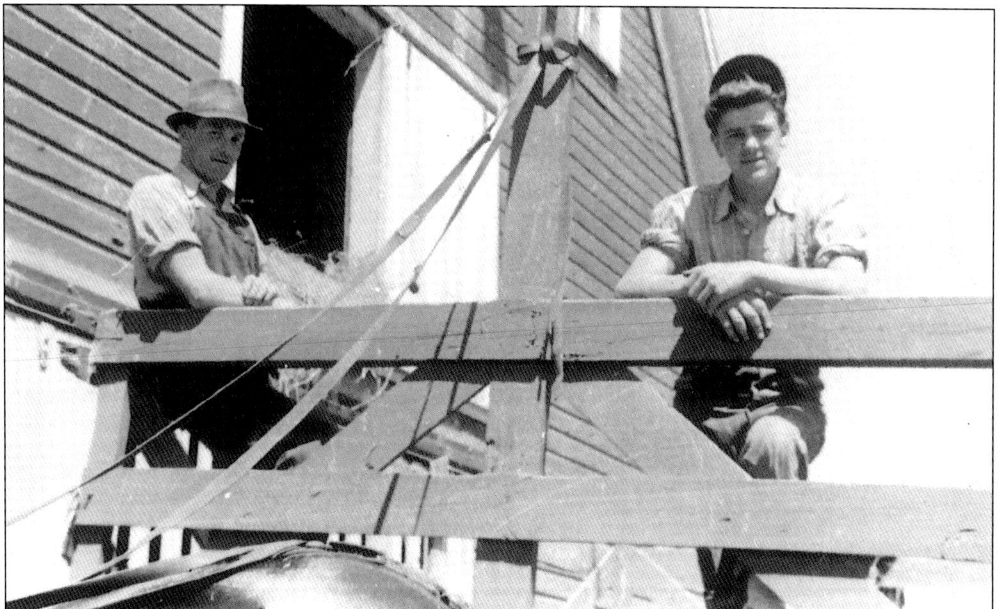

Melvin Eidum and the author didn't like haying, but it had to be done. Mr. Eidum joined the North Dakota National Guard as a private, and ended up a captain at Guadalcanal.

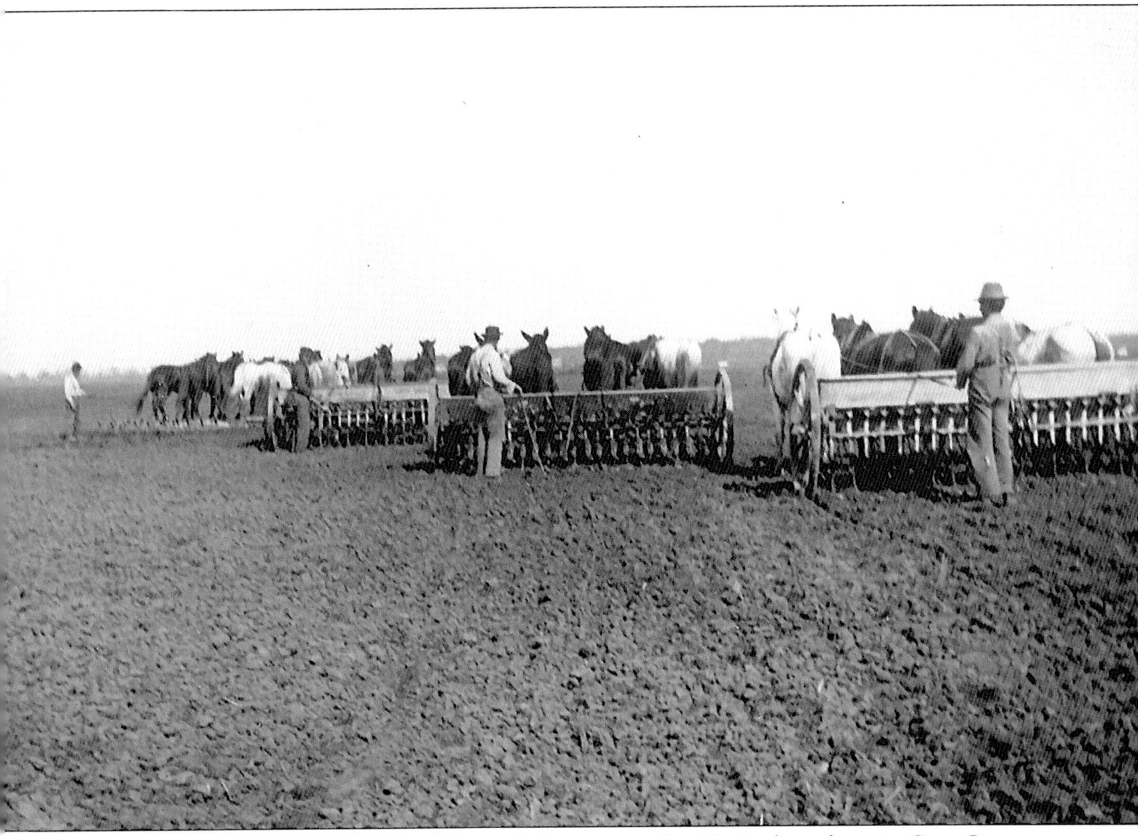

Twenty horses and five men are seeding and plowing on the McAndrew farm in Cass County in 1900. The change from horse farming to tractor farming had many implications—most of them good. The land needed to produce hay and oats for the horses could now be used for cash crops. Fewer hired men would be needed, which meant that the farmer's wife would have fewer mouths to feed. The farm could be expanded. Tractors could—and often were—run all night if necessary, whereas the horses were worn out at sunset and returned to the barn. However, there was a downside as well—you could grow what the horses needed to eat, but you had to pay cash for gasoline to run your tractors, which cost more than horses! Through the years, many farmers have complained about the high cost of farm machinery.

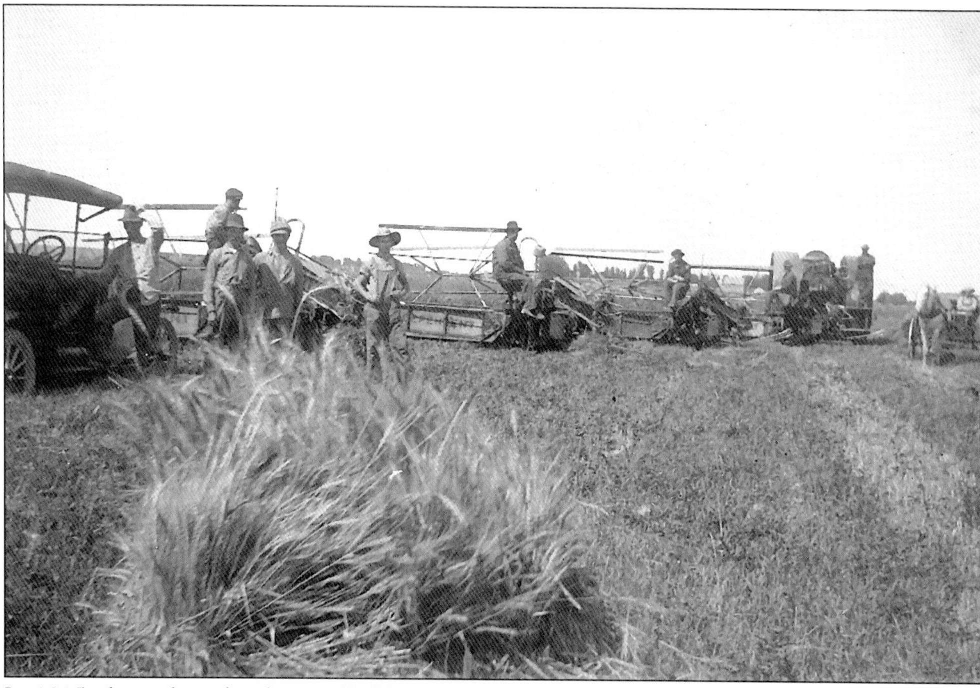

In 1915, these three binders, pulled by a gasoline-powered tractor called the "Big Four," cut a 30-foot swatch at one time. The auto is a 1911 Studebaker. These photographs were contributed by Jim McAndrew who grew up on this farm near the Red River, east of Gardner.

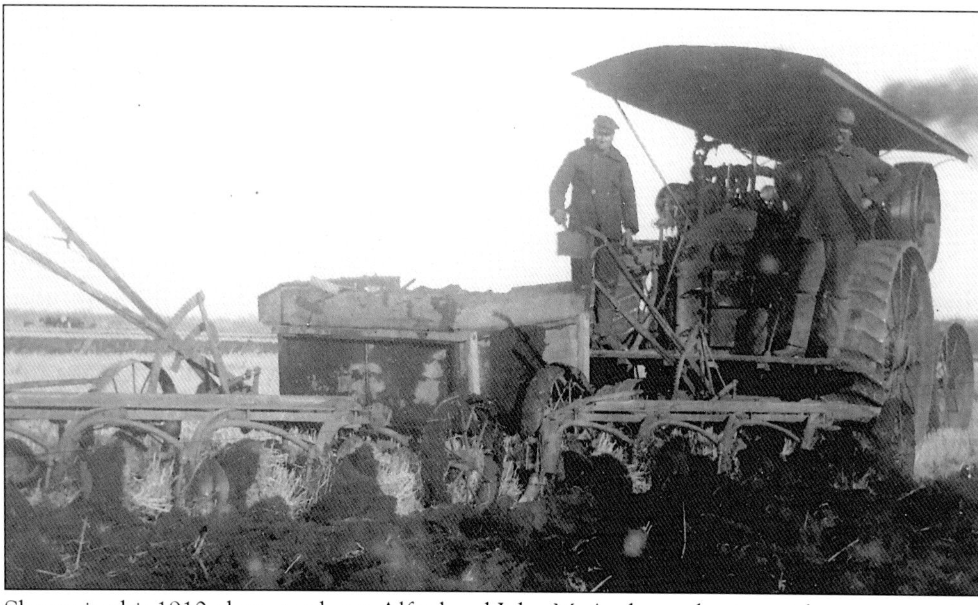

Shown in this 1910 photograph are Alfred and John McAndrew, plowing with a steam engine, which provided the energy before gasoline-powered tractors arrived in North Dakota. These plowshares are sinking deep into the soil and turning over the earth. Today the entire concept of plowing has changed, and the dirt is not turned over—it is scratched or broken up. At this time, the plowshares had to be taken into a blacksmith shop in town quite often for sharpening, but the new tools for plowing do not require sharpening.

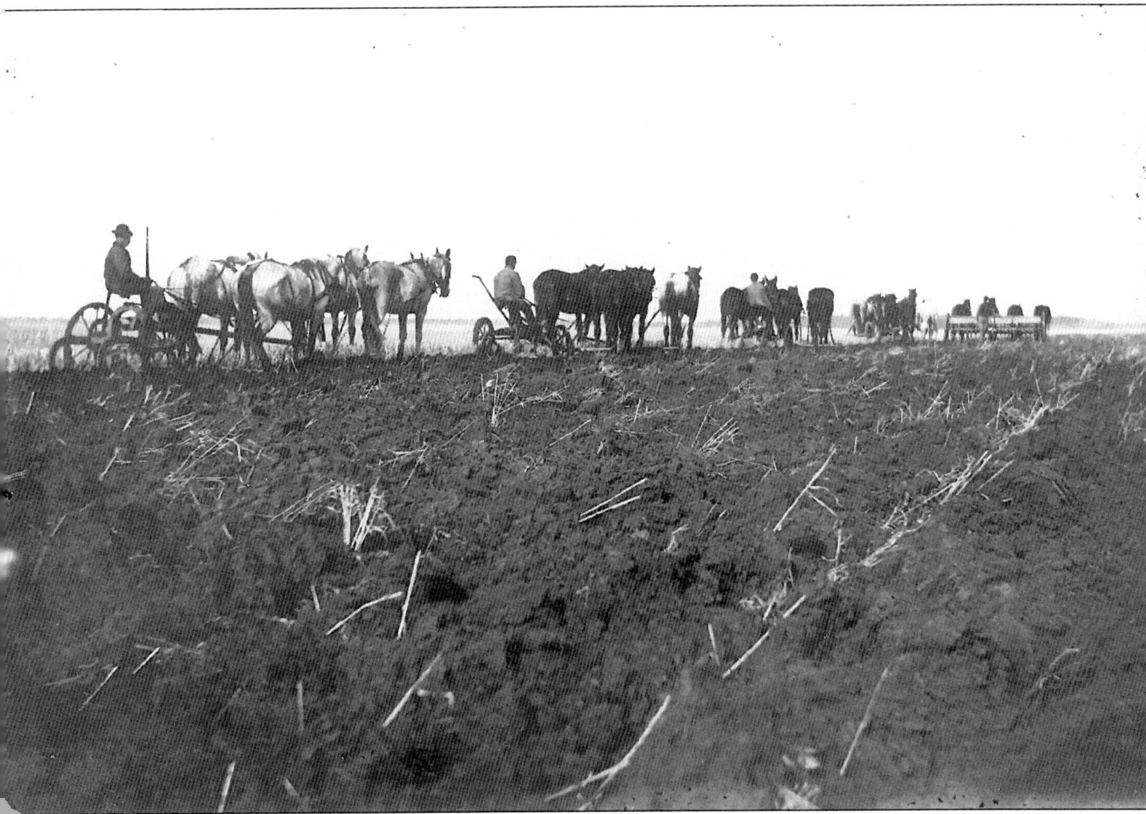

Three drills (planters), twelve horses, and three men are planting wheat on the McAndrew farm, east of Gardner (near the Red River) in 1915. The horses and the hired men required tender loving care—they were doing very hard work all day long in the hot sun.

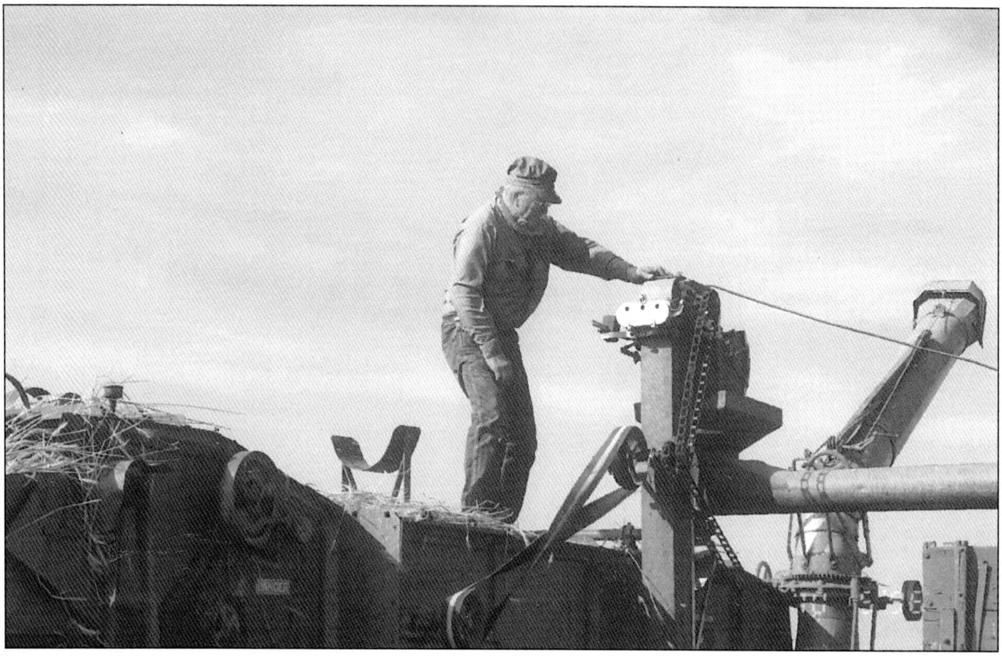

Silhouetted against the North Dakota sky, Jerry Nysveen is pictured working on top of an old grain separator. This might look like a glamorous job, but it is not. It is a dirty, tough job with long hours. There were also many farm injuries during this period. It was not until after 1940 that many safety devices were installed on farm machinery.

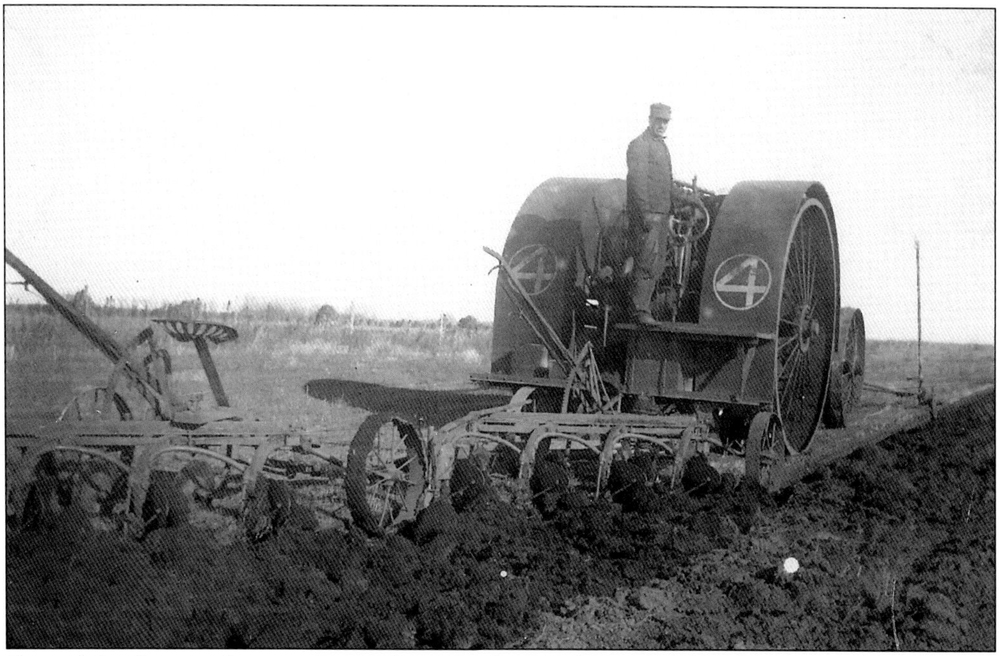

One of the first gasoline tractors to begin replacing the steam engines was the Emerson Big Four, which was made by the Gas Traction Company in Minneapolis. A unique feature of this tractor is that the driver did not really have to steer it too much. A small wheel in the front of the tractor followed the furrow, and this steered the tractor.

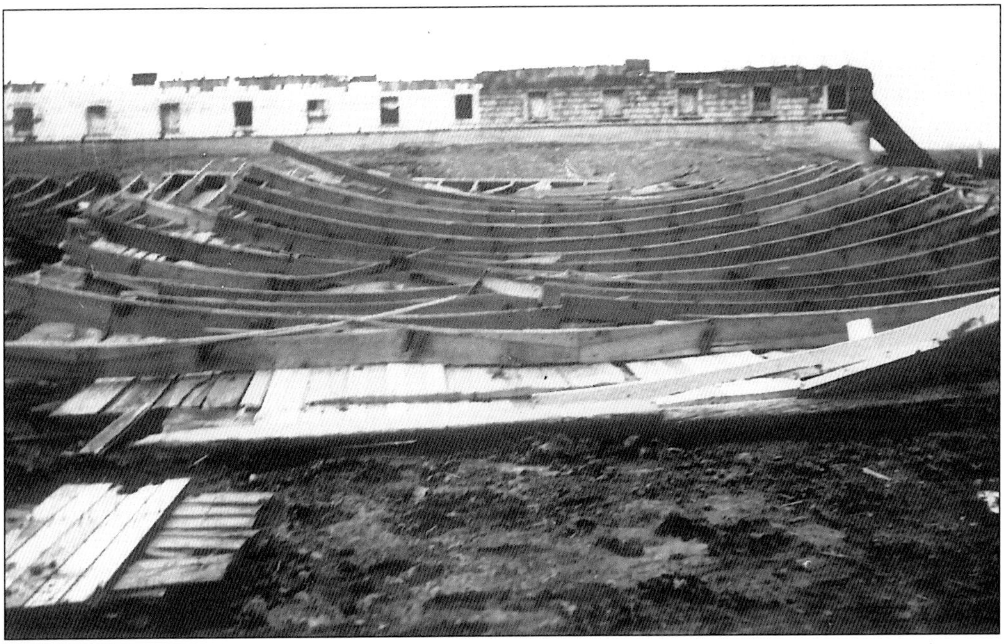

On July 3, 1935, a storm hit eastern North Dakota and took off many barn roofs, like the one pictured above. Pieces of the roof were found a half-mile away.

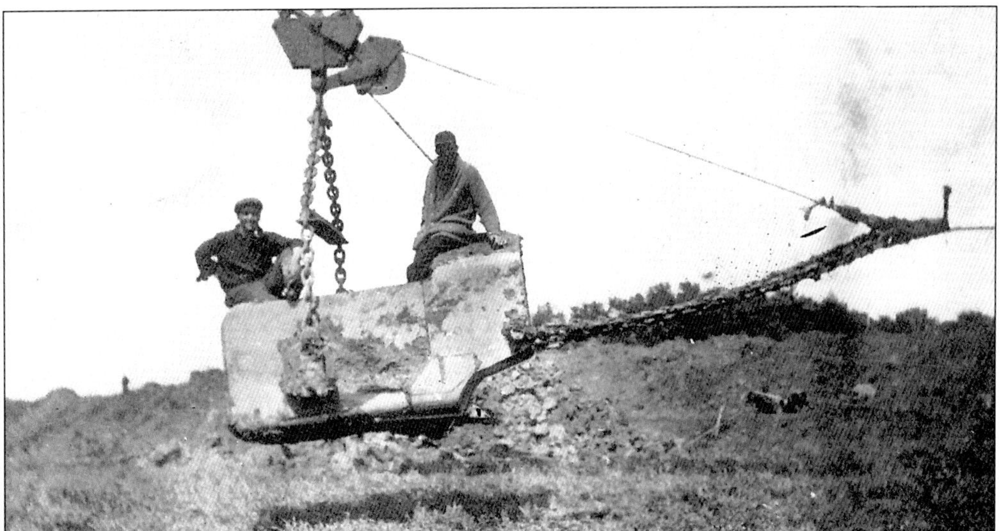

North Dakota has experienced varying water levels over the years. In 1930, this large ditch was dug east of Gardner to drain off excess water. The farmers resented the idea, and one even fought it all the way to the North Dakota Supreme Court only to lose the case.

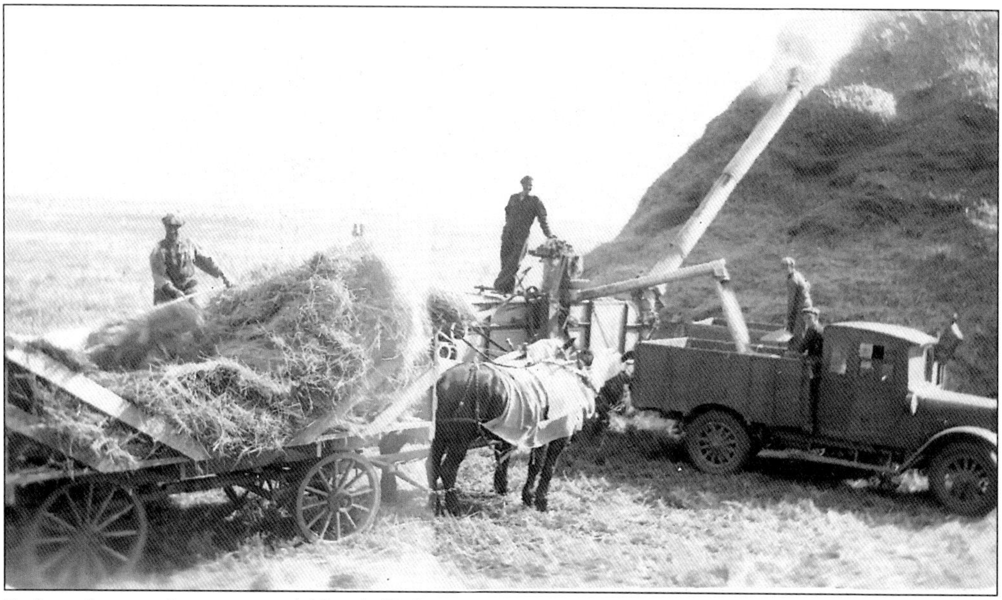

Before the combine entered North Dakota, grain was cut and tied into bundles by a binder. The bundles were then "shocked" and organized in piles with the grain up in the air to dry out. There were about eight bundles to a shock. Two horses pulling a wagon would arrive, then "field pitchers" would throw the bundles in the wagon and take them to the threshing machine, where the grain would be separated from the straw. The grain would be hauled to a granary or an elevator in town, and the straw would be blown into a big pile. These straw stacks might be saved for use in the barn or burned. During the harvest season you might see five to ten straw stocks near your farm going up in flames.

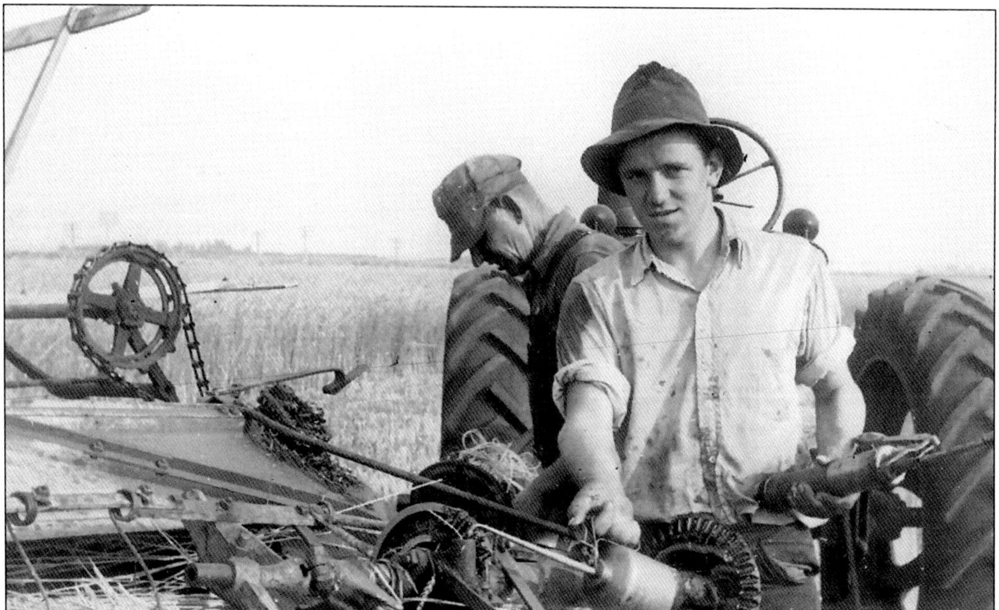

Alfred Brenden and Larry Aasen are oiling and greasing up a binder for cutting and binding wheat in this 1941 photo. About this time, combines were actively replacing binders and threshing machines.

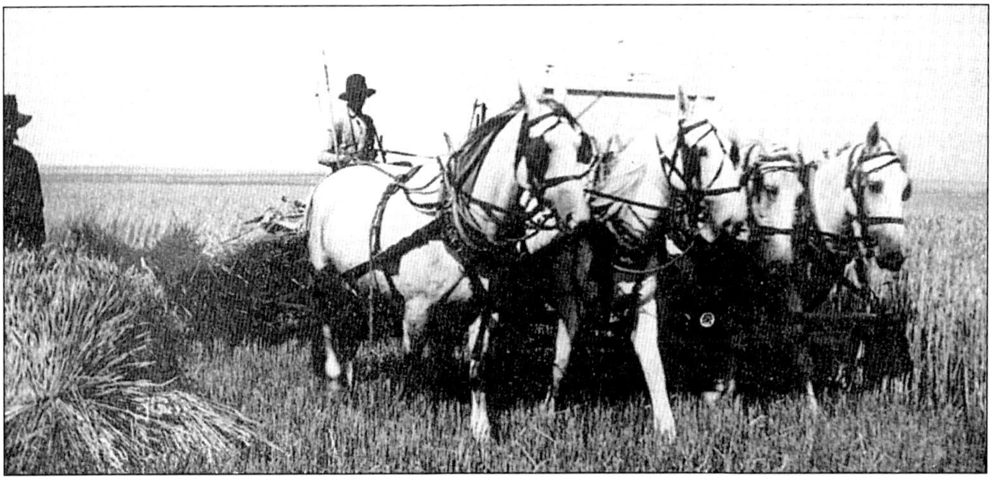

The binder pictured here was pulled by four horses. Note the whip that stands up near the driver. In about 1930, tractors began replacing horses for farm work.

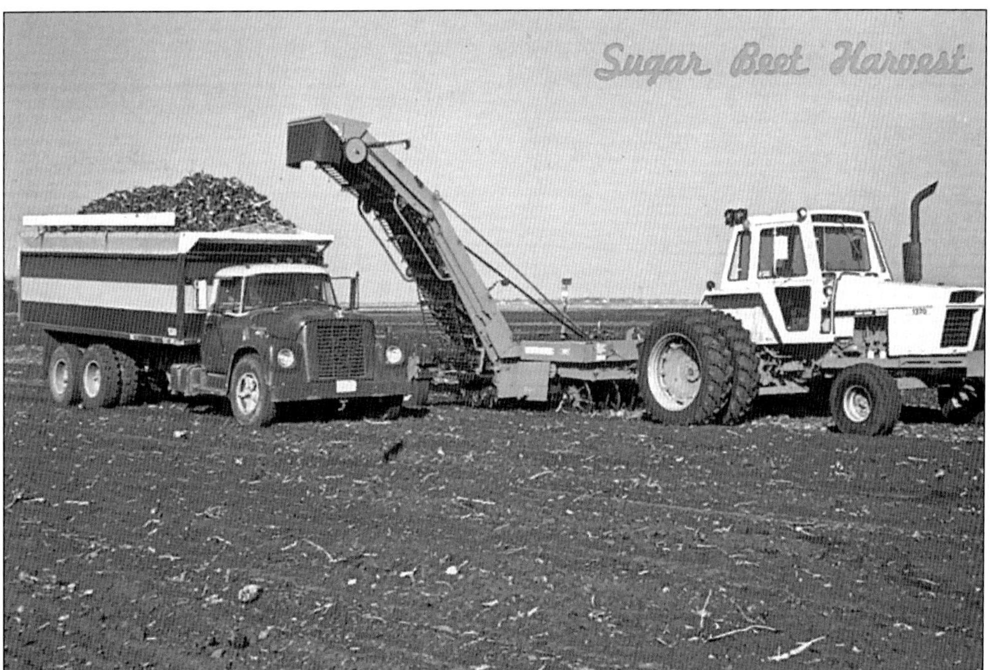

Sugar beets came to North Dakota in about 1930 and have become another leading crop, along with soybeans. The old standby, wheat, costs a lot to grow, and the expenses sometimes outweigh the income, according to agriculture experts.

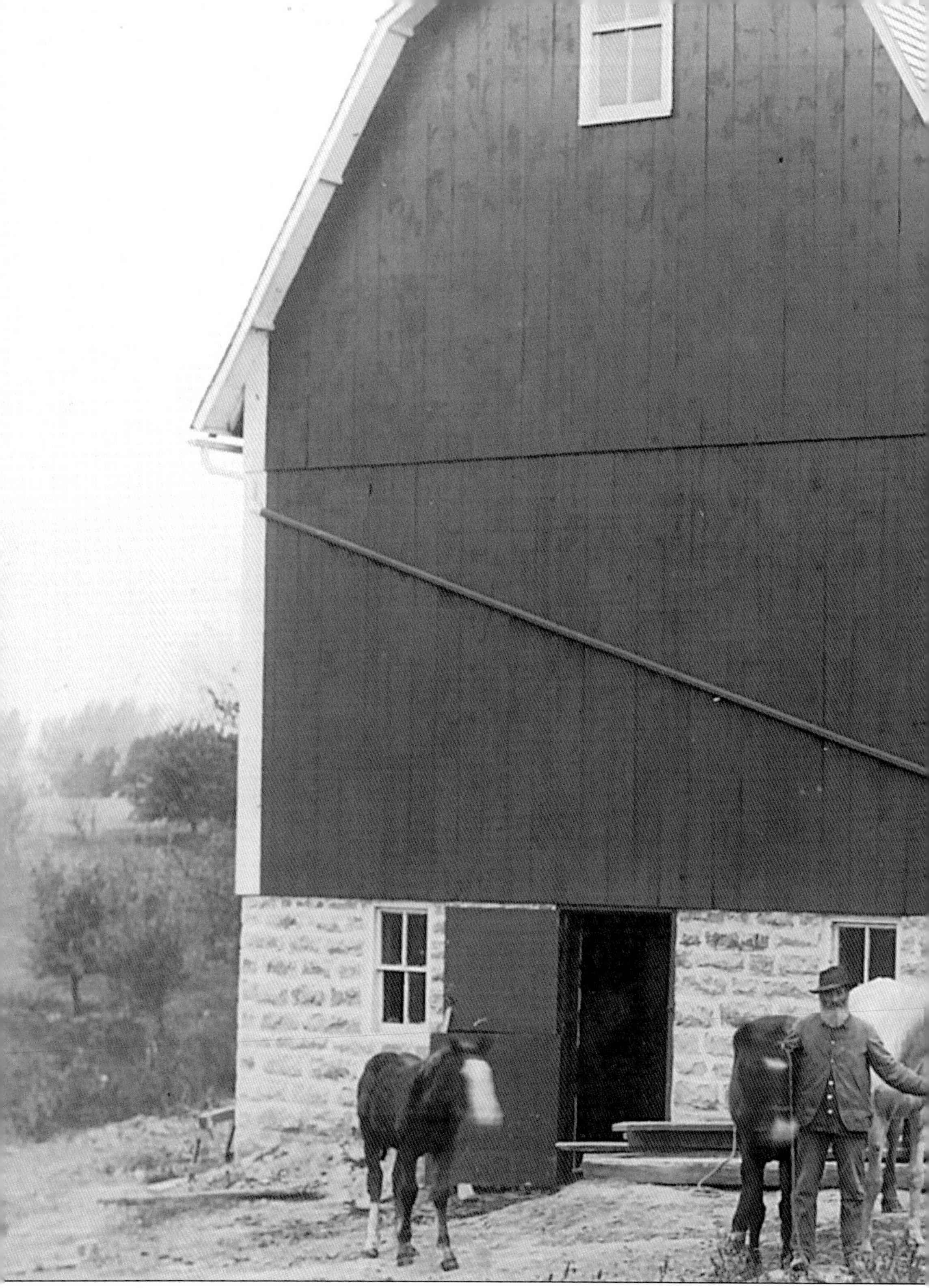

This photo celebrates the construction of a new barn. The proud owners also display their best

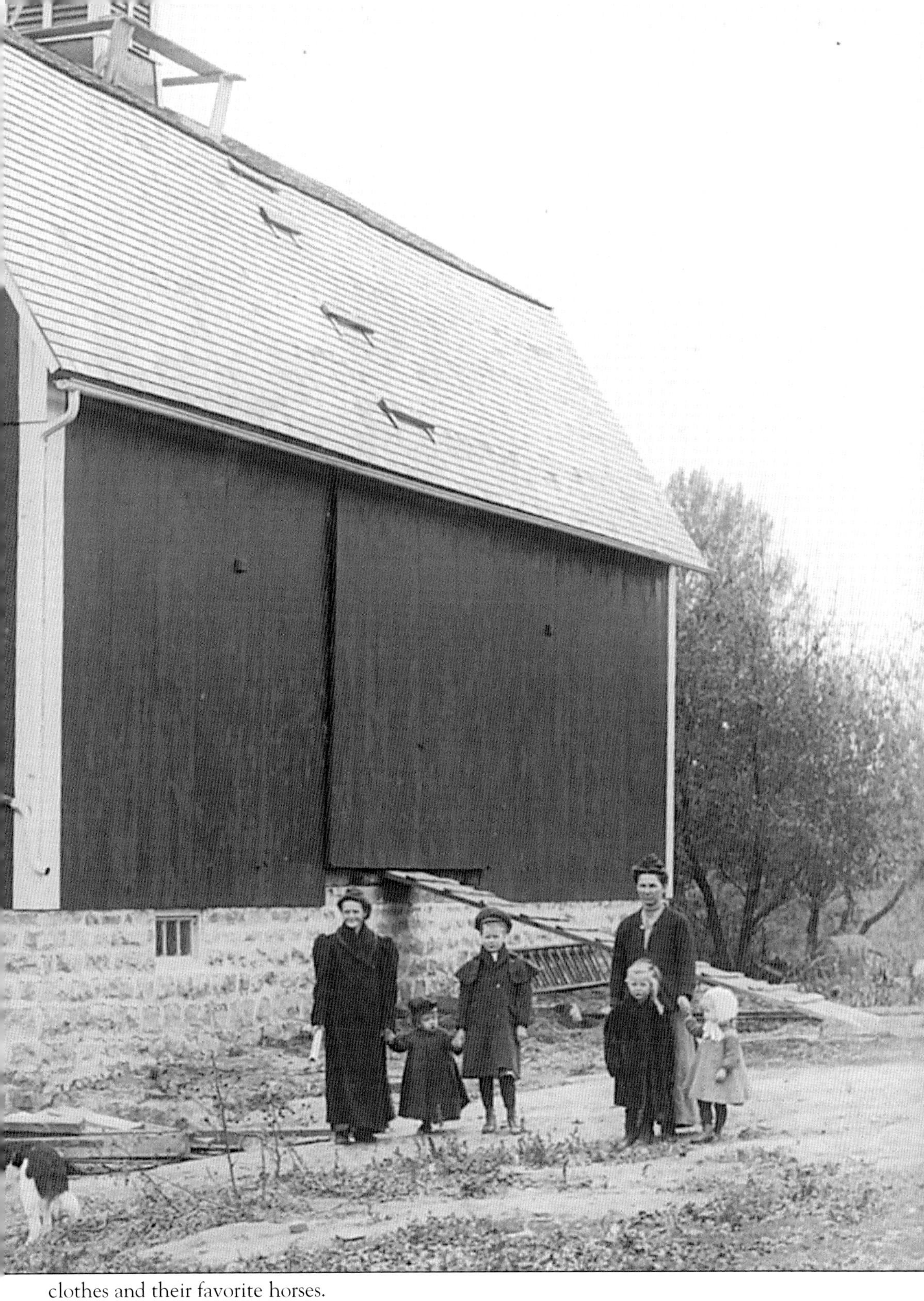

clothes and their favorite horses.

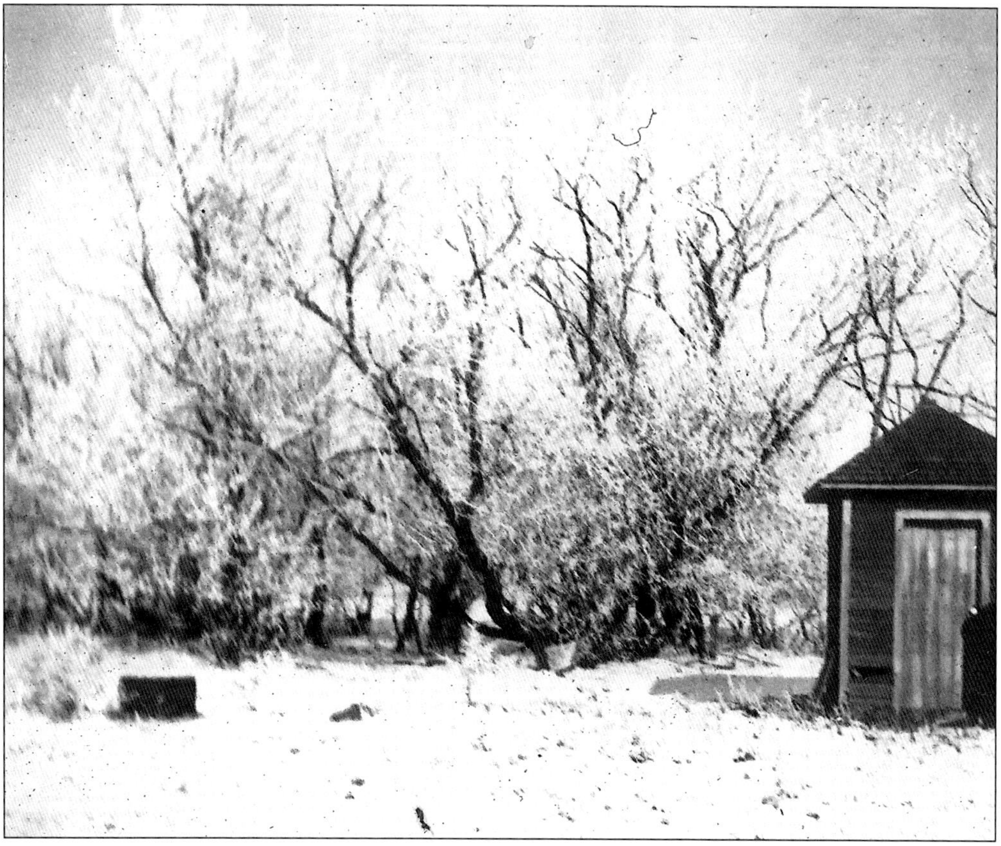

Many farms in the early days contained a smokehouse like this one for curing meat. When the nearby towns installed frozen food lockers, the smokehouses were no longer needed.

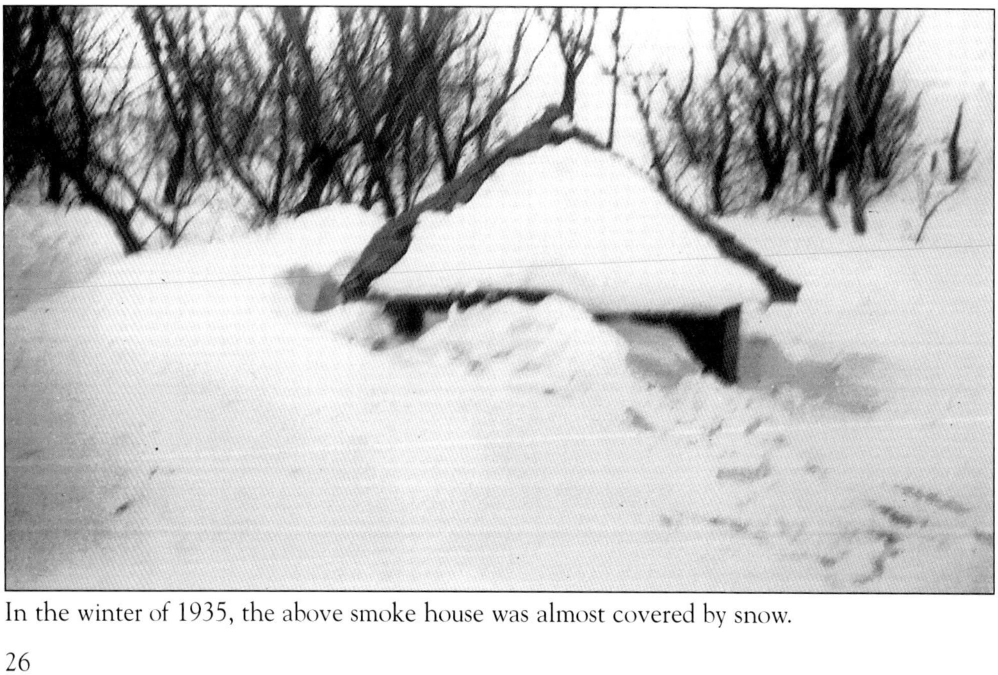

In the winter of 1935, the above smoke house was almost covered by snow.

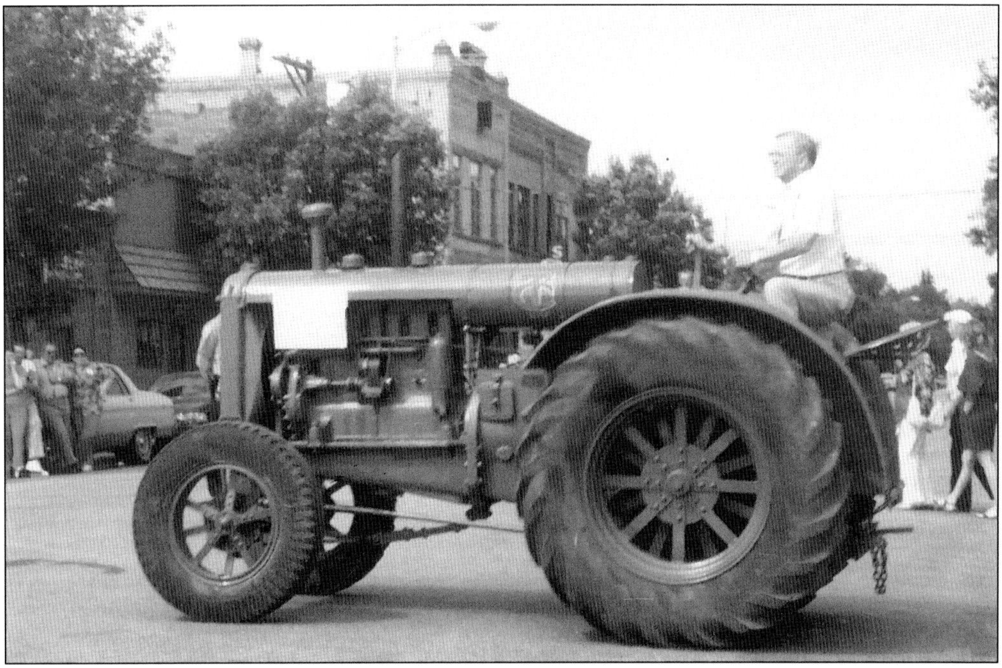

This Twin City Moline tractor was rebuilt in time to take part in the Hillsboro, North Dakota, Centennial Parade in 1991. It was purchased in 1934 and was used for many hours on farms in Eldorado Township, Traill County.

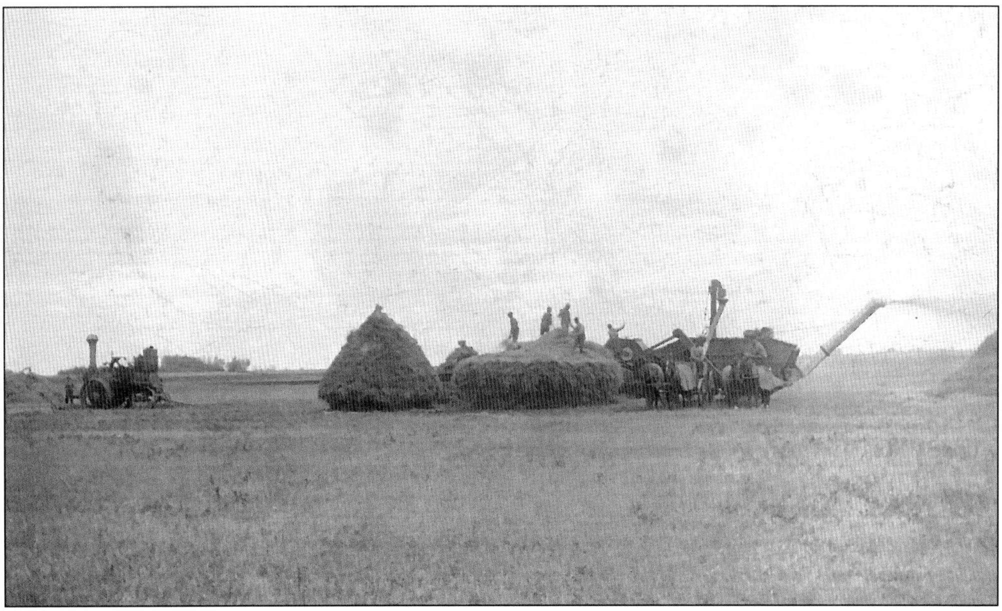

This threshing photo may have been taken before 1900 because the steam engine has the smokestack on the back of the engine, and the engine was pulled to the threshing machine because it could not move itself. The photo also depicts "stack" threshing. The bundles of grain were stacked in a round pile in order to remain dry while the farmer waited for the threshing separator and steam engine to come to his farm. Farmers sometimes had to wait late into the fall since there were not many threshing rigs available.

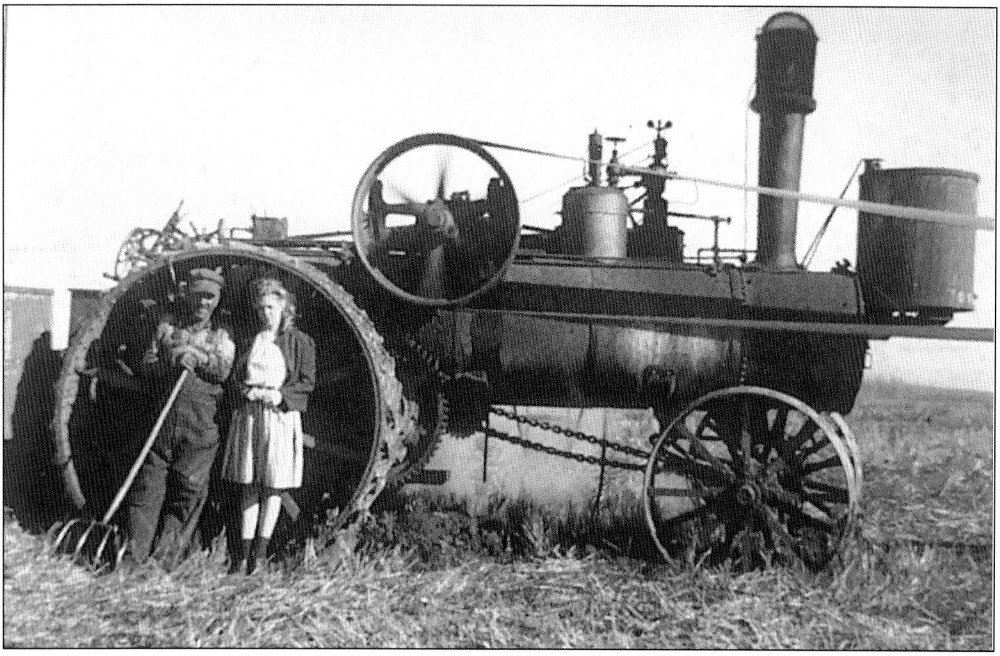

This steam engine was owned by Thinn Smedshammer, who lived in LaMoure County. He threshed (harvested) for himself and for his neighbors, beginning in 1901. This picture shows Bonnie Haugen at age 16 delivering lunch. Bonnie is a sister of June A. Osterberg, a 1949 journalism graduate of UND who contributed this photograph.

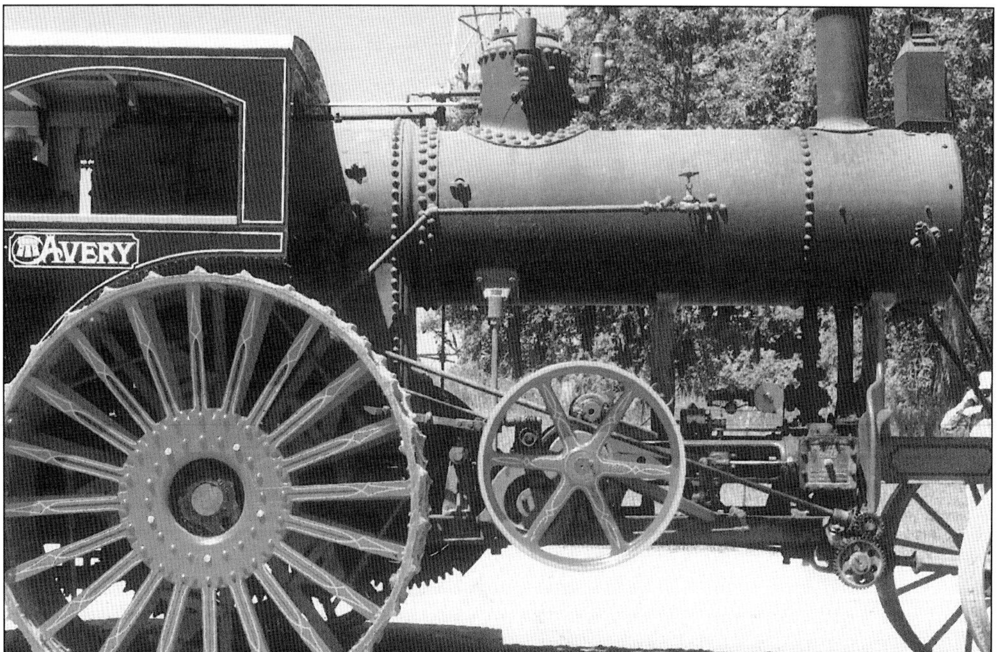

This Avery steam engine was manufactured in about 1920. Steam engines were used on farms before gasoline and kerosene tractors arrived. The steam engine could burn coal, straw, or wood to make a fire that heated the water. The use of steam engines peaked about 1910.

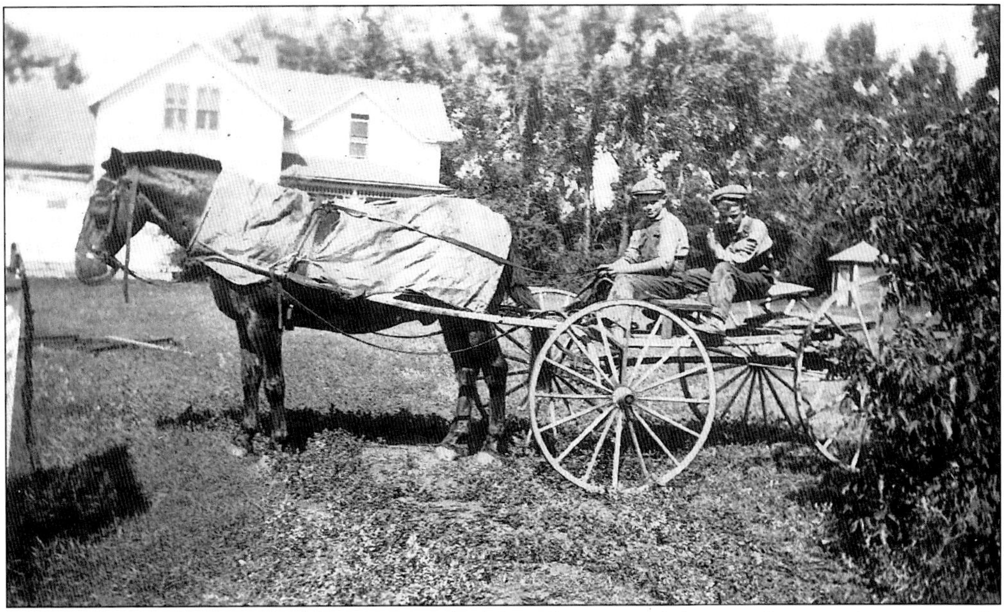

Buggies (even those that had been stripped of their fancy seats), buggy whips, and canvas roofs, were often kept for sentimental reasons.

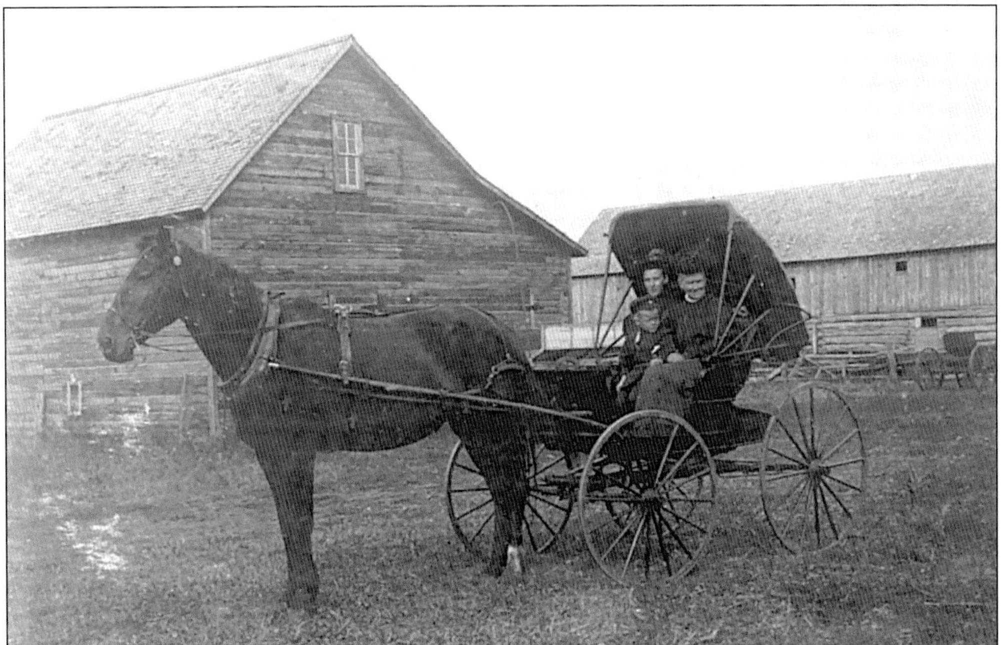

In the early days in North Dakota, city people and farm families all had horses and buggies. They took many shapes and forms, and some were very elaborate.

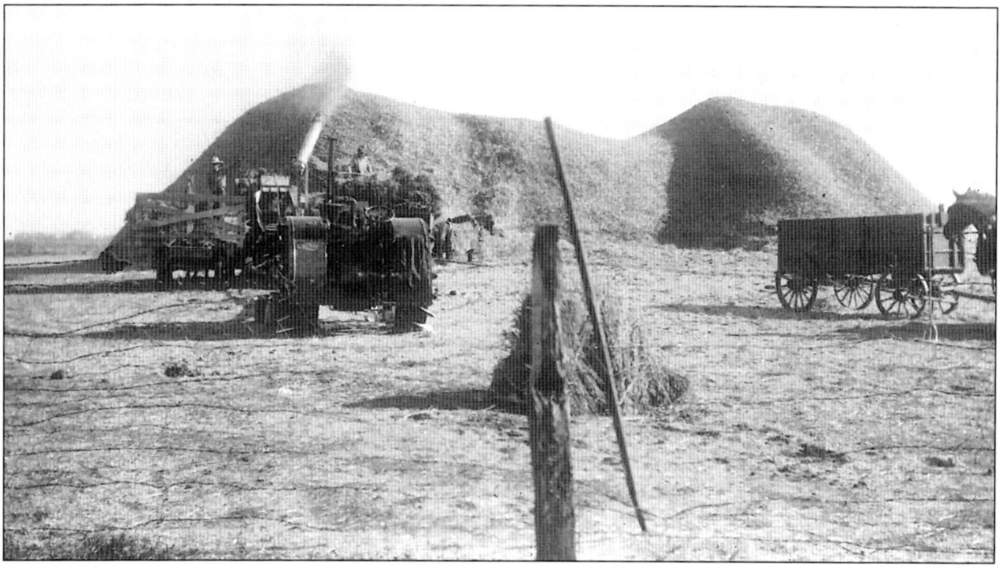

Some farmers took pride in having the largest straw stacks in the township. In 1900, the average size of a North Dakota farm was 343 acres. Today the average farm is 1,292 acres.

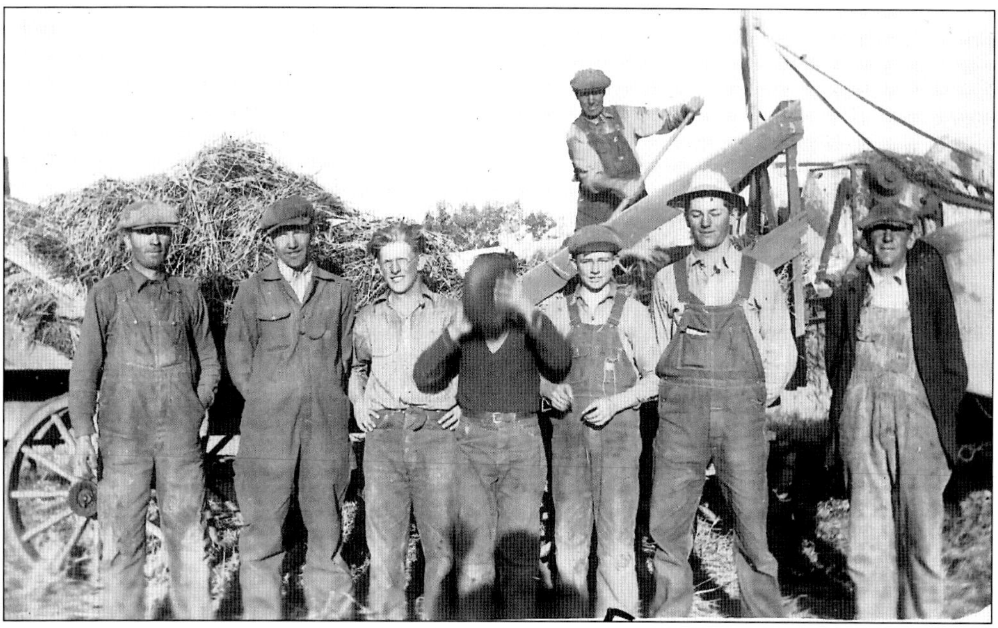

This photo depicts the men who did the heavy lifting in dusty fields in the hot sun. The men, hired for about a month, would come from Minnesota, South Dakota, and some from as far away as Chicago. As a rule, they slept on the hay in the barn or in crude bunkhouses. The workday lasted from sunup to sundown. They looked forward to Saturday night, when many of them would get drunk. Sunday was for sleeping, but when they were bone tired during the week, they prayed for rain!

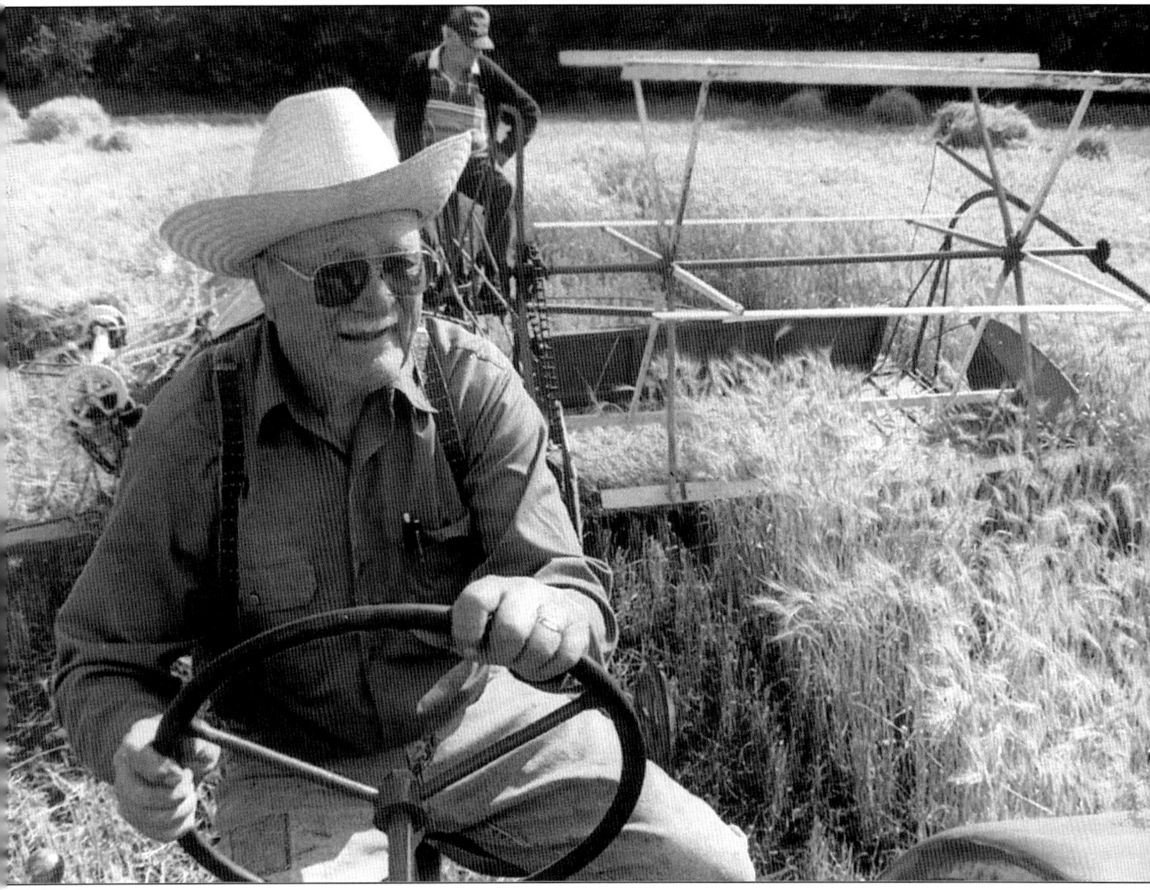

The ways of old-fashioned farming are often restaged at North Dakota historical events. Jerry Nysveen (on the tractor) and Alvin Nelson (on the binder) demonstrated to the people in Hillsboro that this old-fashioned machinery could still do the job. In 1900, there were 45,332 farms in North Dakota, and today there are 30,500.

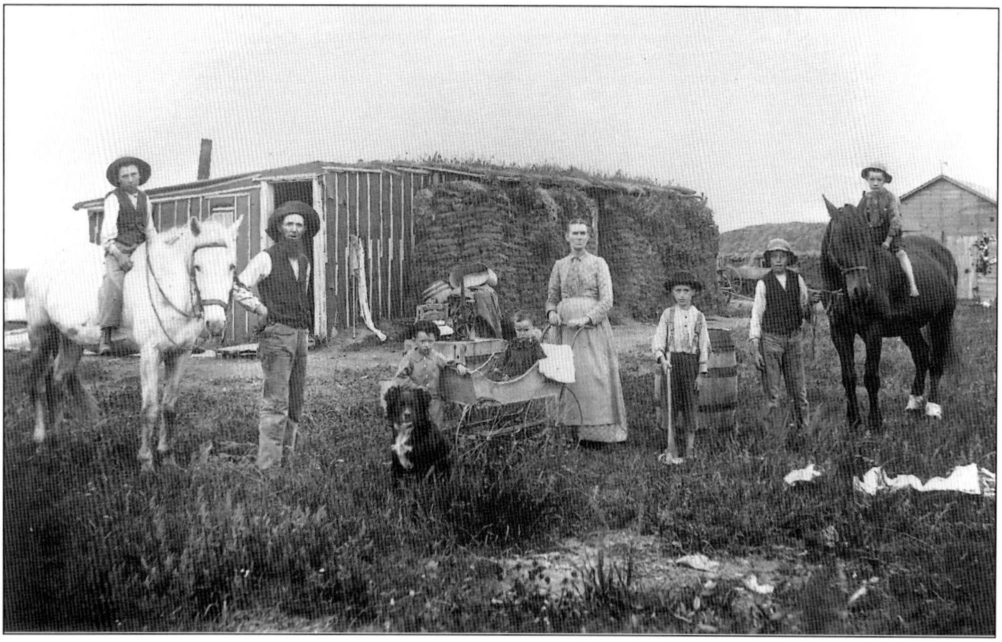

The Towner County family of Joseph and Annie Burkholder gather in front of their new home with their horses, babies, and buggy in this 1901 photo. Tarpaper and sod were used on the house in an attempt to keep out the cold when winter came.

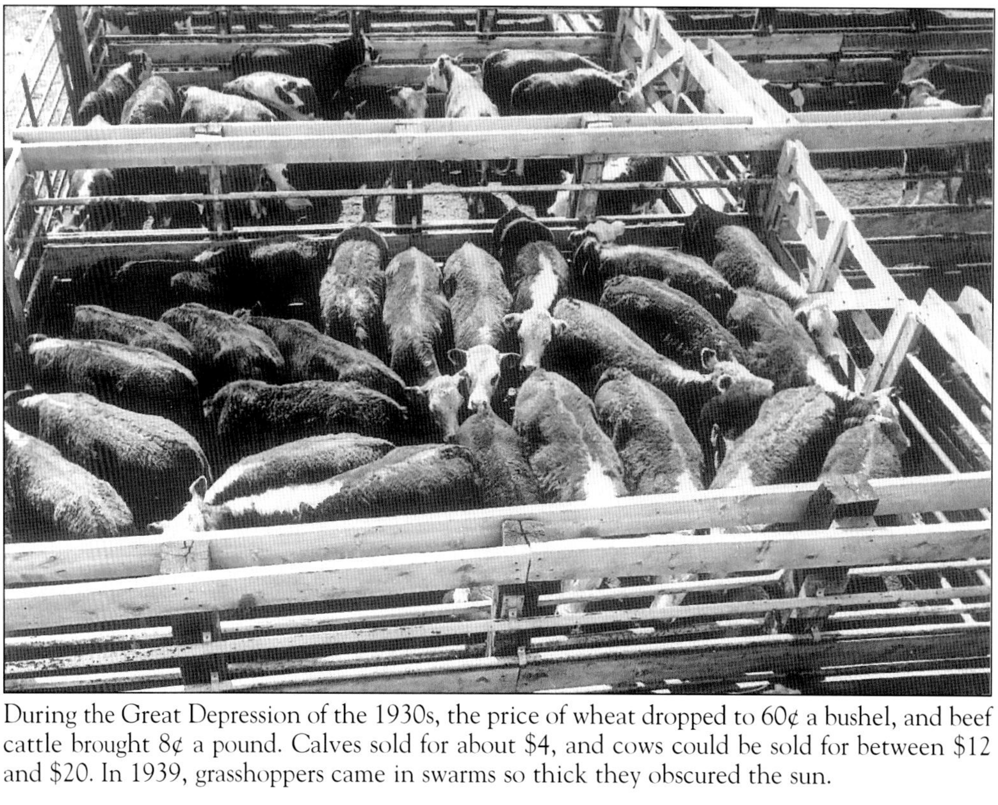

During the Great Depression of the 1930s, the price of wheat dropped to 60¢ a bushel, and beef cattle brought 8¢ a pound. Calves sold for about $4, and cows could be sold for between $12 and $20. In 1939, grasshoppers came in swarms so thick they obscured the sun.

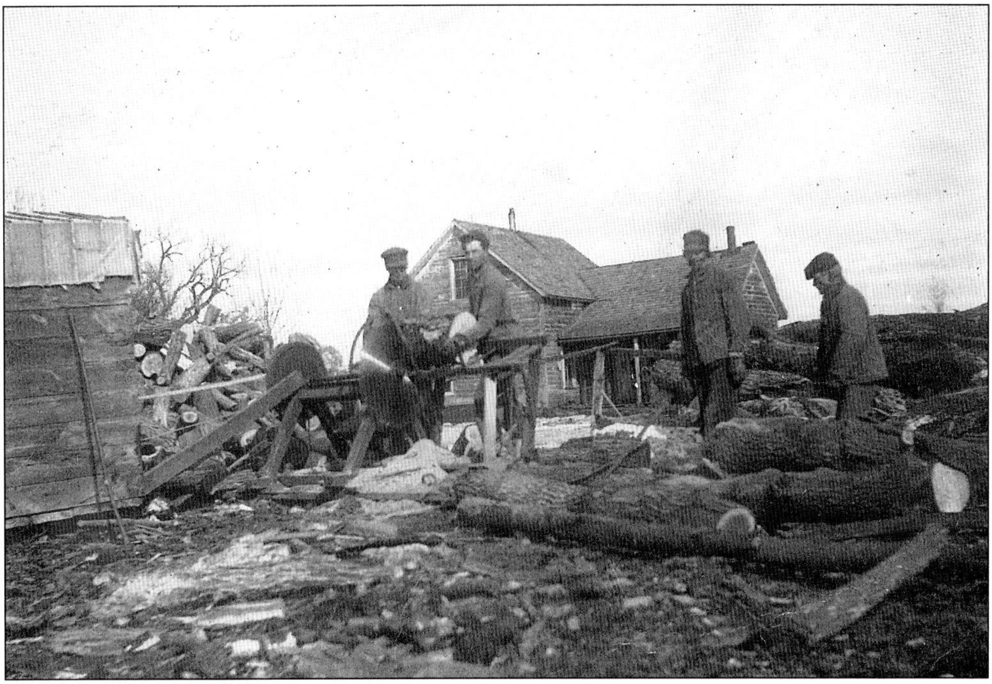

There was always work to do on the farm, even in winter. Farmers would saw trees for firewood, fix machinery, repair buildings, shovel snow, repair harnesses, and clean barns and chicken coops—and that was just work outside the house. Inside, the women were cooking, canning, quilting, mending and patching clothes, taking care of kids, knitting socks, making beds, and killing bed bugs.

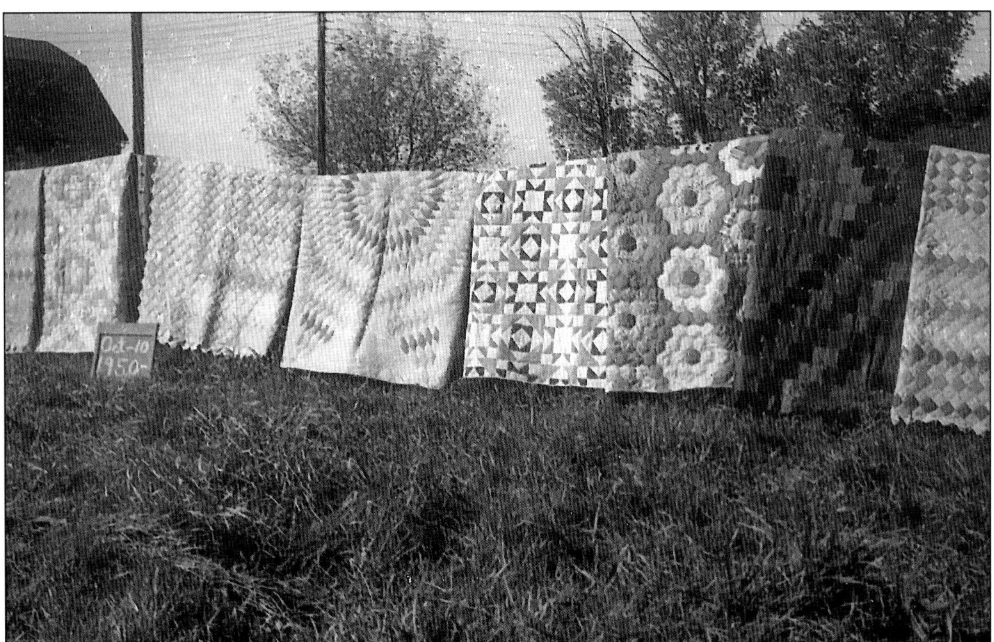

Every summer more and more quilts would be hung on a fence to be photographed.

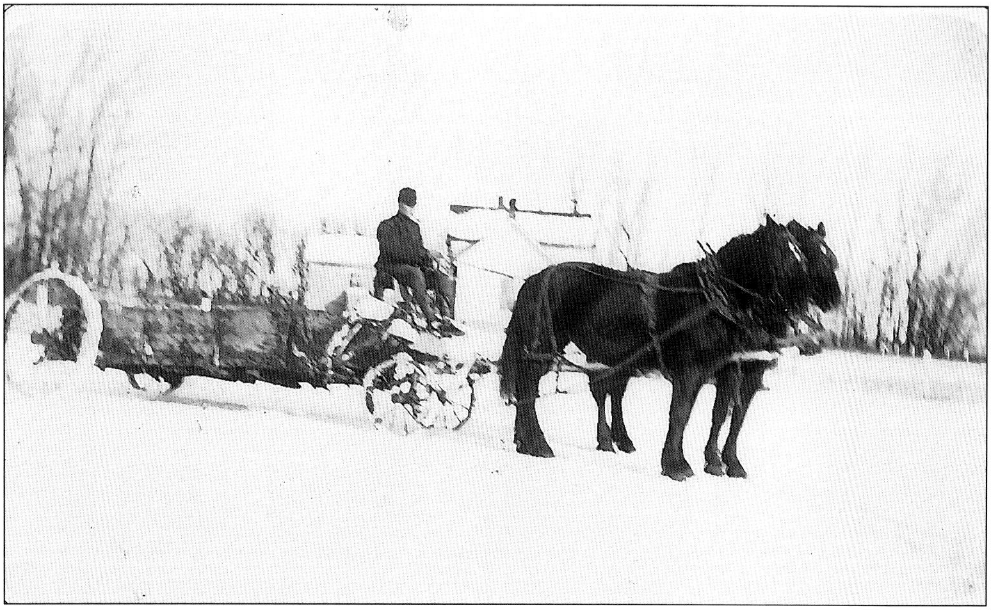

From 1900 to 1940, most of the barns in North Dakota were full of cows and horses in the winter. This meant that the farm's manure spreader was used every day, no matter what the weather was like. Now most of these barns are empty or have been blown down.

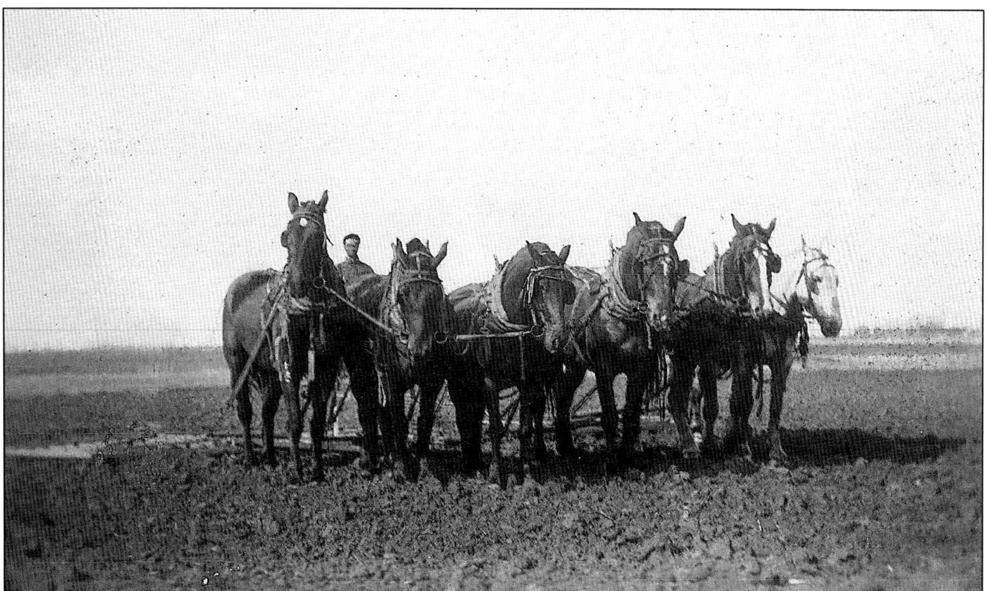

It took six sturdy workhorses to pull seven sections of a drag. The drags had steel spikes, which broke up the soil to get it ready for seeding.

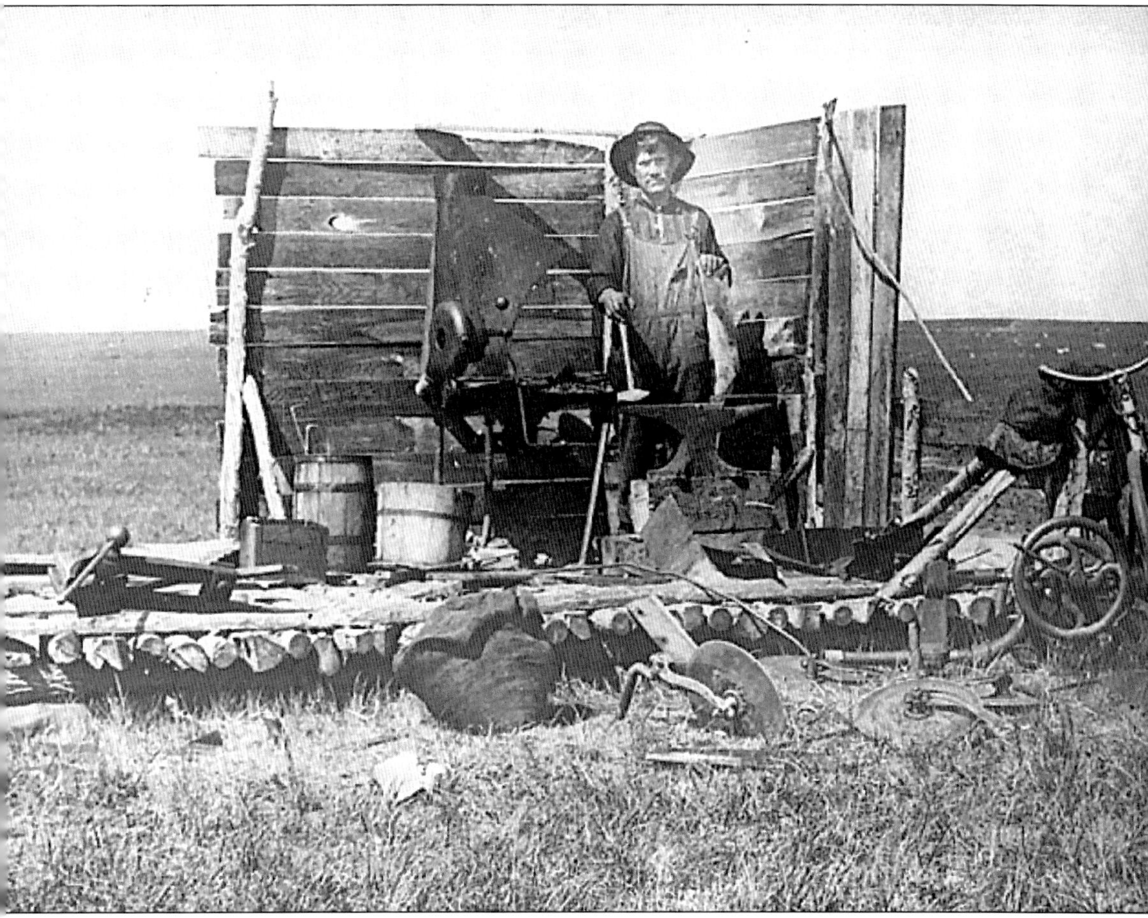

This pioneer blacksmith was a clever businessman. His shop was on a stoneboat, which could be pulled from farm to farm. In this period, every small town had a blacksmith shop for sharpening plowshares, welding, and other tasks. Some of the larger farms even had their own blacksmith shop. These shops began to disappear around 1980. Stoneboats were also used by early farmers to haul rocks off their land. Breaking the prairie sod and hauling off the rocks was no easy task.

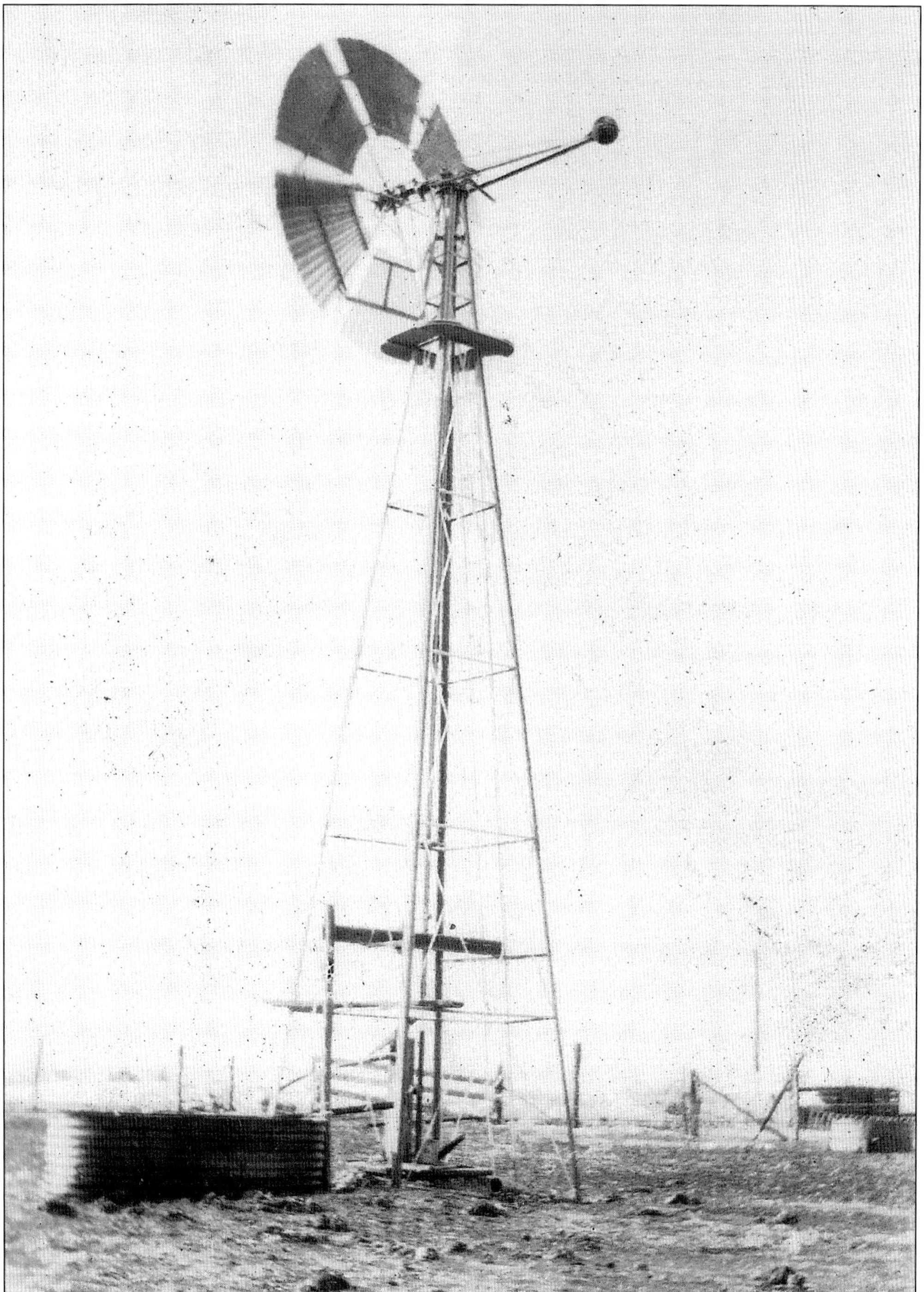

Long before the energy experts began to utilize windmills for power, they were used on almost every farm in North Dakota to pull water up to water tanks for the farm animals. Today you see windmills in many parts of the U.S. and Europe. North Dakotans have known for many years that wind is an abundant source of energy.

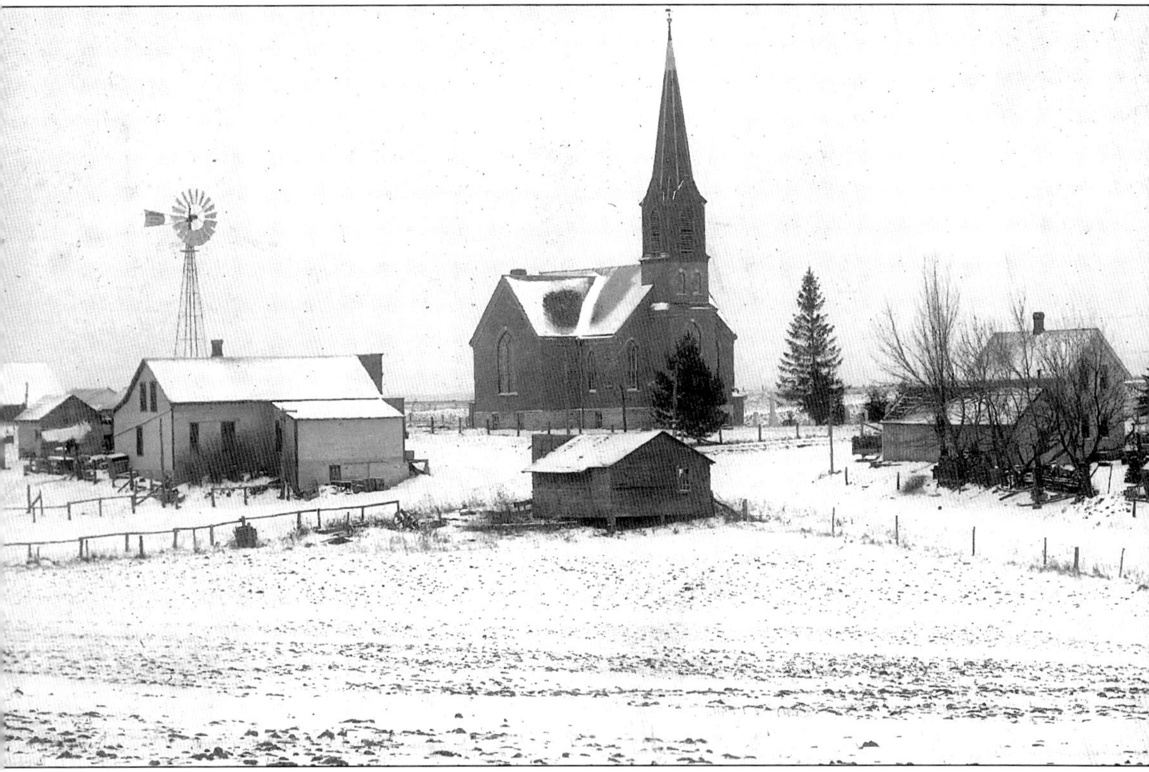

Black Hammer, Minnesota, is a small town near Spring Grove, and many people from this area moved up to North Dakota. This photograph shows that the windmill was constructed near the church. Small towns did not have planning and zoning commissions.

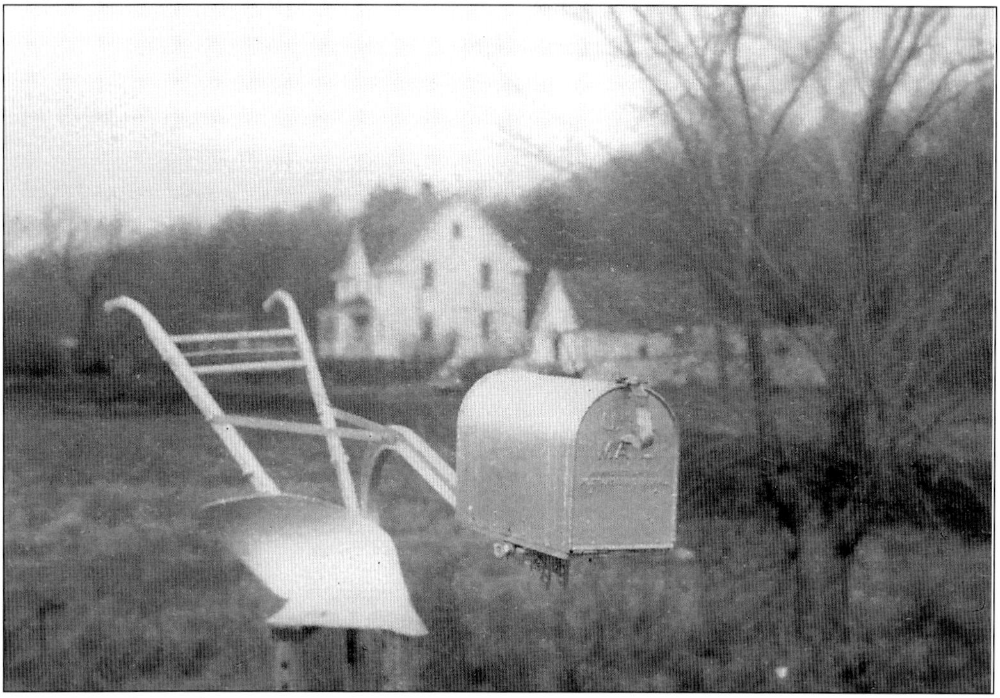

This old walking plow was turned into an art object and used as part of the mailbox.

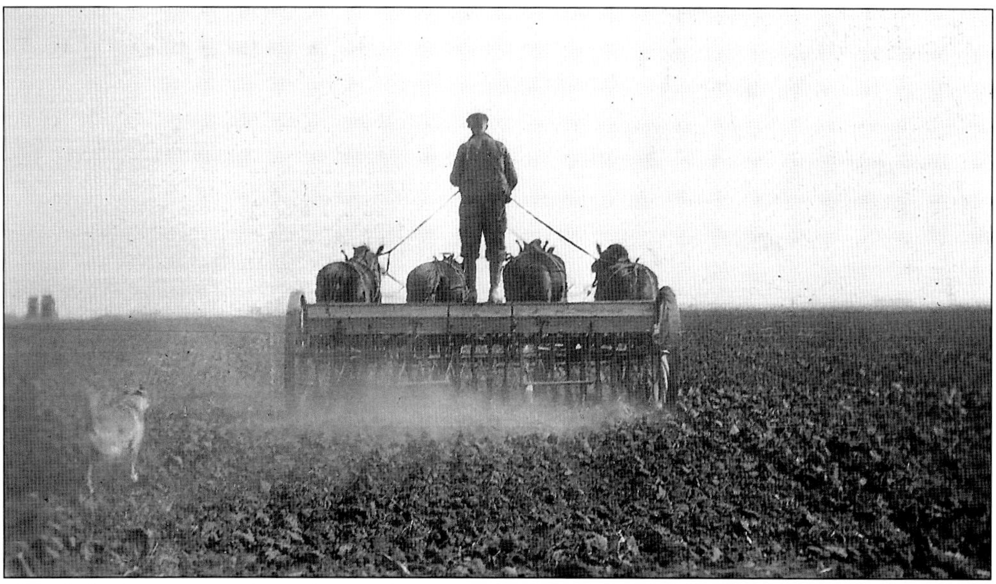

This drill planter is seeding wheat. There is a platform for the driver to stand on, but in order to get a better view over the horses, the driver balances himself on top of the drill and holds on tightly to the reins. His faithful dog and the town of Taft are visible on the left.

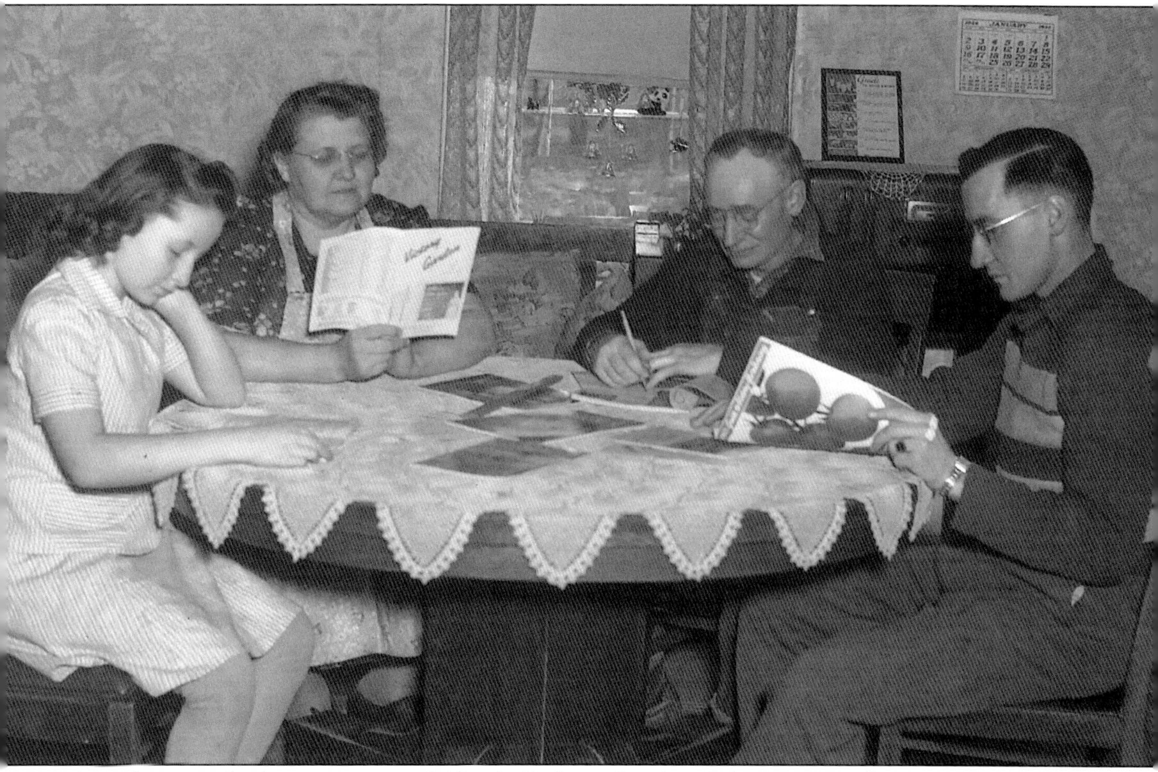

This photograph depicts a typical North Dakota family of the 1940s. There is a radio—television is still a few years off—and the telephone on the wall is certainly nothing like a cell phone! Today many farm families utilize computers.

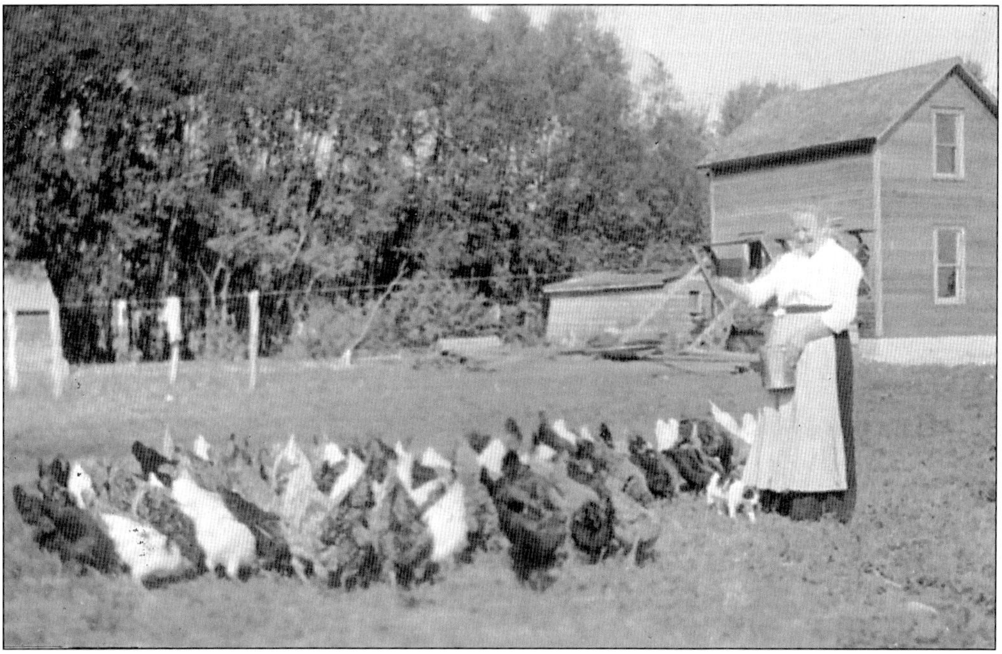

In the 1920s and '30s, it was common for people in towns to raise chickens in their back yards. Today, local zoning laws would probably not allow this. Some people even kept cows in town. In 1906, there were some two hundred cows still being milked in Bismarck.

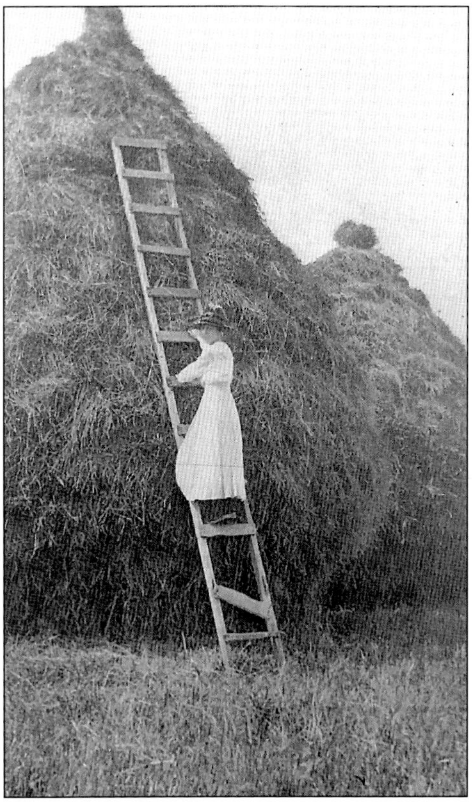

While the farmer waited for the threshing crew to arrive at his farm, he often stacked his grain in piles like this to keep it dry and accessible to the threshing crew. This young woman is making a personal inspection of the stack, apparently unaware that the second step of her ladder is broken!

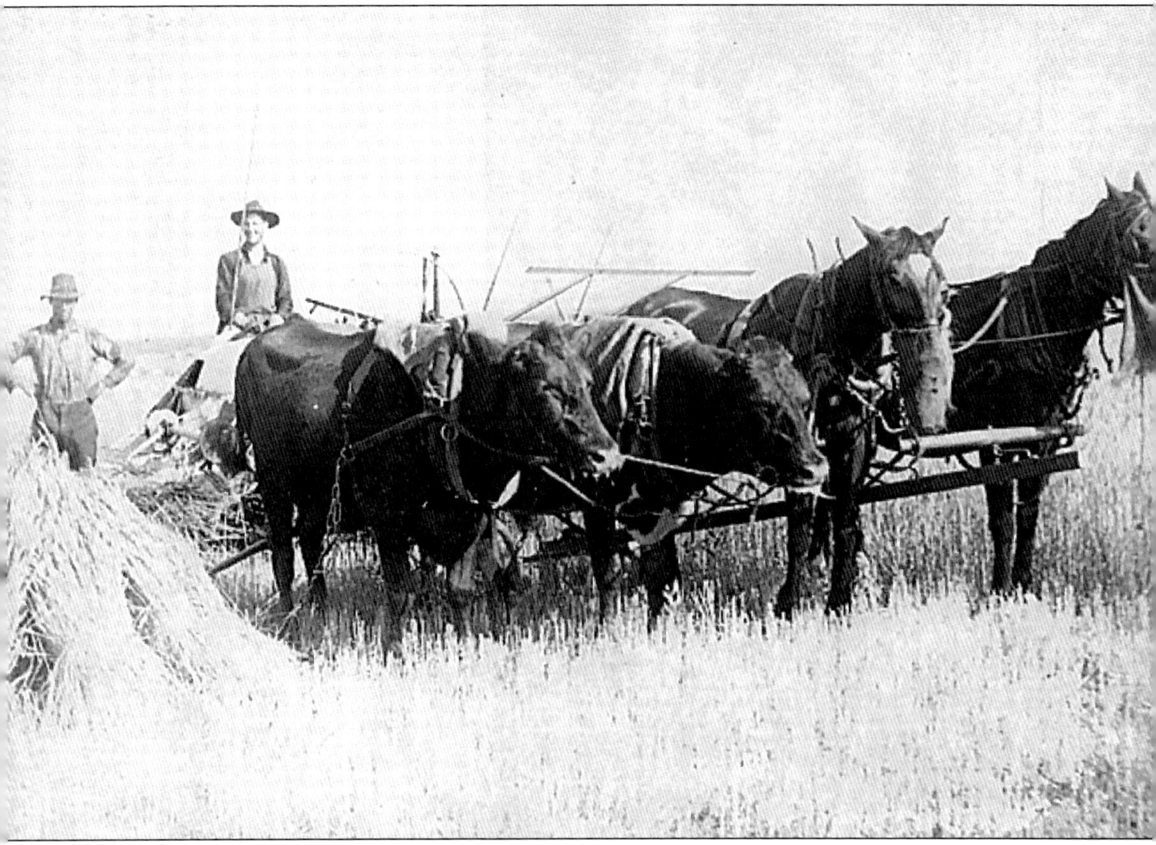

Early settlers had to be creative. In this case, one farmer put two horses and two cows to work. Now that is an interesting merger!

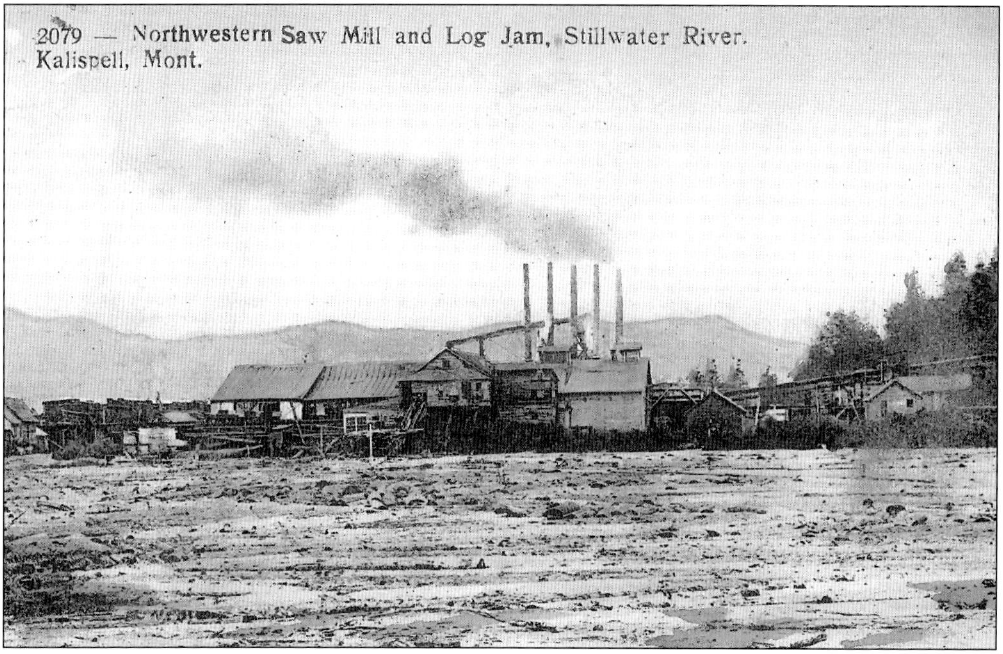

During the winter, some farmers ventured out-of-state to make some money. Some went to work in this sawmill in Kalispell, Montana, and others went elsewhere in Montana to "harvest" blocks of ice from frozen rivers. These blocks were stored in warehouses, covered with sawdust, and saved for use the next summer.

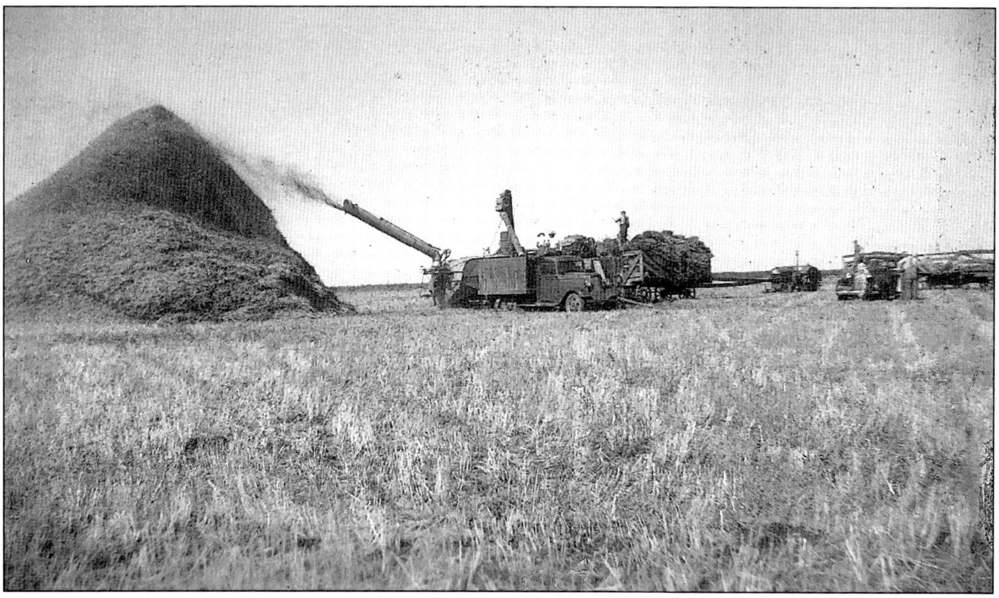

This strawstack has a very sharp peak at the top. However, this was not a natural occurrence—the boss in charge adjusted the blower like a paintbrush! This 1938 photograph shows wheat being threshed at the McAndrew Farm in Cass County.

Three

Young People

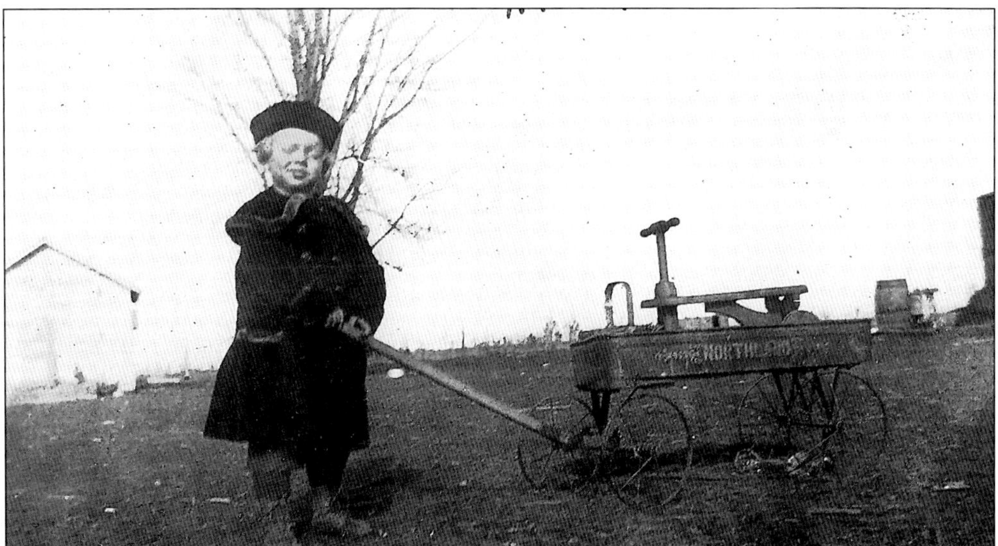

This little farm boy did well for himself on Christmas in 1921. He got a wagon with metal wheels, and a new homemade coat with a fur collar. The wooden tricycle would eventually be passed down to younger brothers.

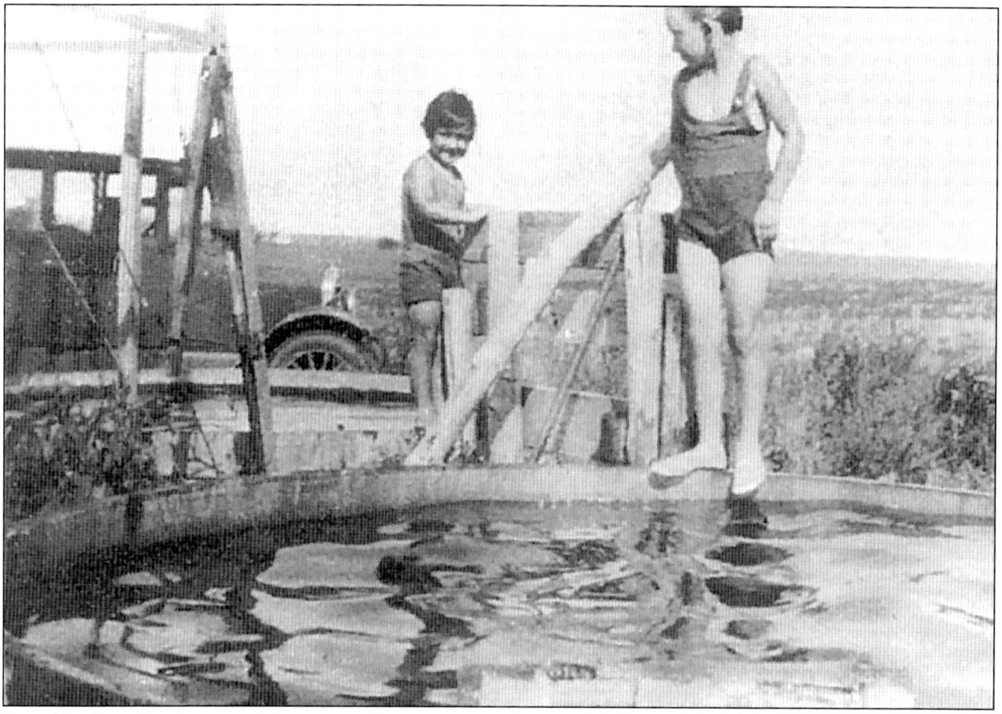

Lois Phillips Hudson and her sister Patty get ready to swim in a neighbor's stock tank. Lois has written many books and articles about her life in North Dakota. She was born in Jamestown and lived on a farm near Cleveland in Stutsman County.

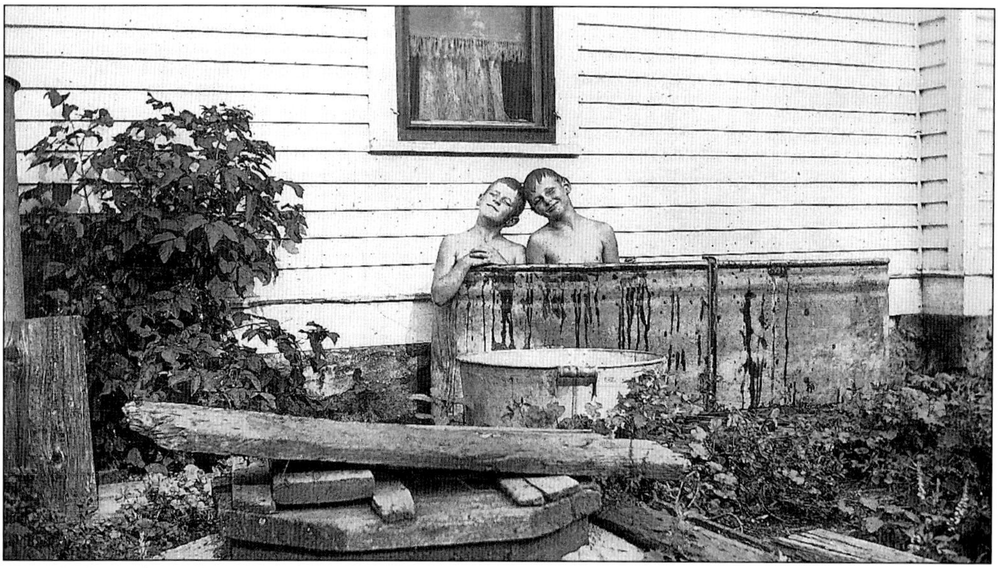

Farm kids—when they were not forced to work in the fields—had a good time. They could go for a swim in the cow's water tank, or they could hook up a horse to a buggy. They might also build a secret shack in the woods where they could hide to get out of doing farm work. The shack was also a good place to conceal forbidden magazines and corn tassel, which they were not supposed to smoke! One kid would always be posted as a lookout in case a parent appeared.

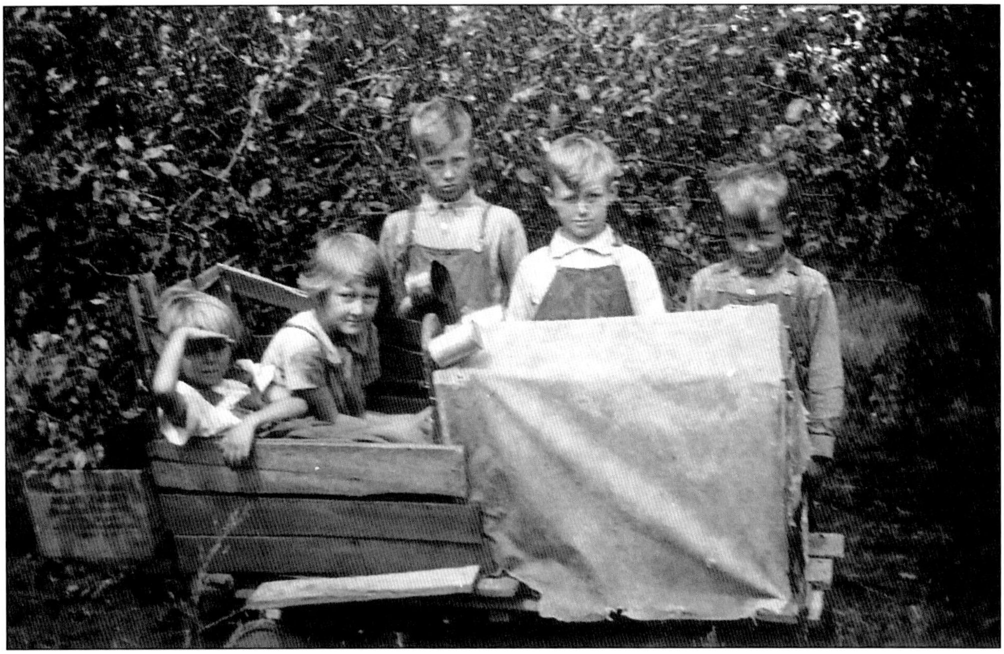

In 1927, toys in North Dakota did not come from F.A.O. Schwarz. Instead, kids made their own. Boards and canvas and a few tin cans made a pretty good car, like this speedy-looking one pictured above.

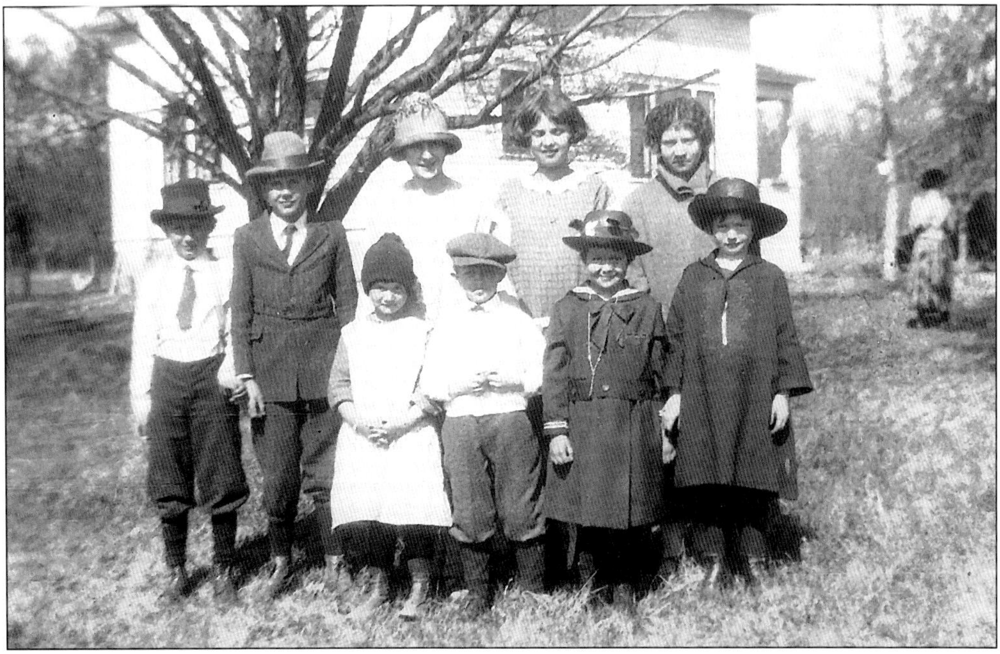

This was an important day—the annual school picnic. All of these kids attended a one-room school. The lady with the hat (in the center) is the teacher. During the Great Depression, many teachers were paid in promissory notes. Some stores would cash them, but others would not. Many school districts were so poor that they were forced to use volunteers to teach. Other schools simply closed down.

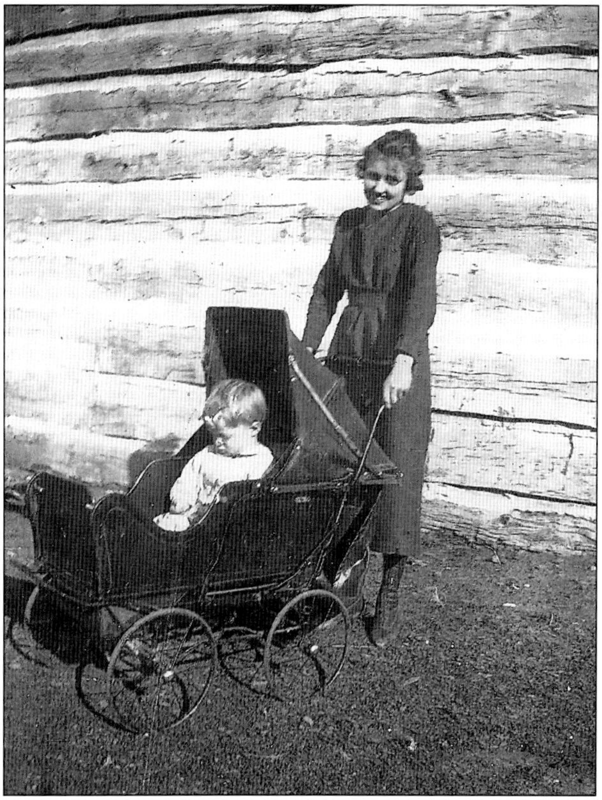

This young fellow is getting a ride in a state-of-the-art buggy pulled by a pretty young lady in this 1918 photo. Note her smile and her high button shoes. They both lived in the log house shown in the background.

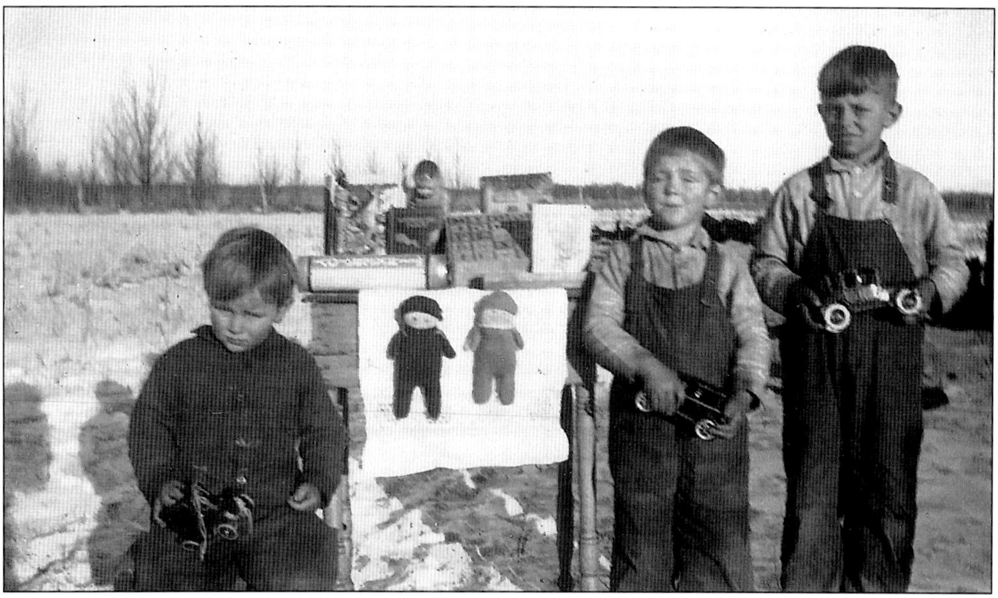

It was Christmas Day in 1925, and this photo had to be taken outside in the cold, as the flash camera was not yet common. The toys probably came from Montgomery Ward and were hidden under a bed until they could be placed under the Christmas tree. Next to the toys, the best gift was the sack of hard candy they would get at the annual Christmas church service. Real candles would decorate the Christmas tree, as electricity was not readily available.

Happiness is a little girl with two dolls! Note her high buckle shoes and her expression—not a care in the world.

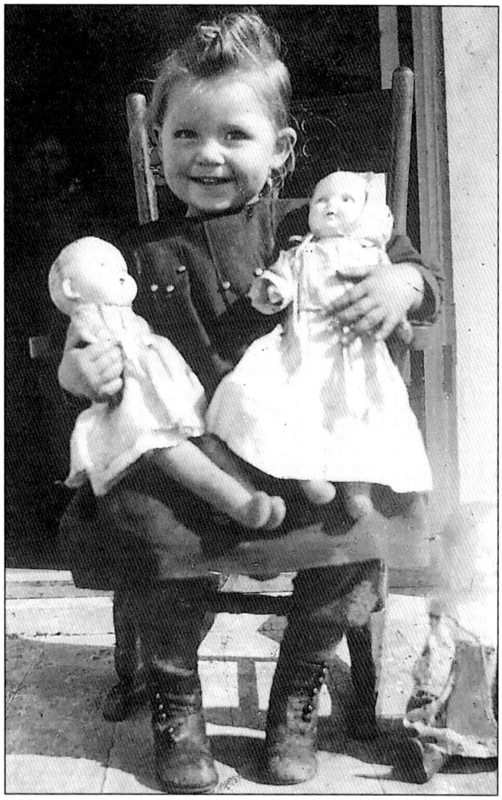

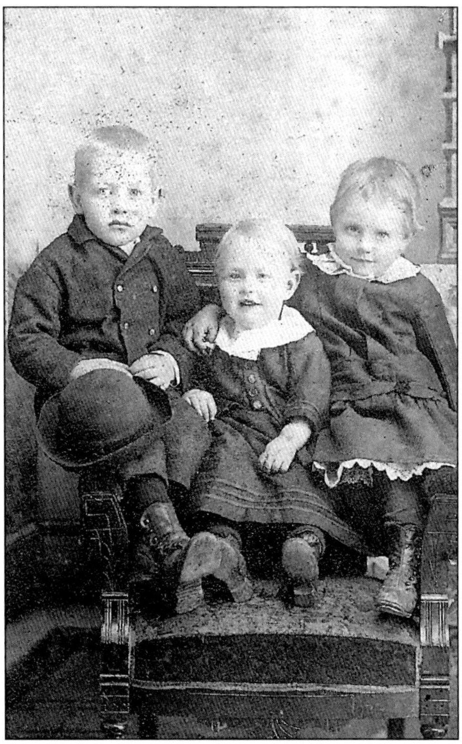

This is the way the young folks dressed up for the photographer around 1900. J.L. Skrivseth took this photograph at his studio in Hillsboro. On the back, he printed "Duplicates can be had at any time." Many of his photographs have appeared in centennial books published throughout North Dakota.

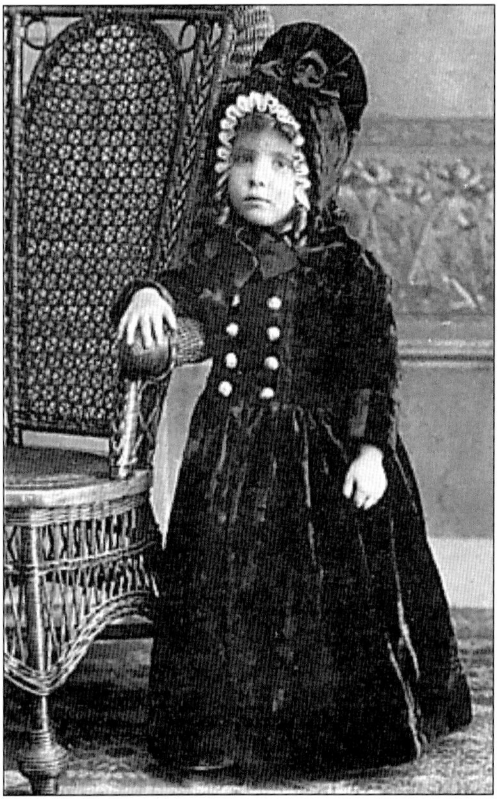

This young lady is all dressed up for Sunday school.

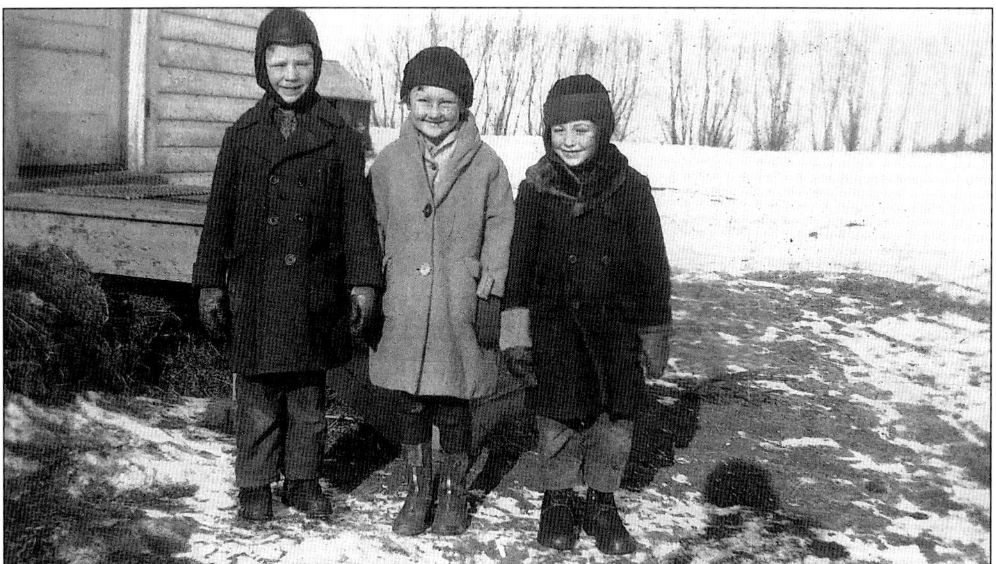

These three second-graders do not seem to be bothered by the weather in this 1927 photo. They are, from left to right: James McAndrew, Myrtle Johnson, and Milton Aasen of River School 108 in Noble Township, Cass County.

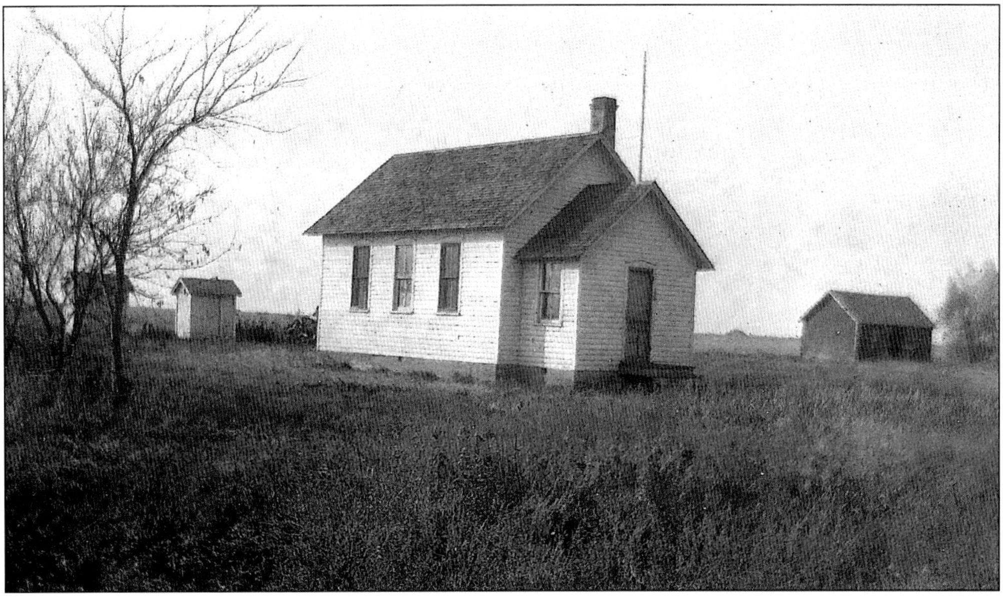

From 1900 to 1930, North Dakota had hundreds of one-room schools like this one in Cass County.

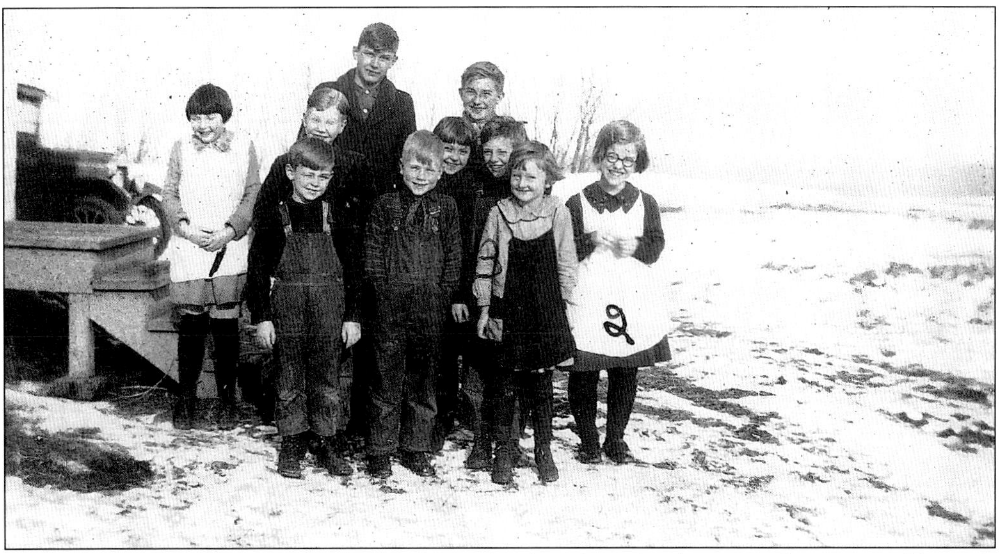

In 1928, these kids all attended a one-room school. Judging by the snow, this was a cold North Dakota day. However, the kids probably did not mind too much—they were probably all wearing long johns.

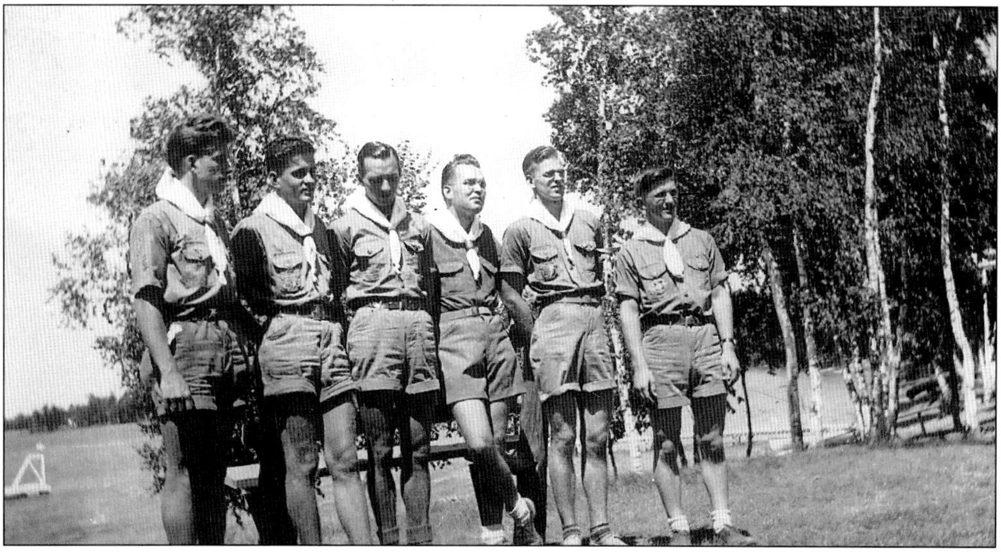

According to the Boy Scouts of America, scouting has always been a popular activity in North Dakota. Because of the sparse population of the state, many of the kids participated in the "Lone Scout" program since there were often not enough kids to form a troop. Many boy scouts from the Fargo area and throughout eastern North Dakota would go to Camp Shawondasee on Long Lake, near Detroit Lakes. For the farm kids lucky enough to get to this camp, it was like a paradise after coming from the dusty plains of North Dakota.

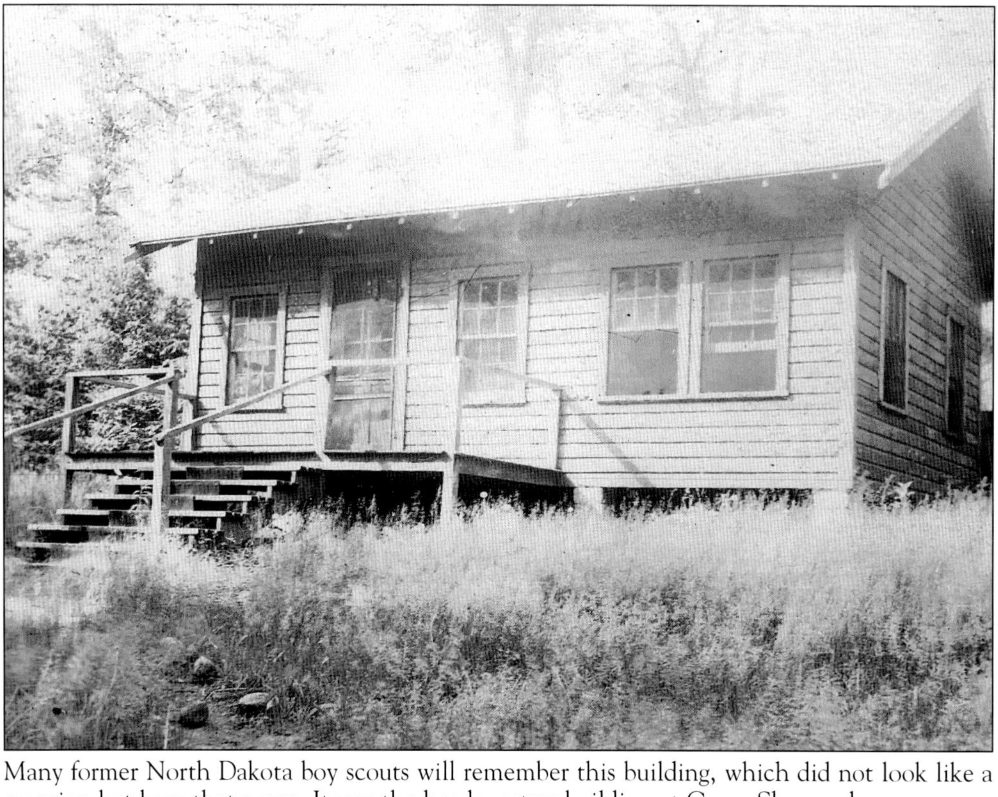

Many former North Dakota boy scouts will remember this building, which did not look like a mansion but bore that name. It was the headquarters building at Camp Shawondasee.

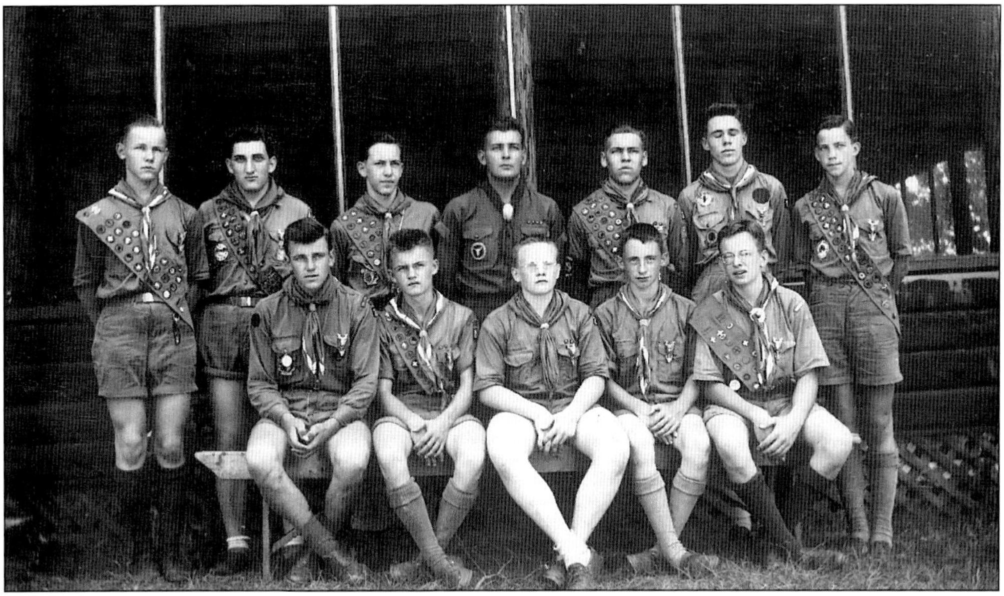

These North Dakotans were part of an Eagle Scout troop. This photograph was taken in 1941.

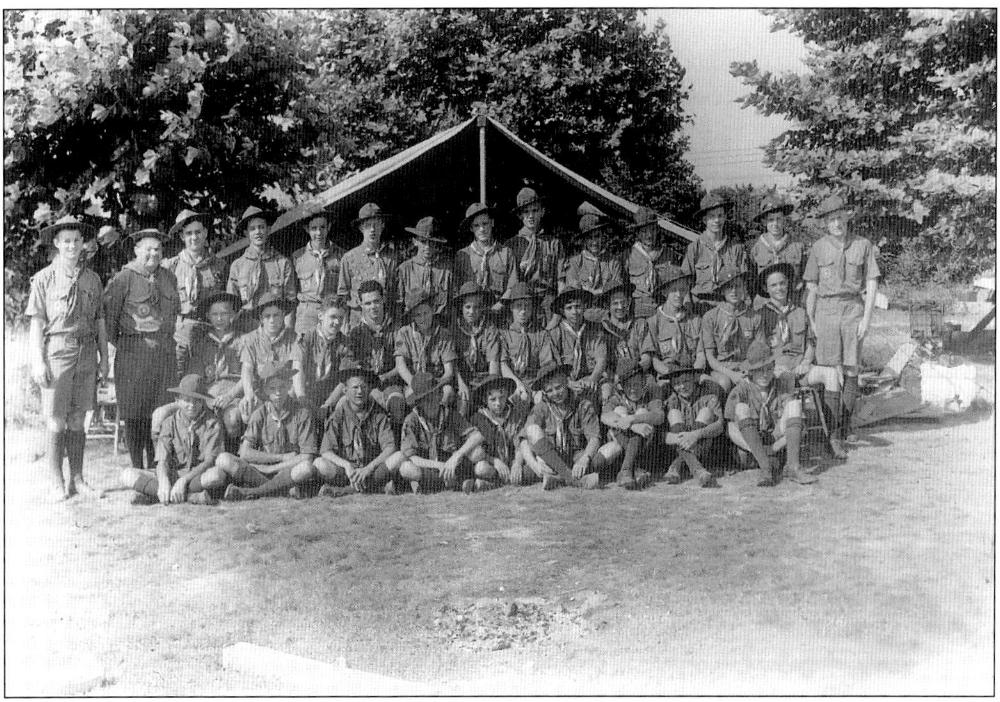

These scouts represented North Dakota at the national Boy Scout Jamboree in Washington, D.C. in July of 1937.

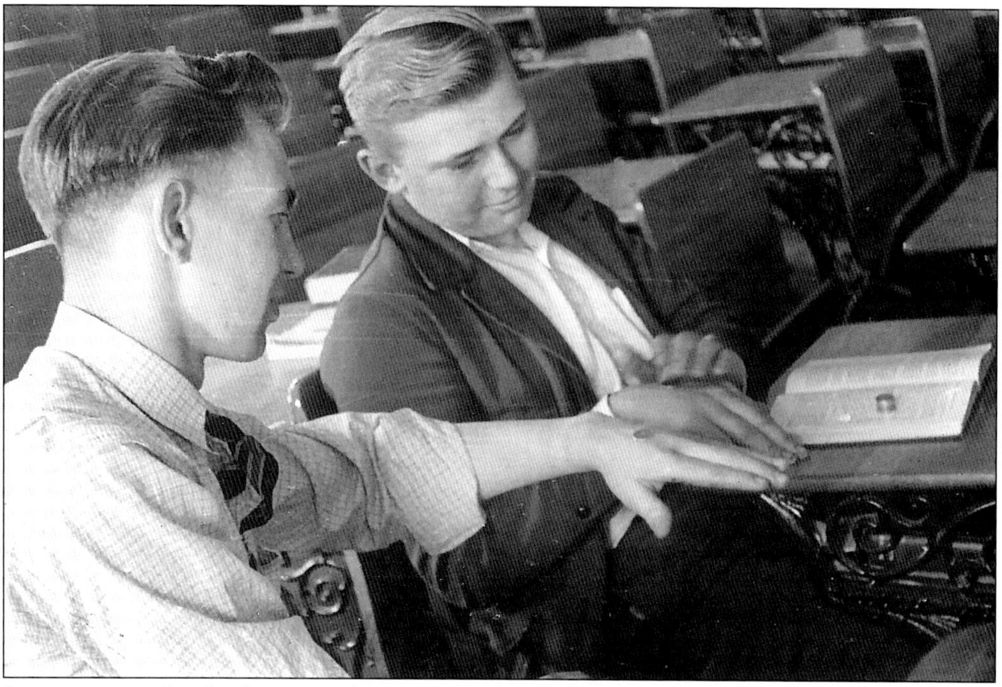

It was against school rules to match pennies in the study hall at Hillsboro High School, but Lyle Henning and Darrel Sorum were caught by an alert photographer and reported!

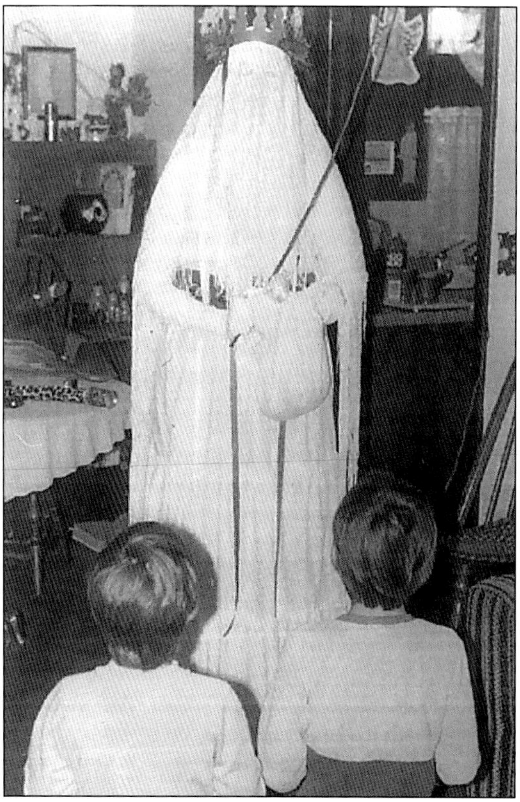

German-Russian children kneel before the veiled "Krischtkindl" on Christmas. The female masquerader carries a willow switch in one hand and a bag of sweets in the other.

Four

POLITICS

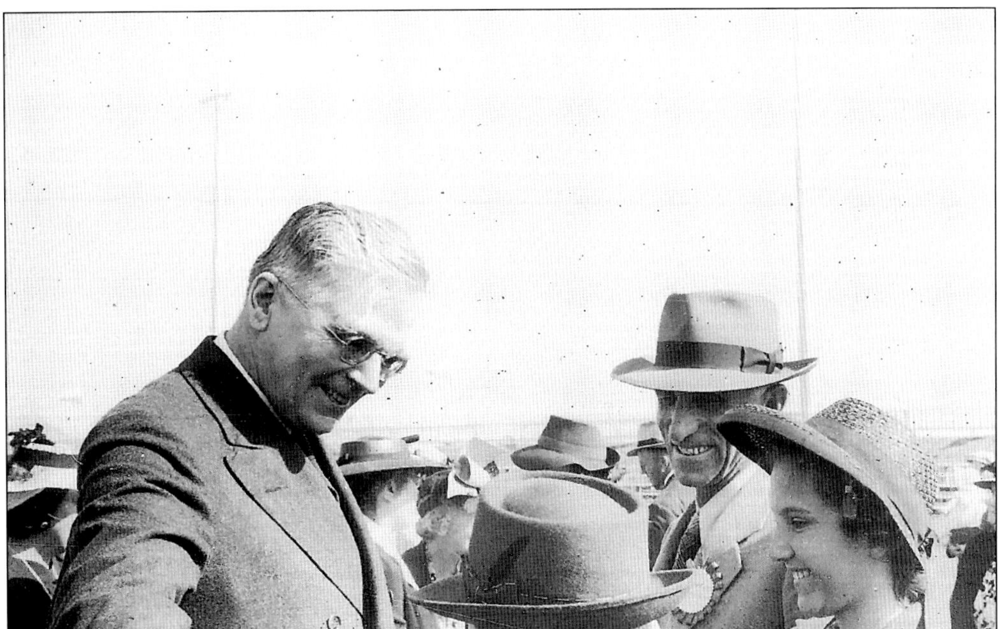

North Dakota governor John Moses was photographed here at an event in Mayville. He served from 1939 to 1944. He towered over his audience—a great political asset.

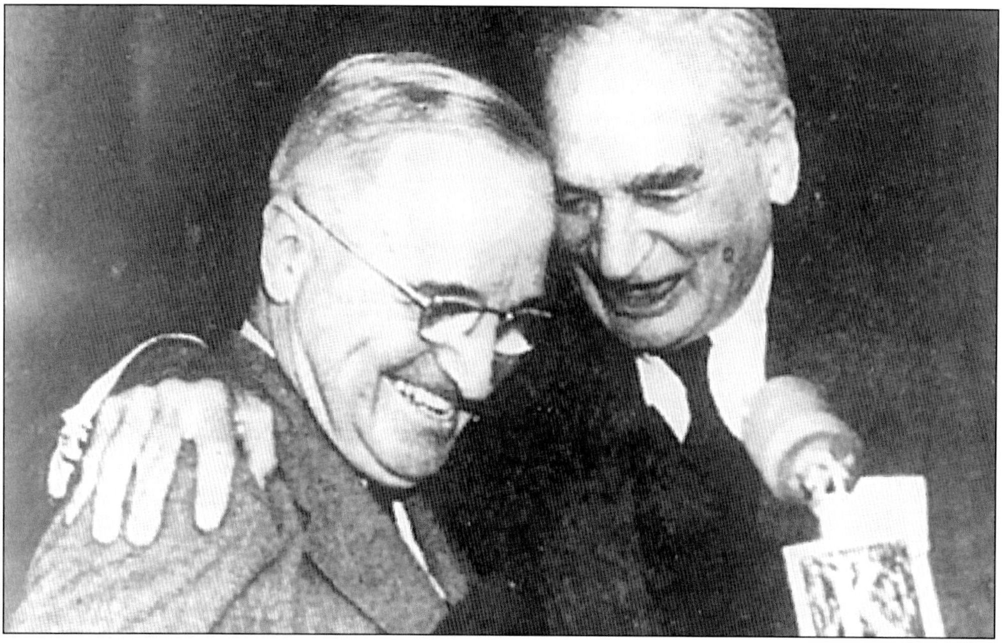

President Harry Truman was a Democrat and Bill Langer a Republican, but they had no problems understanding each other.

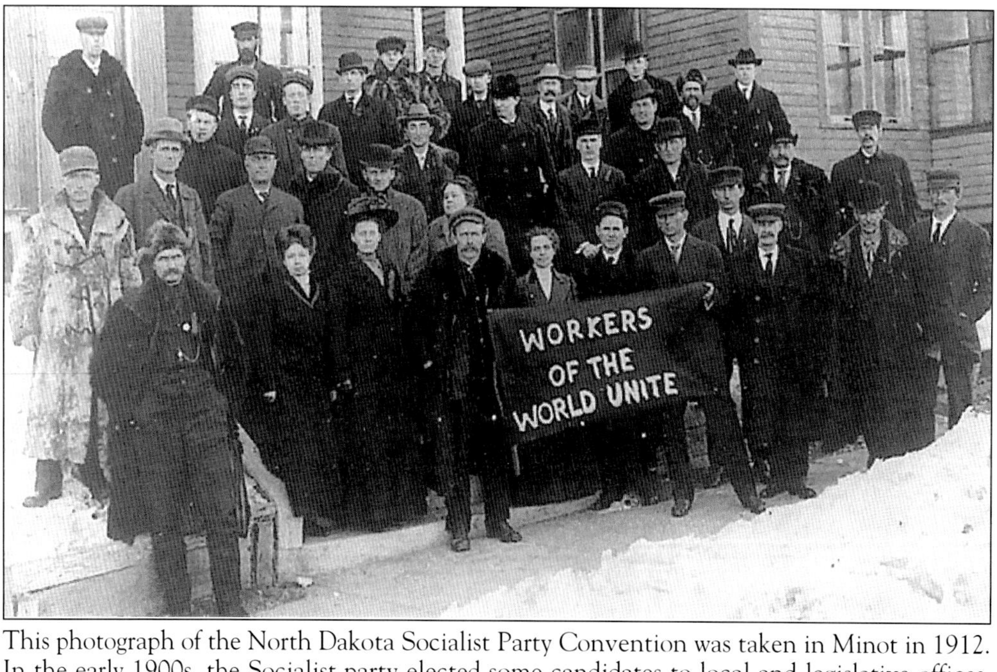

This photograph of the North Dakota Socialist Party Convention was taken in Minot in 1912. In the early 1900s, the Socialist party elected some candidates to local and legislative offices, but lost strength during World War I.

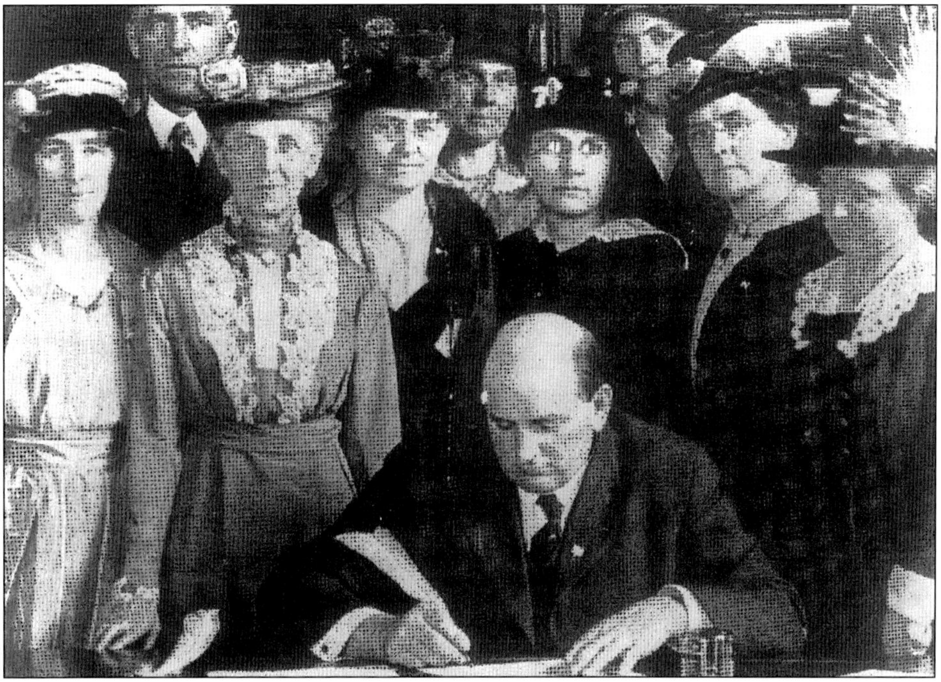

Governor Lynn J. Frazier signs the women's suffrage bill on January 23, 1917, giving North Dakota women the right to vote. This milestone law was stubbornly resisted, which may surprise some readers of this book.

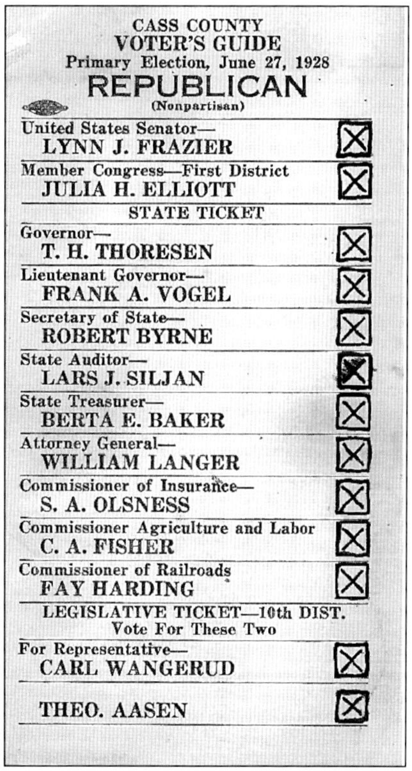

CASS COUNTY
VOTER'S GUIDE
Primary Election, June 27, 1928
REPUBLICAN
(Nonpartisan)

United States Senator—
LYNN J. FRAZIER

Member Congress—First District
JULIA H. ELLIOTT

STATE TICKET

Governor—
T. H. THORESEN

Lieutenant Governor—
FRANK A. VOGEL

Secretary of State—
ROBERT BYRNE

State Auditor—
LARS J. SILJAN

State Treasurer—
BERTA E. BAKER

Attorney General—
WILLIAM LANGER

Commissioner of Insurance—
S. A. OLSNESS

Commissioner Agriculture and Labor
C. A. FISHER

Commissioner of Railroads
FAY HARDING

LEGISLATIVE TICKET—10th DIST.
Vote For These Two

For Representative—
CARL WANGERUD

THEO. AASEN

Lynn Frazier ran on this ticket and was elected.

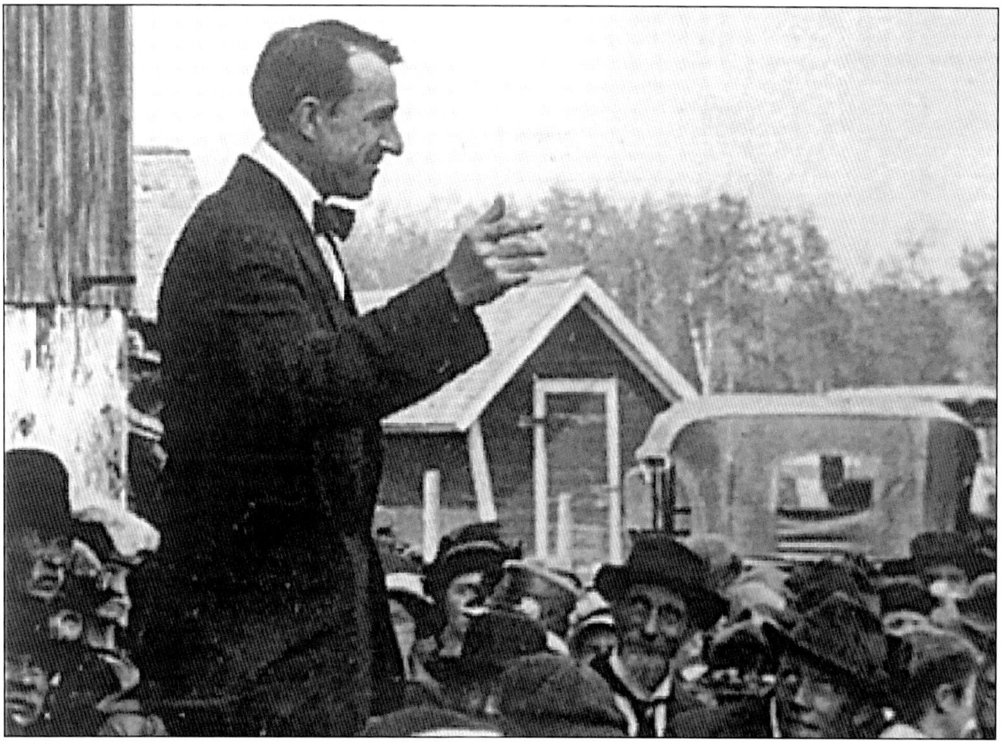

Two of the most colorful politicians in North Dakota were A.C. Townley (above), the founding father of the Nonpartisan League, and William Langer (below), governor and senator, and a participant in many political brawls.

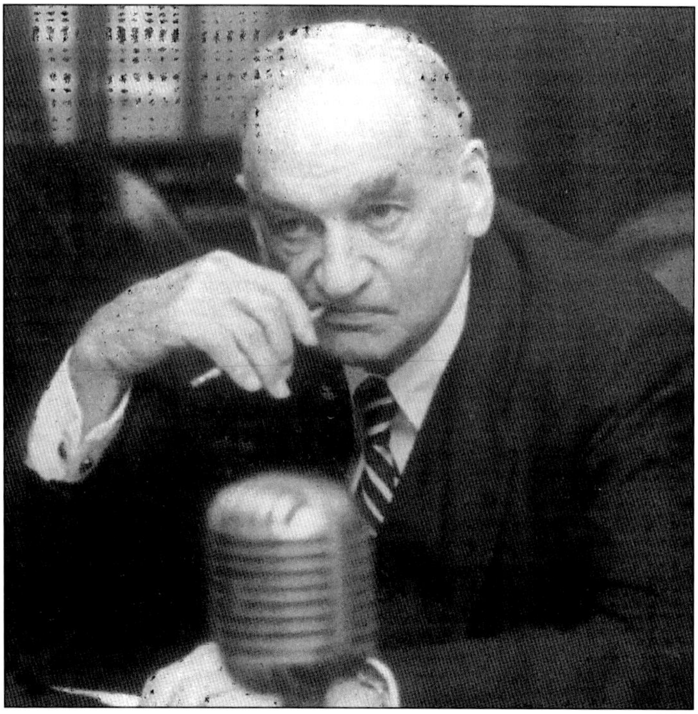

Five

WAR

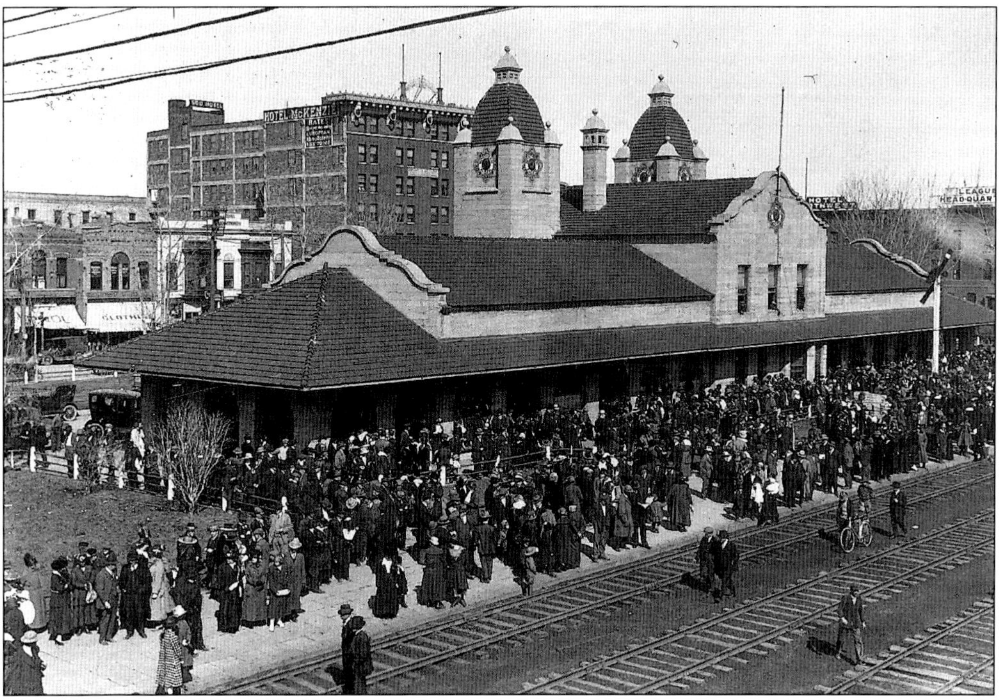

In 1917, this crowd gathered at the Bismarck railroad depot to see World War I soldiers off to war. Unfortunately, this scene was held again around North Dakota for World War II and other wars to follow.

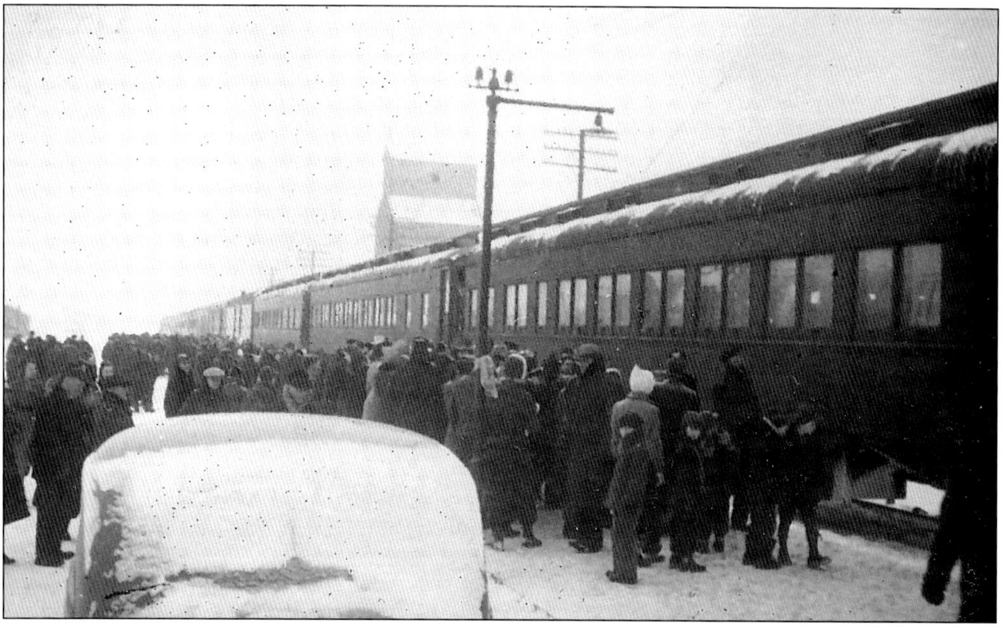

On February 26, 1941, a special train pulled into Hillsboro, North Dakota, to pick up Company L of the 164th North Dakota National Guard. The regiment trained at Camp Claiborne, Louisiana. They were then shipped to the South Pacific, where they fought the Japanese at Guadalcanal and Bougainville. Other North Dakota towns with soldiers in the 164th regiment included Bismarck, Fargo, Devils Lake, Harvey, Bottineau, Cavalier, Grafton, Rugby, Cando, Williston, Carrington, Valley City, Jamestown, Edgeley, Wahpeton, Dickinson, Grand Forks, and Hillsboro. Soldiers from all over Traill County belonged to Hillsboro's Company L.

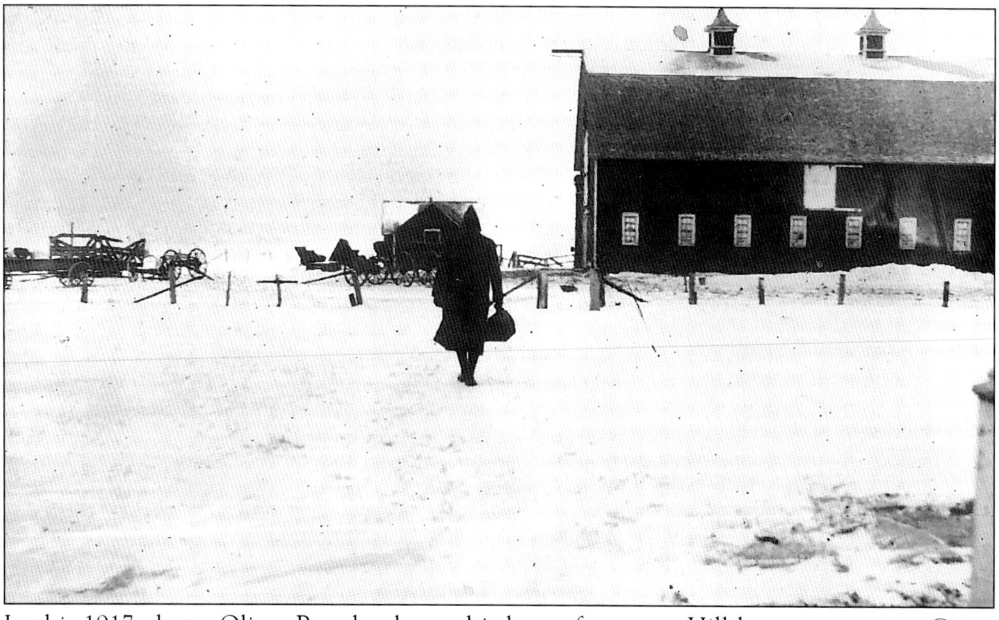

In this 1917 photo, Oliver Brenden leaves his home farm near Hillsboro to return to Camp Dodge, Iowa, and then to sail to France. He died in 1922 as a result of poison gas used by the enemy.

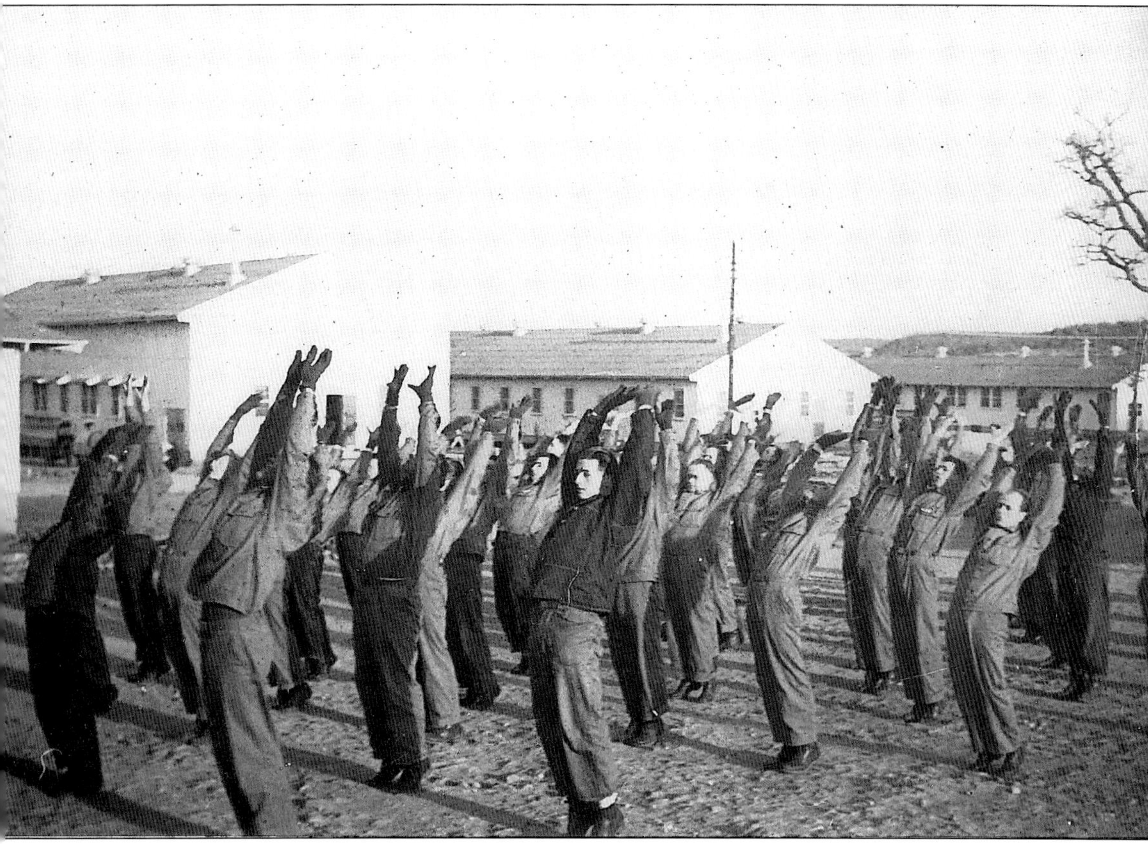

North Dakota's 164th Infantry regiment fought in Mexico, France, and at Guadalcanal. It suffered very heavy losses in Guadalcanal, being the first army group there not having the support it needed. Nearly 30,000 North Dakotans served in World War I. Approximately 70,000 served in World War II.

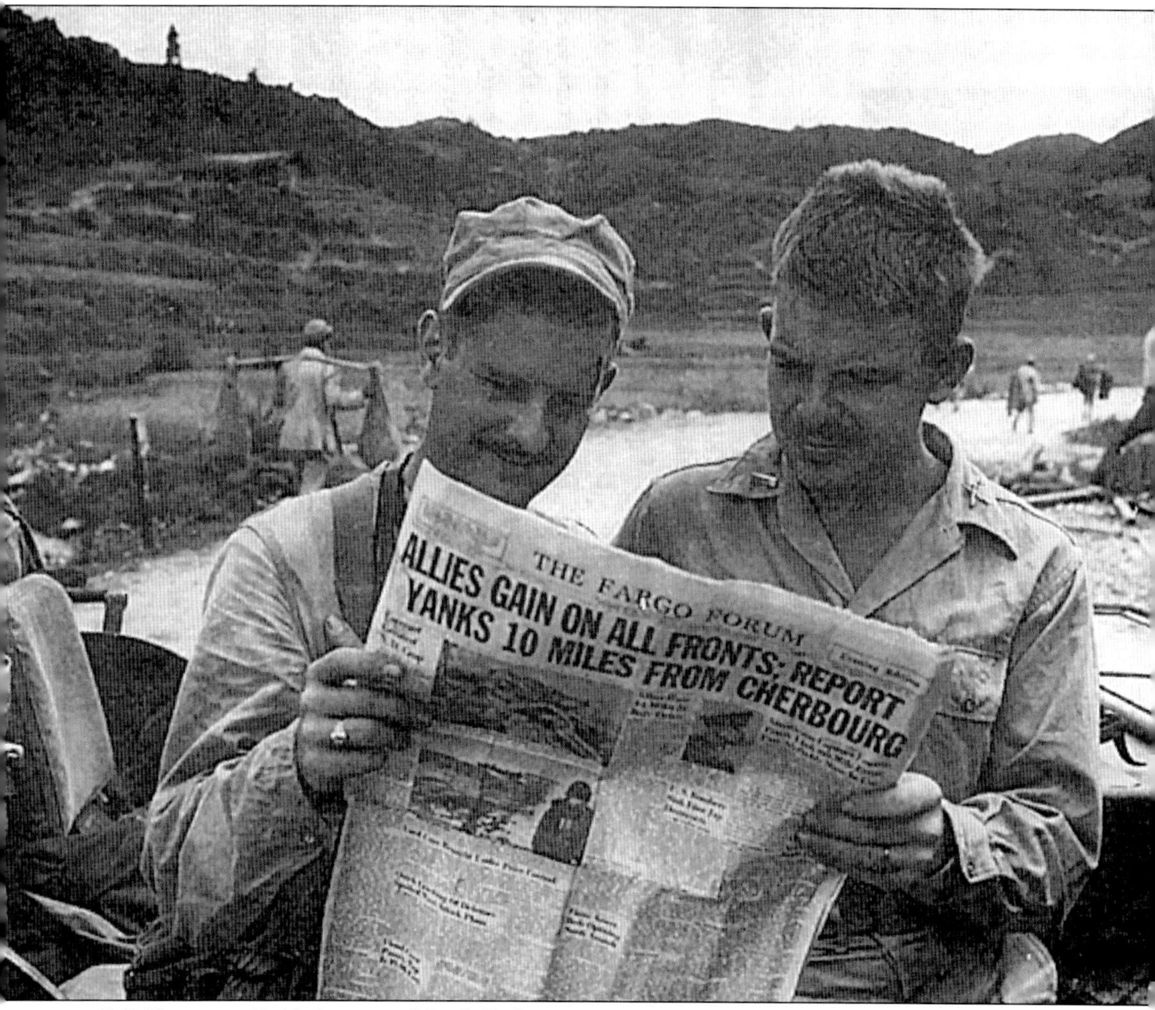

Bill Shemorry (left), longtime North Dakota newspaperman and writer, is pictured here reading the *Fargo Forum* while in China during World War II. Lt. John Sanders is on the right. Mr. Shemorry provided a number of photos and words for this book. He has written many books and articles about North Dakota.

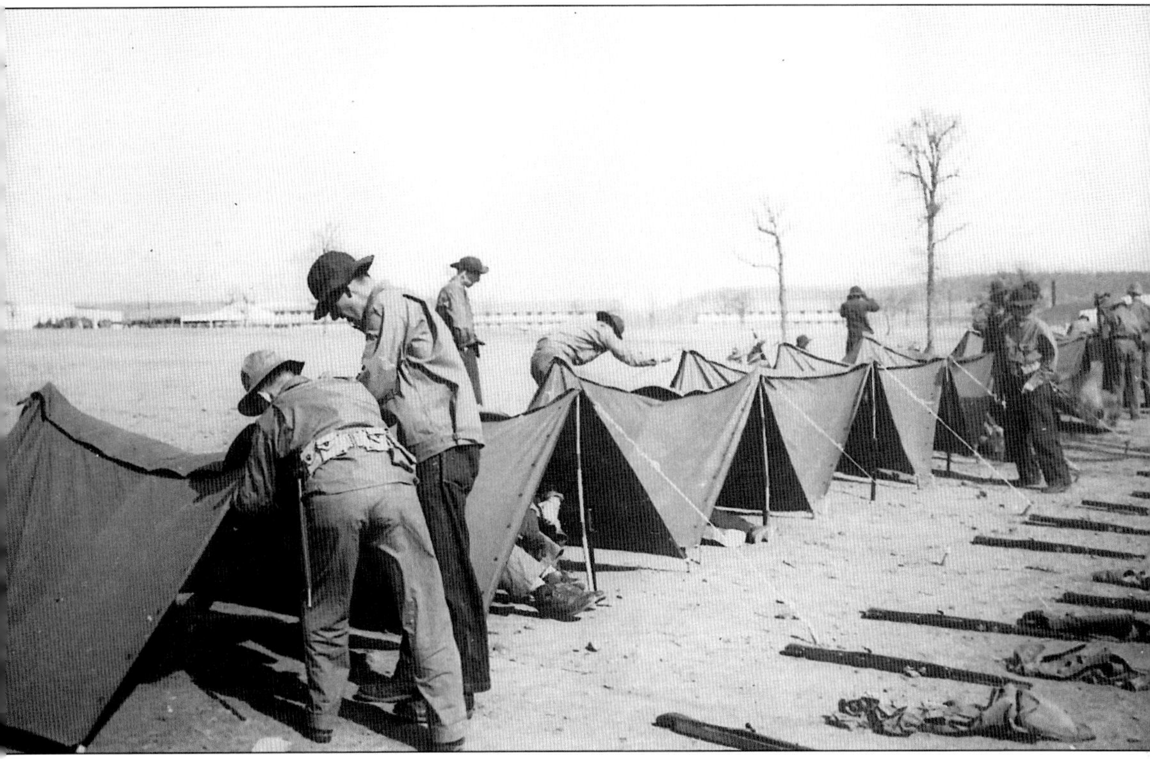

Many young North Dakota men were drafted during World War II and sent to Camp Wolters in Texas, among other training camps, most of which were located in southern states. This forced the North Dakota soldiers to learn about chiggers, grits, and heat reaching above 100 degrees. A colonel in a training camp once told the author of this book that North Dakotans made good soldiers because they were familiar with machinery, hard work, and were used to inclement weather.

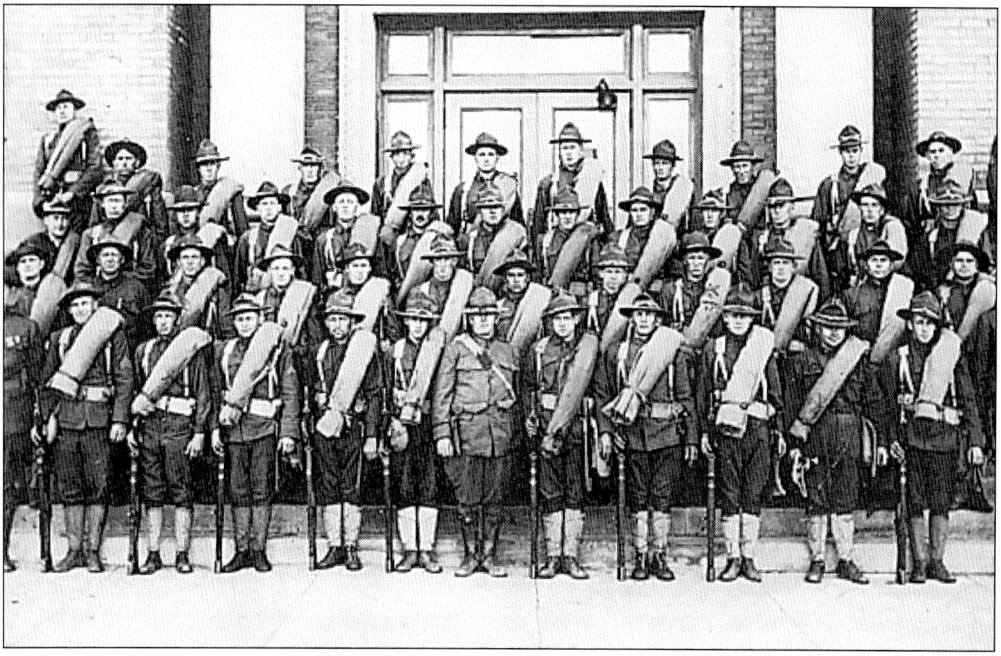

Pictured here is Company L of the 164th Infantry in a photo taken before going off for training at Camp Greene, North Carolina, in 1917. On Christmas Day of that year, they were somewhere in France. Eight were killed and forty were wounded from Company L during that war. Note the bedrolls wrapped around the soldiers.

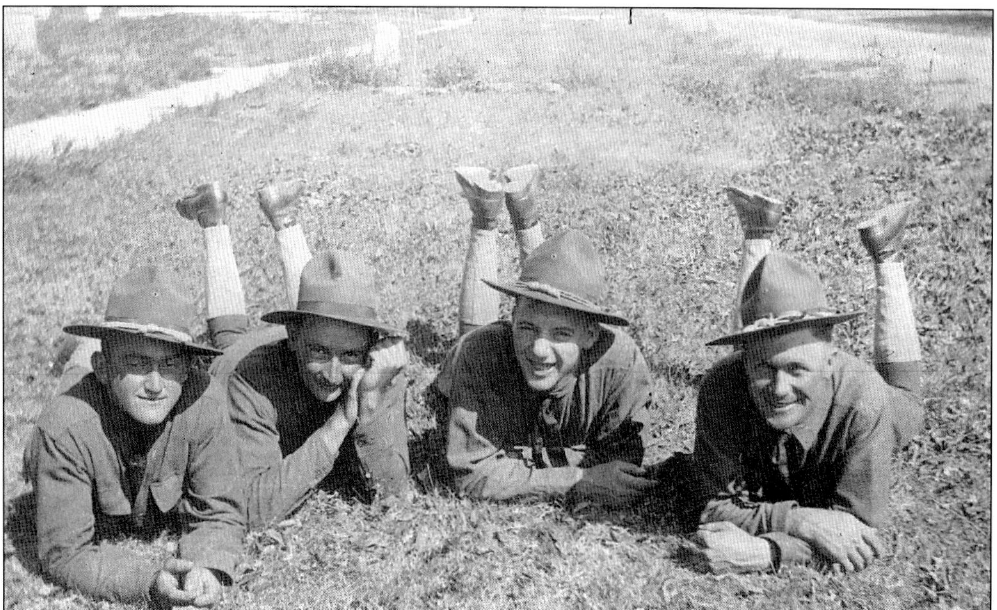

These World War I soldiers are relaxing on the grass in Hillsboro before heading off to the bloody trench warfare in France. The body of one Hillsboro soldier was found 18 years later and was returned to Hillsboro with full military honors.

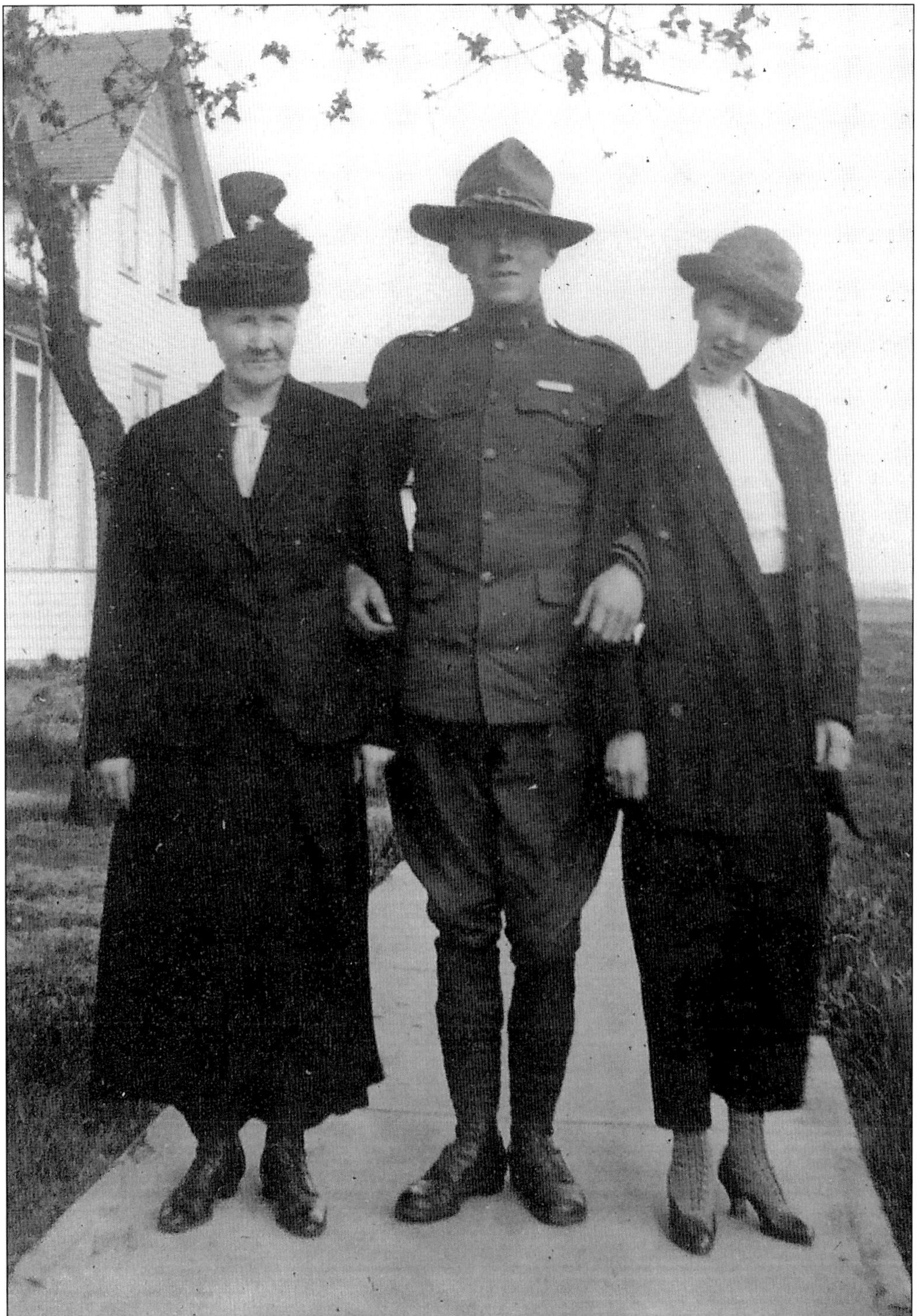

World War I soldier George Robinson was greeted on his return from France by his wife Clara, and mother-in-law Ann. Note the jaunty tilt of the campaign hat, popular during that war.

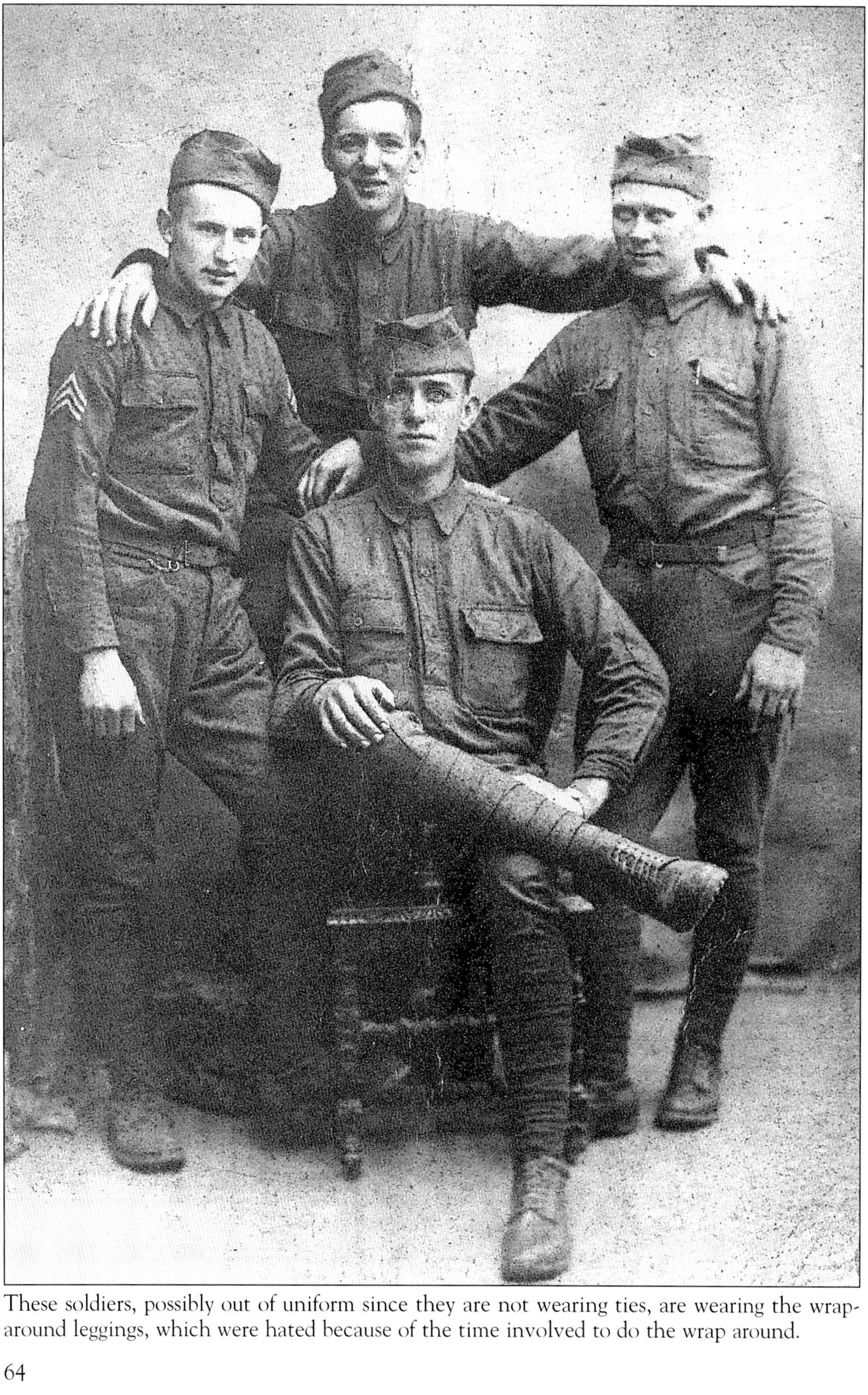

These soldiers, possibly out of uniform since they are not wearing ties, are wearing the wrap-around leggings, which were hated because of the time involved to do the wrap around.

Six

TRANSPORTATION

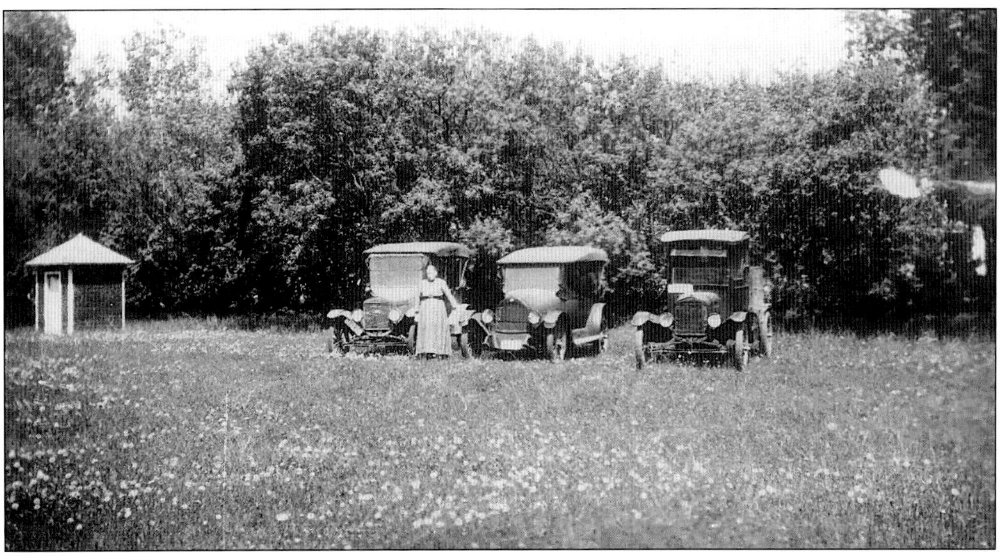

Transportation in North Dakota was difficult during the first part of the twentieth century. Dirt and gravel roads were not the swiftest routes for travel. Although they were well-paid for their efforts, the Great Northern and the Northern Pacific Railroads contributed greatly to the settlement of North Dakota. At one time, the railroads were given one-fourth of all the land in the state. The railroad depots in every town were the center of action with people and freight constantly coming and going. Now many of the depots stand empty, made obsolete by trucks, cars, and airplanes. Here Mrs. Torger Brenden inspects three cars that her sons have purchased. The cars are early Overlands and Fords. The building on the left is a smokehouse for curing hams.

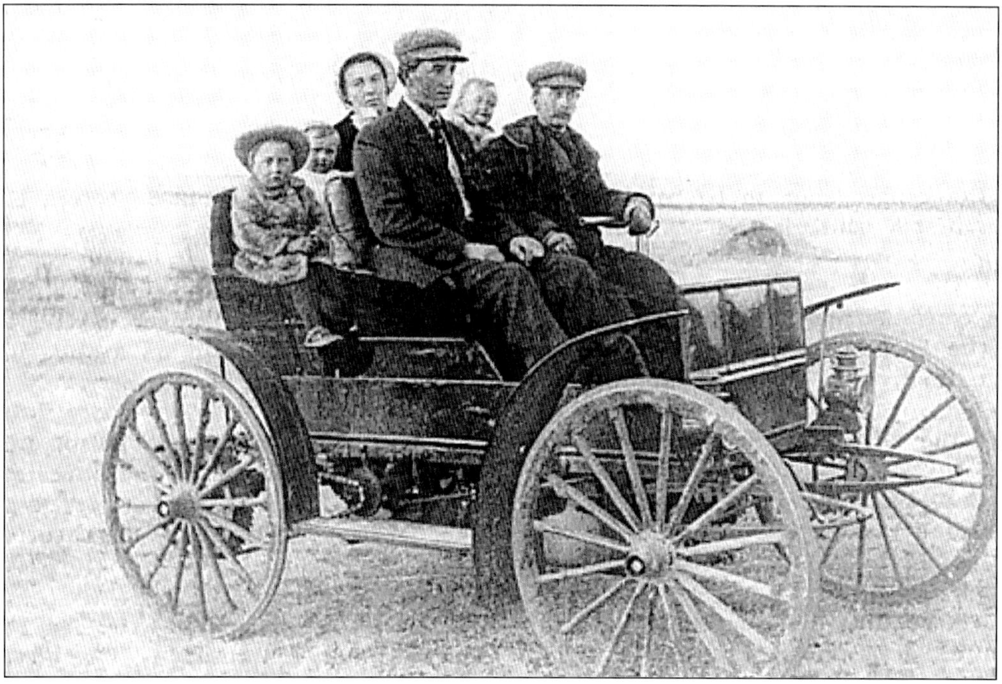

This "high wheeler" was probably one of the first cars in North Dakota. There was no air in the tires.

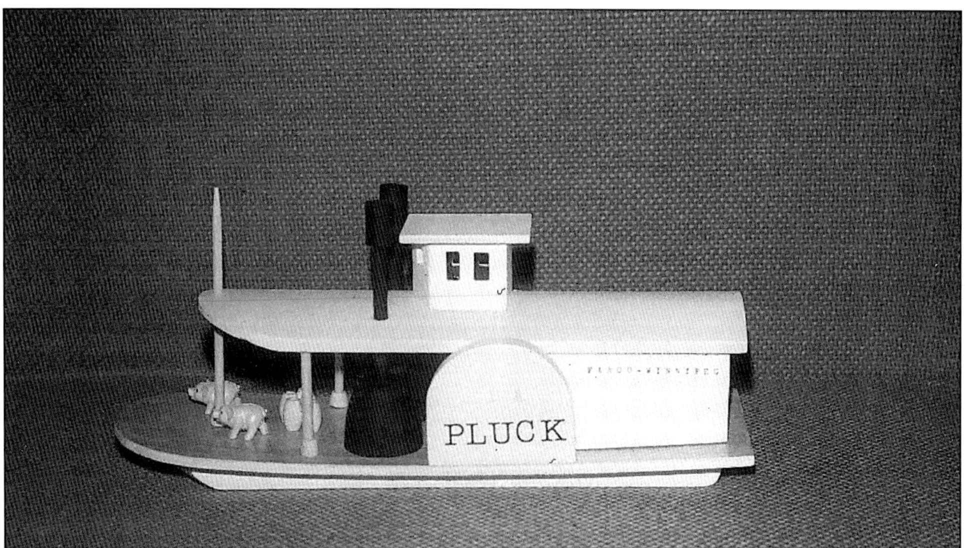

This is a model of the river steamer *Pluck* that operated between Fargo, North Dakota, and Winnipeg, Manitoba, Canada around 1859.

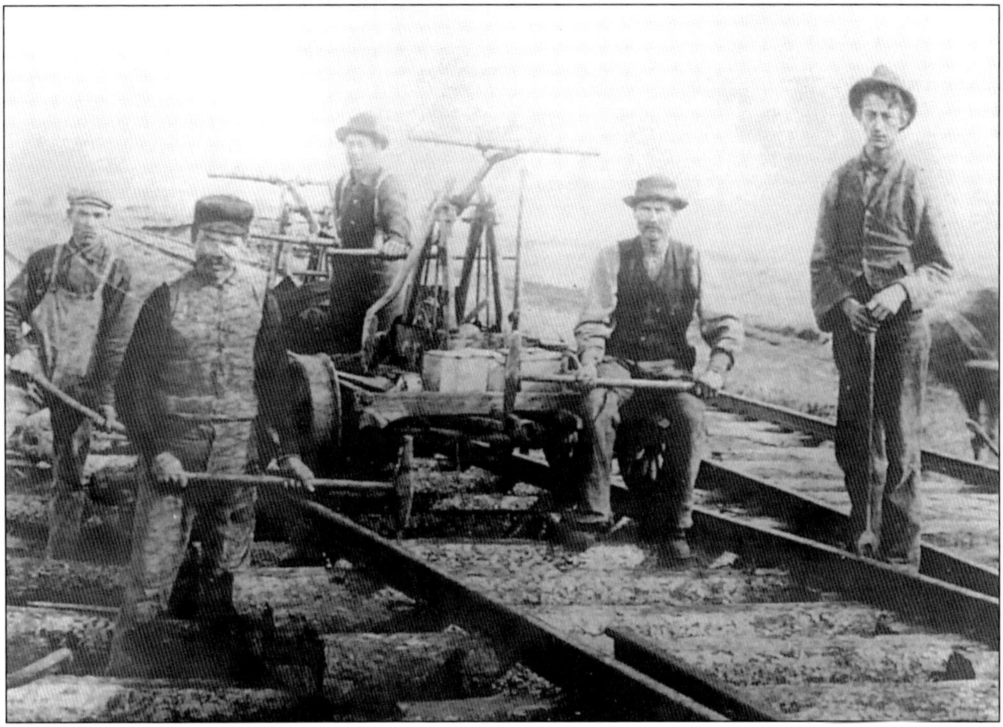

This railroad work crew was photographed constructing a sidetrack near Bathgate. Some early homesteaders worked part-time building the railroad to earn some cash.

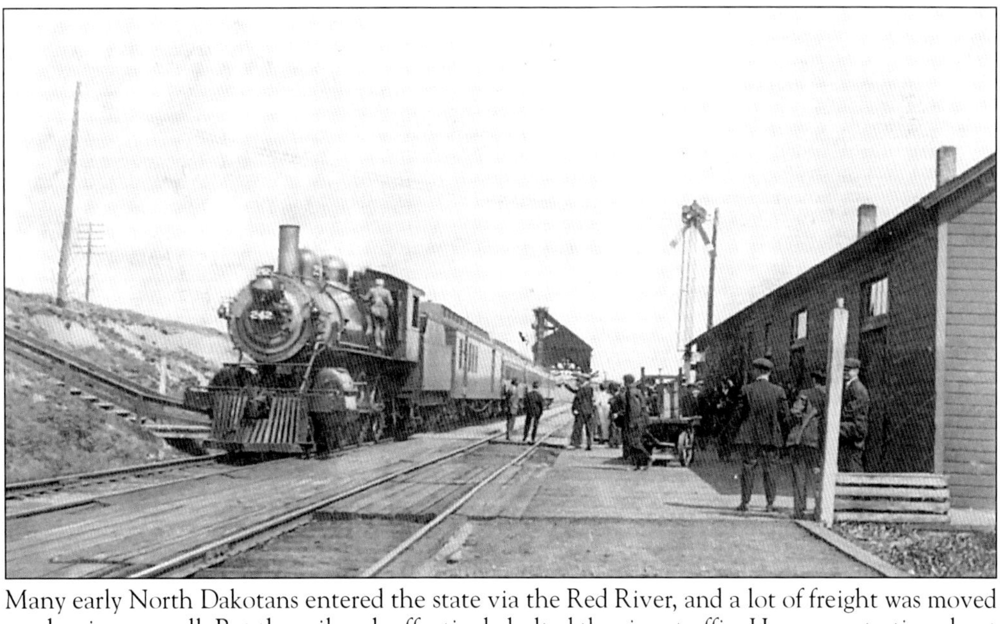

Many early North Dakotans entered the state via the Red River, and a lot of freight was moved on the river as well. But the railroads effectively halted the river traffic. However, starting about 1940, big trucks on the highways began taking business away from the railroads.

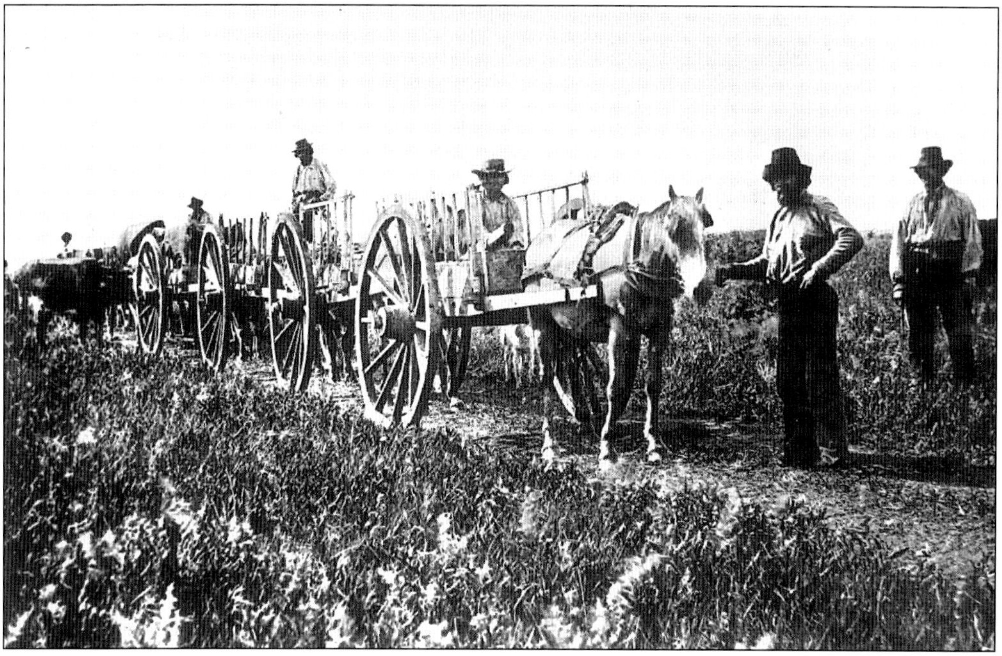

Red River carts made their way from St. Paul, Minnesota, to Pembina, North Dakota, and into Canada. They carried furs to St. Paul, and in turn brought supplies to the settlers and the Native Americans. Built of wood, the carts were a marvel of engineering simplicity and required little maintenance, although they did have quite a squeak! The ruts from the wagon wheels are still visible along the Red River.

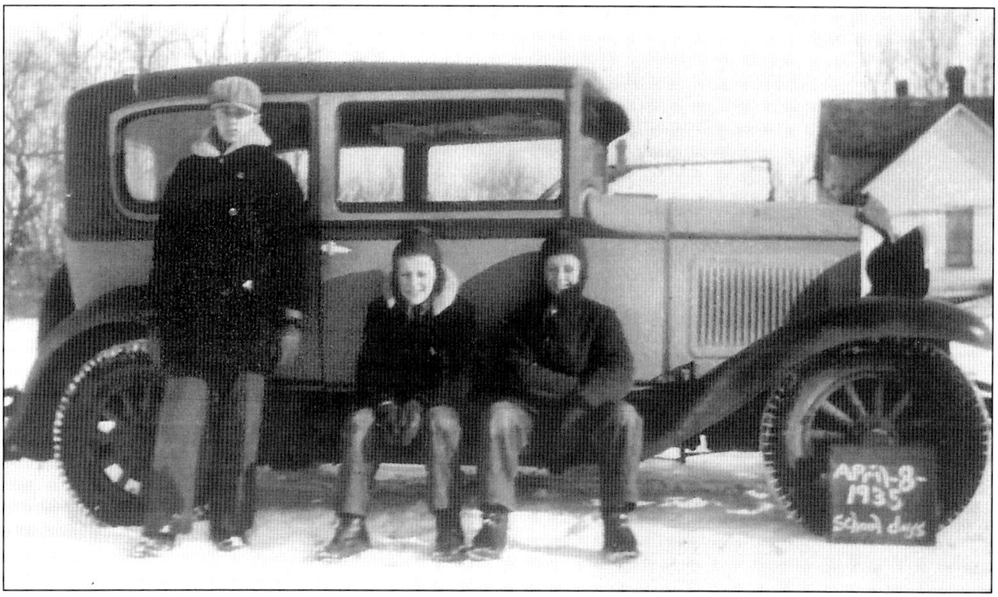

This 1929 car, called a Whippet after the small, swift dog, was made by the Willys Overland Corporation. It was a four-cylinder car that looked like a Model A Ford. It carried the three Aasen boys to school for many years. In the winter, the oil had to be drained from the Whippet every night and kept warm in the kitchen. The battery got the same treatment. When its speedometer stopped working, it read over 120,000 miles—a bargain at $495!

Seven

THE WAY IT WAS

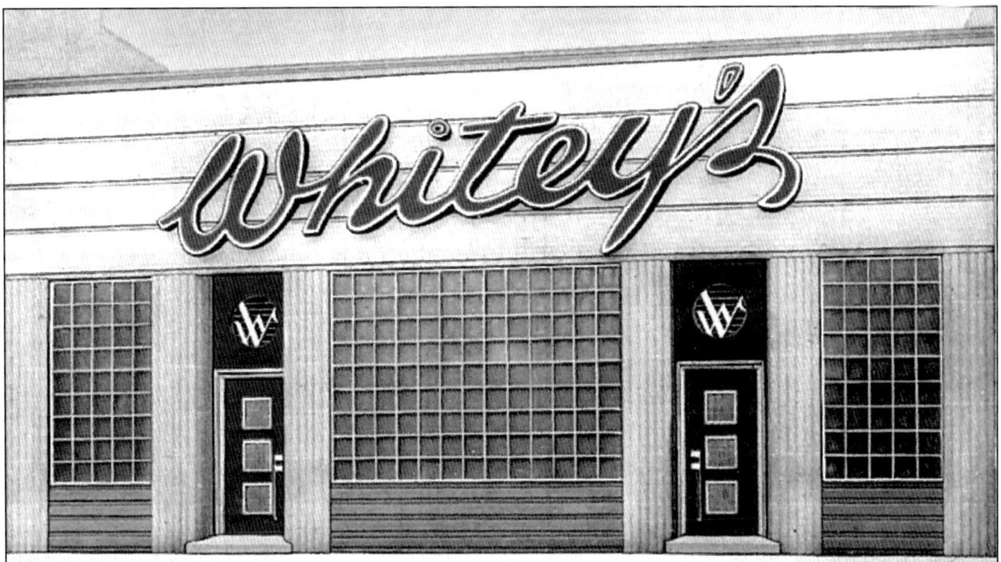

Whitey's Bar in East Grand Forks, Minnesota, has been popular with North Dakotans since 1930. It was known for its good food, great service, friendly waiters, gambling, and liquor (which was not always readily available in North Dakota). College students, businessmen, farm workers—all were welcome and well-treated here. In the early days, it was alleged that Whitey's had slot machines and gambling devices that could quickly be removed if necessary. Although hurt by the flood of 1997, Whitey's has moved a few blocks and is still serving the men and women of North Dakota and Minnesota. Whitey's breaded pork chops were (and are) worth driving many miles to enjoy!

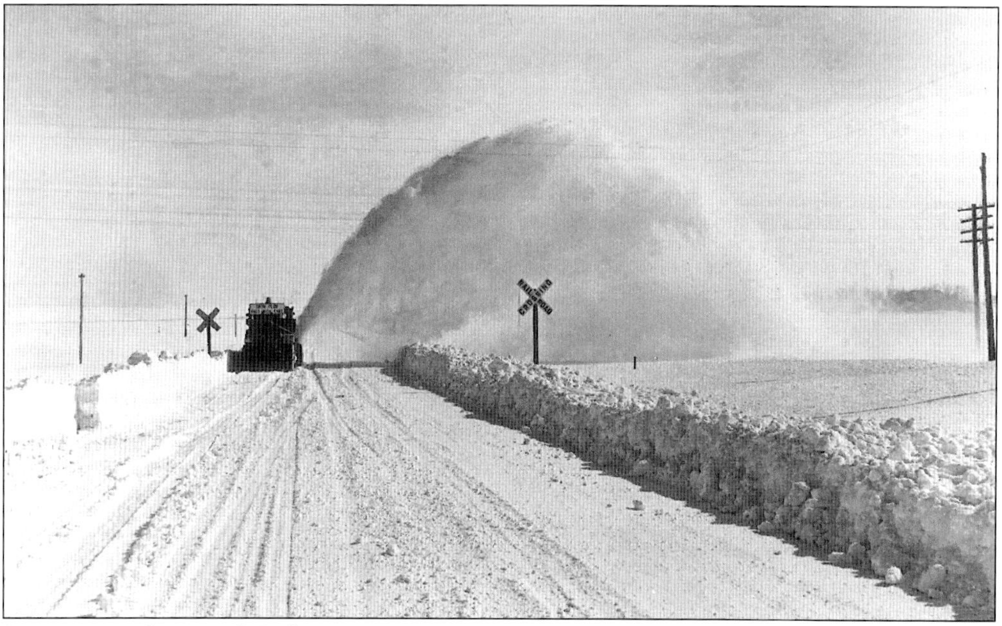

Snow removal in North Dakota is a constant winter challenge, but the new machines do send up a beautiful spray!

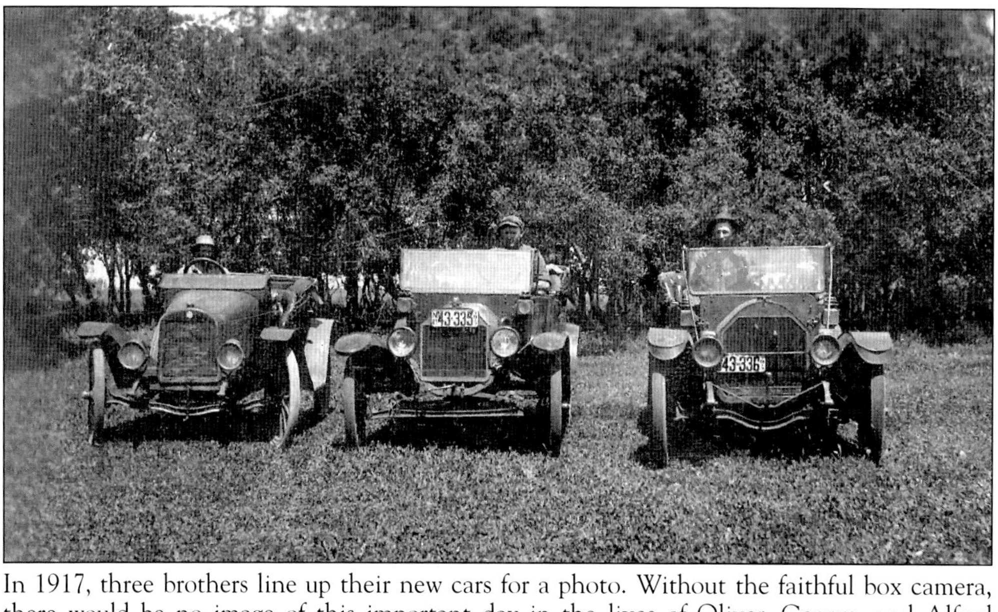

In 1917, three brothers line up their new cars for a photo. Without the faithful box camera, there would be no image of this important day in the lives of Oliver, George, and Alfred Brenden.

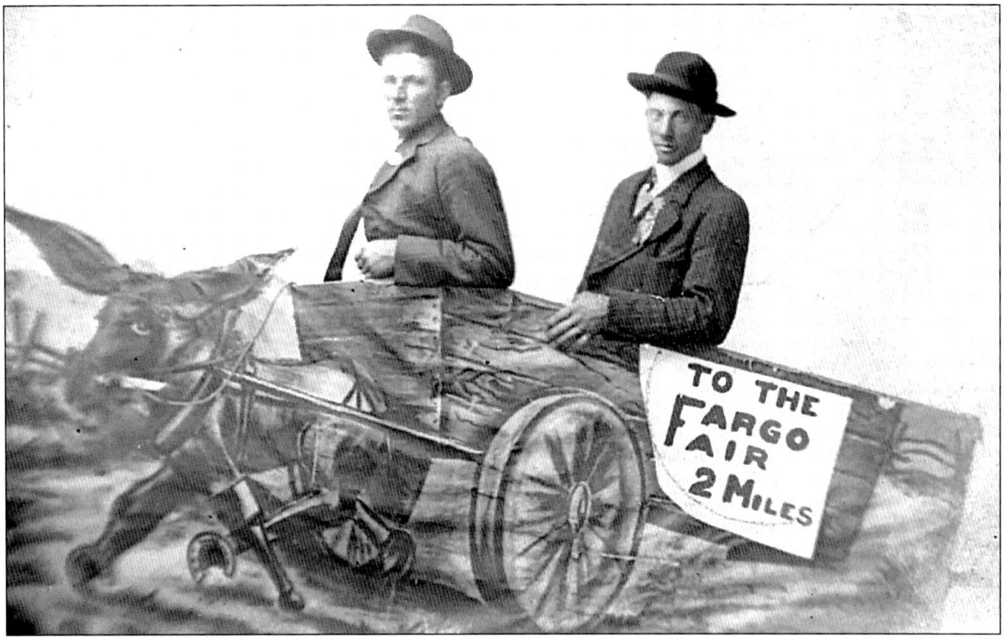

Fun times in the early days came with the annual county and state fairs. You could have comical photos taken of yourself (like the one above), or enter cattle, quilts, or home-canned goods in the competitions, ride the Ferris wheel or the merry-go-round, or just walk around eating cotton candy. It was a chance to put on a clean white shirt, see your friends, catch up on the gossip, check out the girls, and get away from the farm work for a day or two. Quite often a carnival man would try to pull some scam on the country boys, and sometimes the carnival man would be run out of town! During the week the hired men would whisper about the "girlie shows" they had seen.

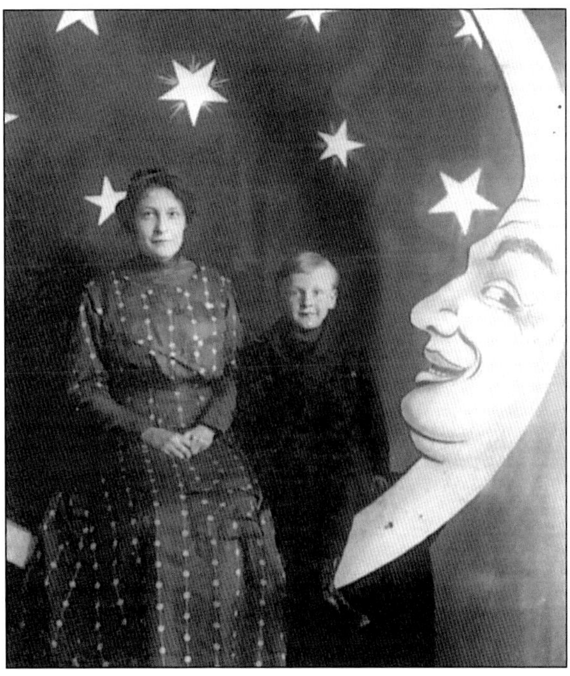

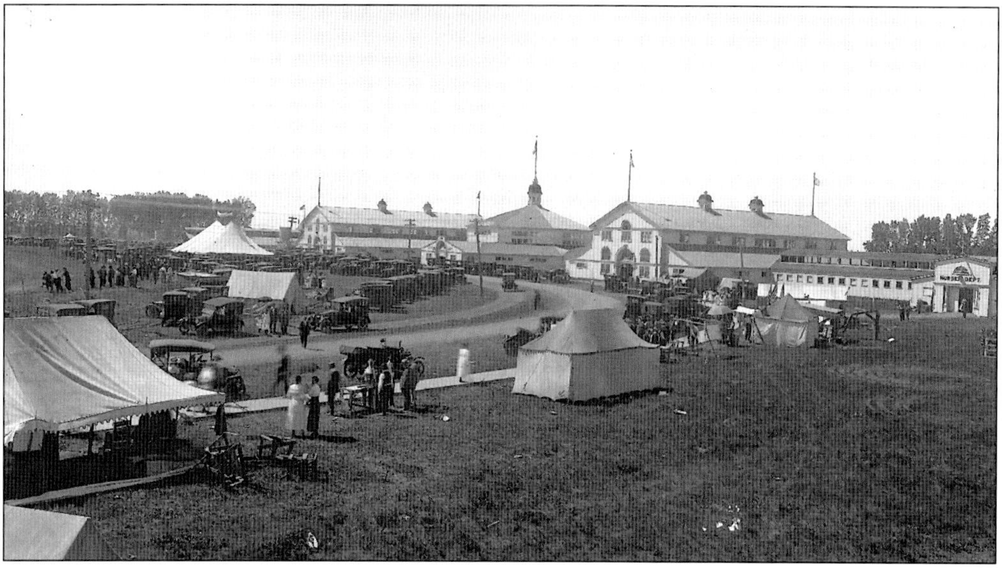

Many North Dakotans attended events at the Red River Valley Fairgrounds in Fargo, shown here in a July 1918 photo. Fargo North High School now occupies this site.

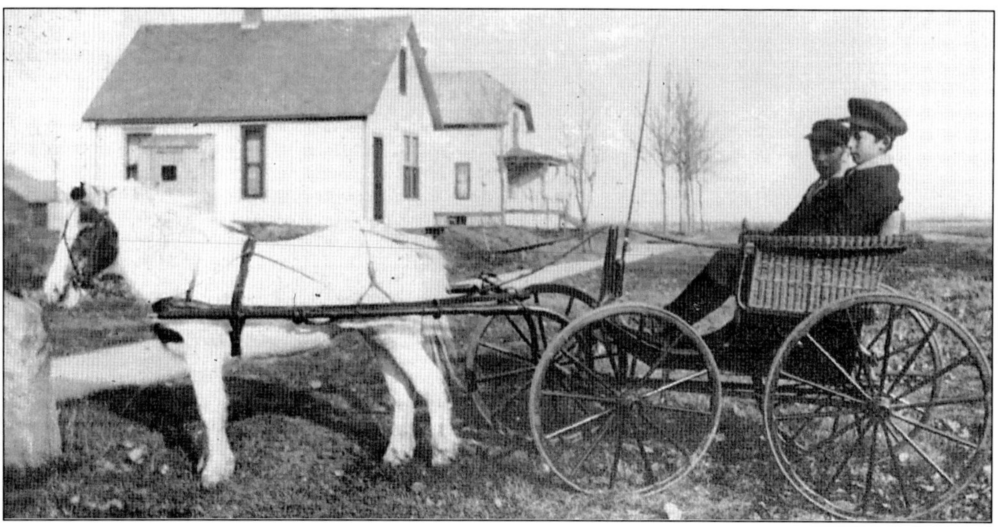

Most kids in the first half of the century did not have cars, but they had a lot of fun with horses and Shetland Ponies hooked up to buggies of various sizes.

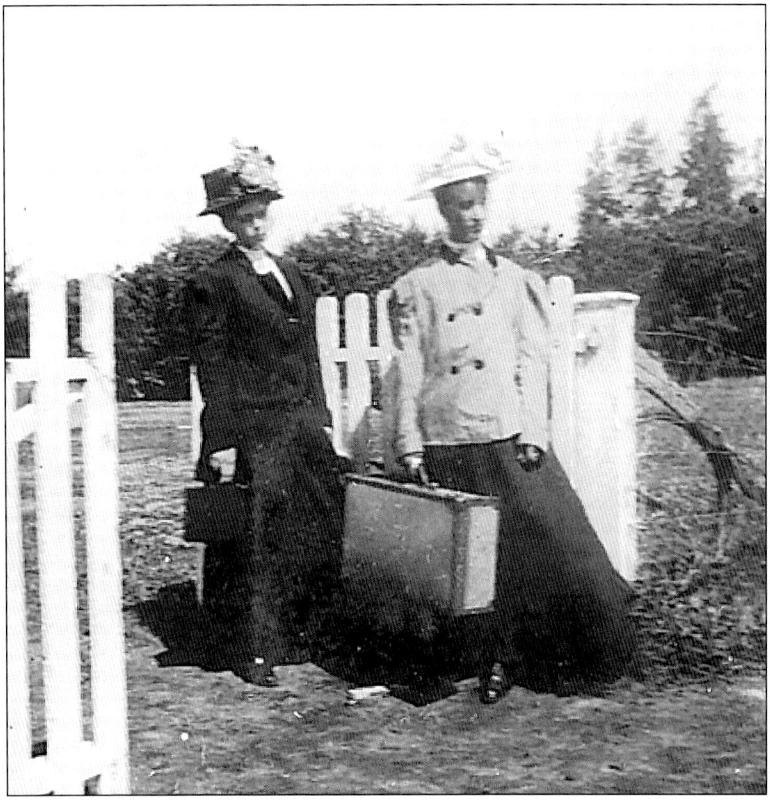

Box cameras were loaded with fresh film when a trip was planned. Many traveled within the state, but sometimes travelers would venture east into Minnesota, or west into Montana. Not as many ventured into South Dakota, as it was quite difficult to travel that direction because most major roads ran east-west. As you can see from these photos, when people traveled they dressed up—no tank tops or hip-huggers!

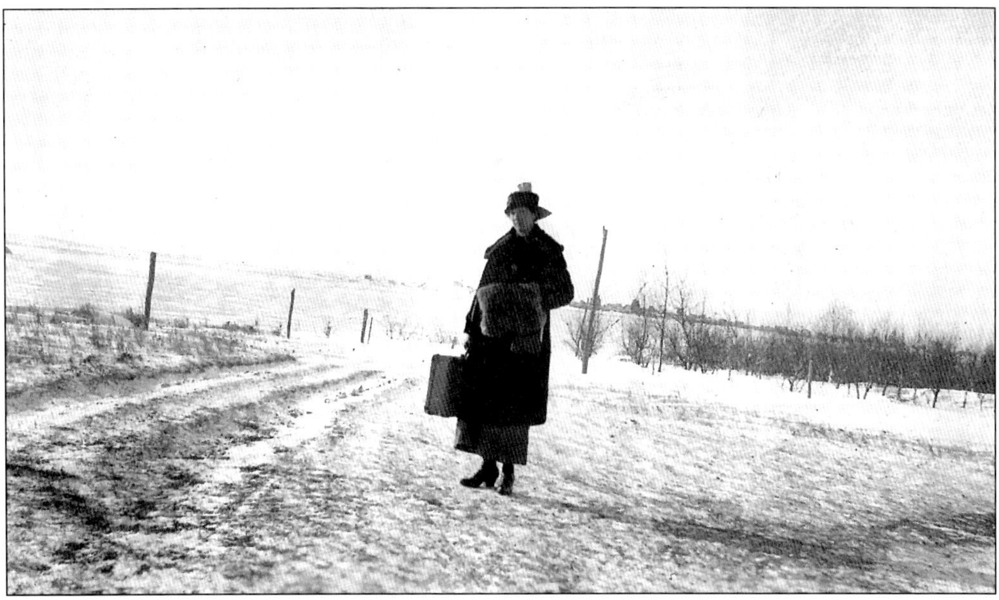

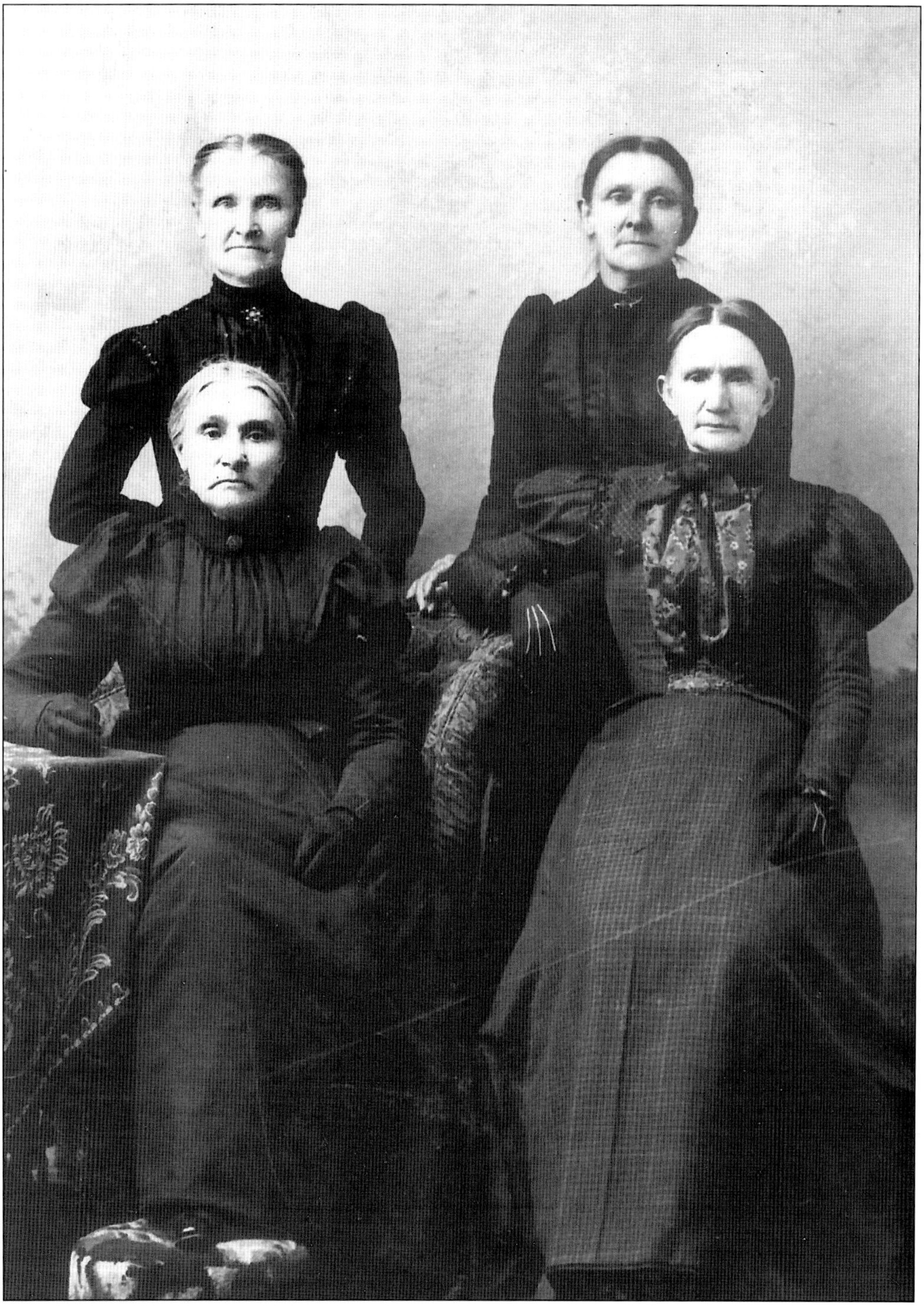

Life expectancy was not very long in the early Dakota days. The flu epidemic of 1918 killed 2,500 North Dakotans. One writer claims that the reason so many women wore black was because they had so many funerals to attend.

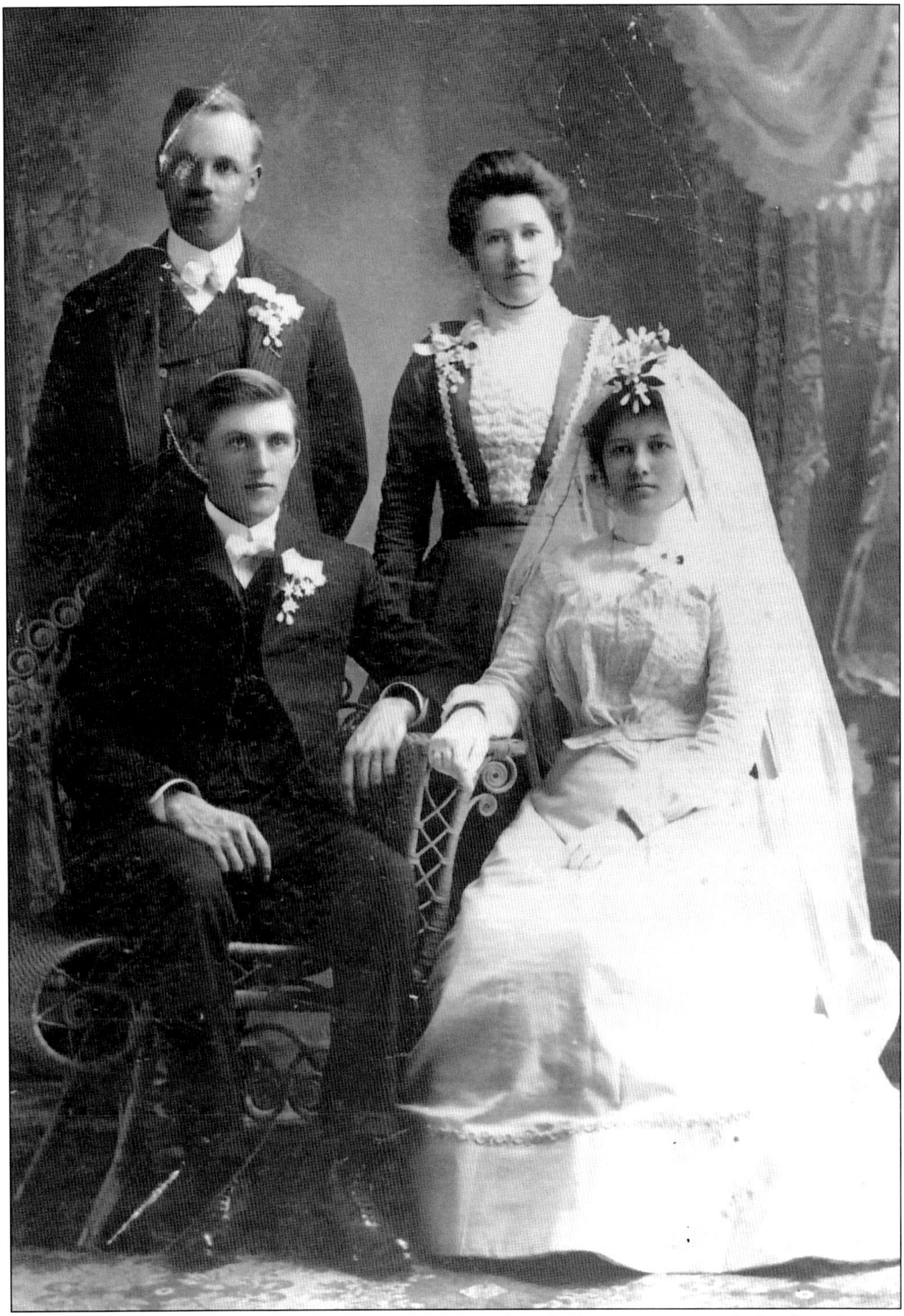

Wedding photos were quite formal. They were a cherished possession, and the first thing a family tried to save if there was a fire. During this period, fire protection, especially on the farms, was very poor.

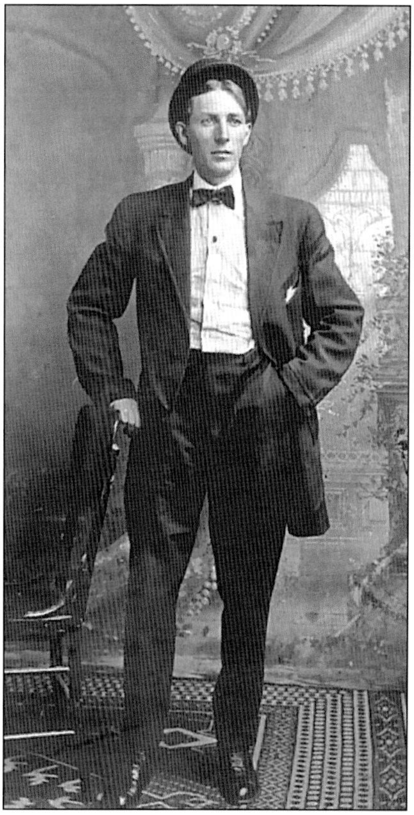

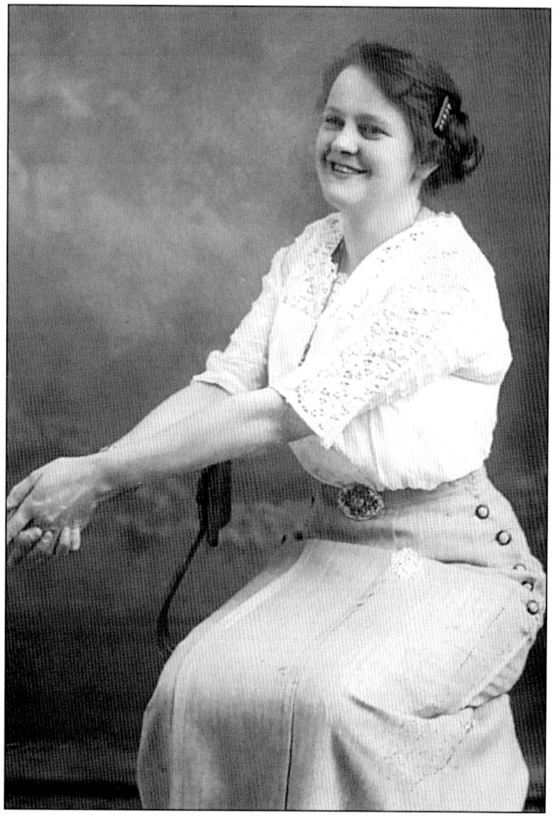

These 1911 photographs portray two well-dressed people living in Spring Grove, Minnesota. Many people from this little town in southeastern Minnesota migrated up to North Dakota to get free land, or to buy bigger farms. Some made the 300-mile trip by covered wagon.

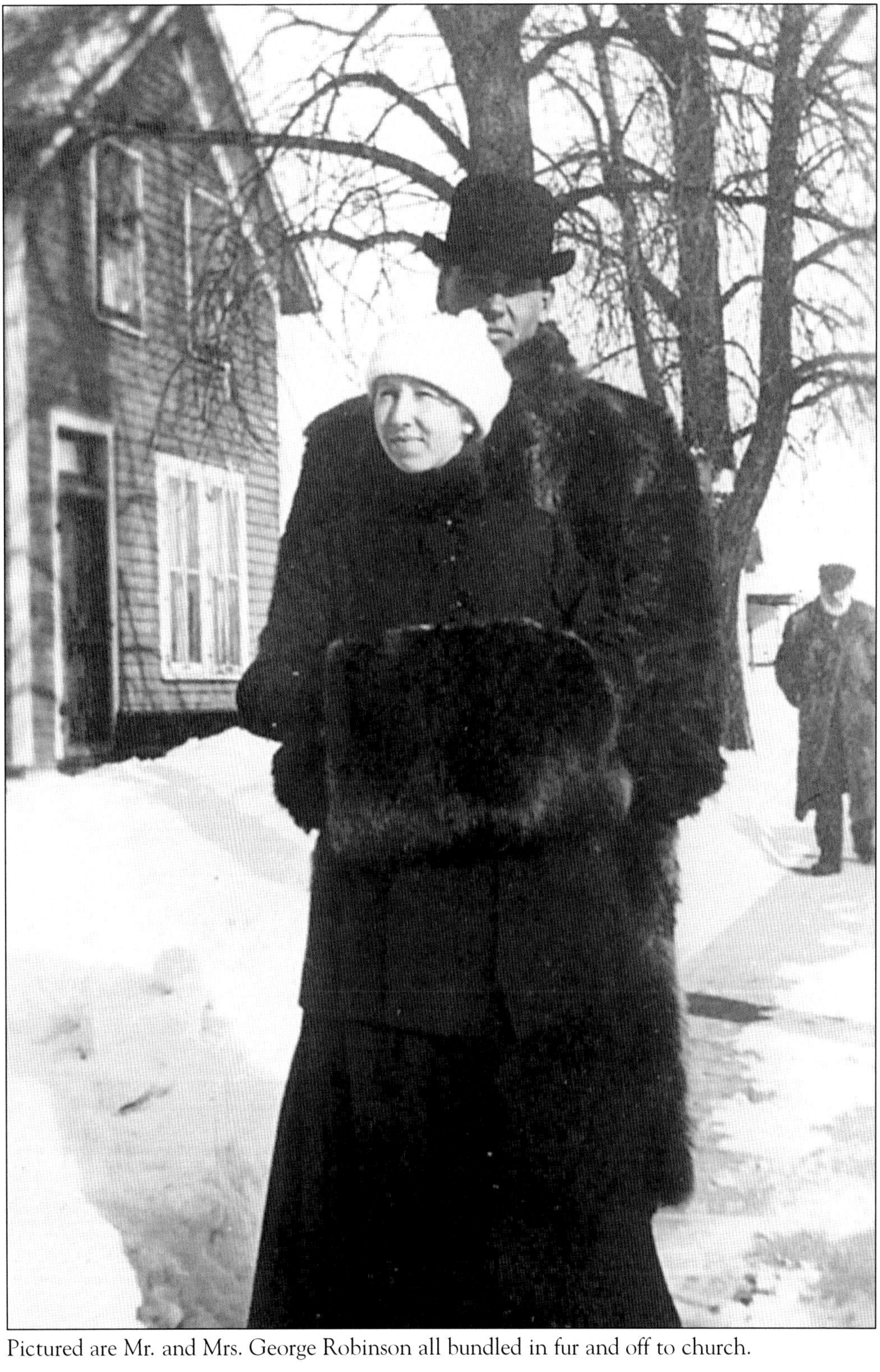

Pictured are Mr. and Mrs. George Robinson all bundled in fur and off to church.

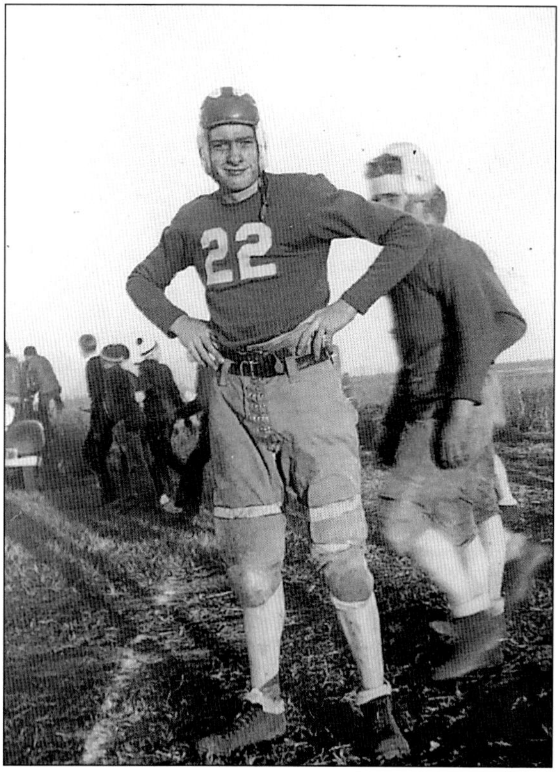

Hillsboro's Tommy Kelly was an All-State fullback in 1938, but his football uniform was held together by tape. Note the old-fashioned soft leather helmet.

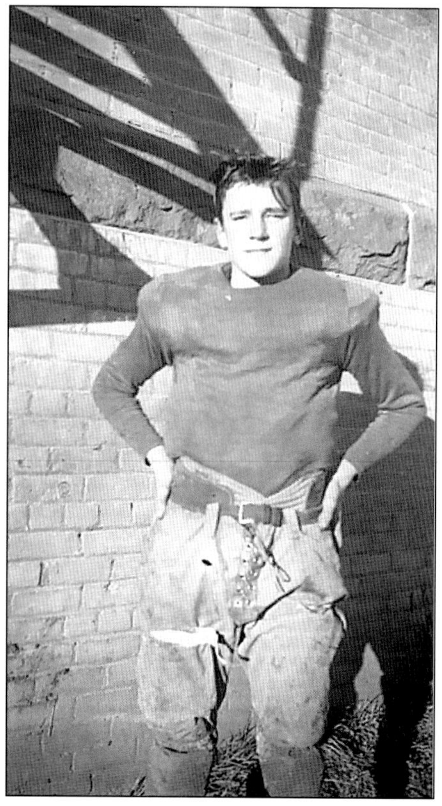

The ragged football suit shown here was probably donated to Hillsboro High School by the North Dakota State University team when they got new equipment.

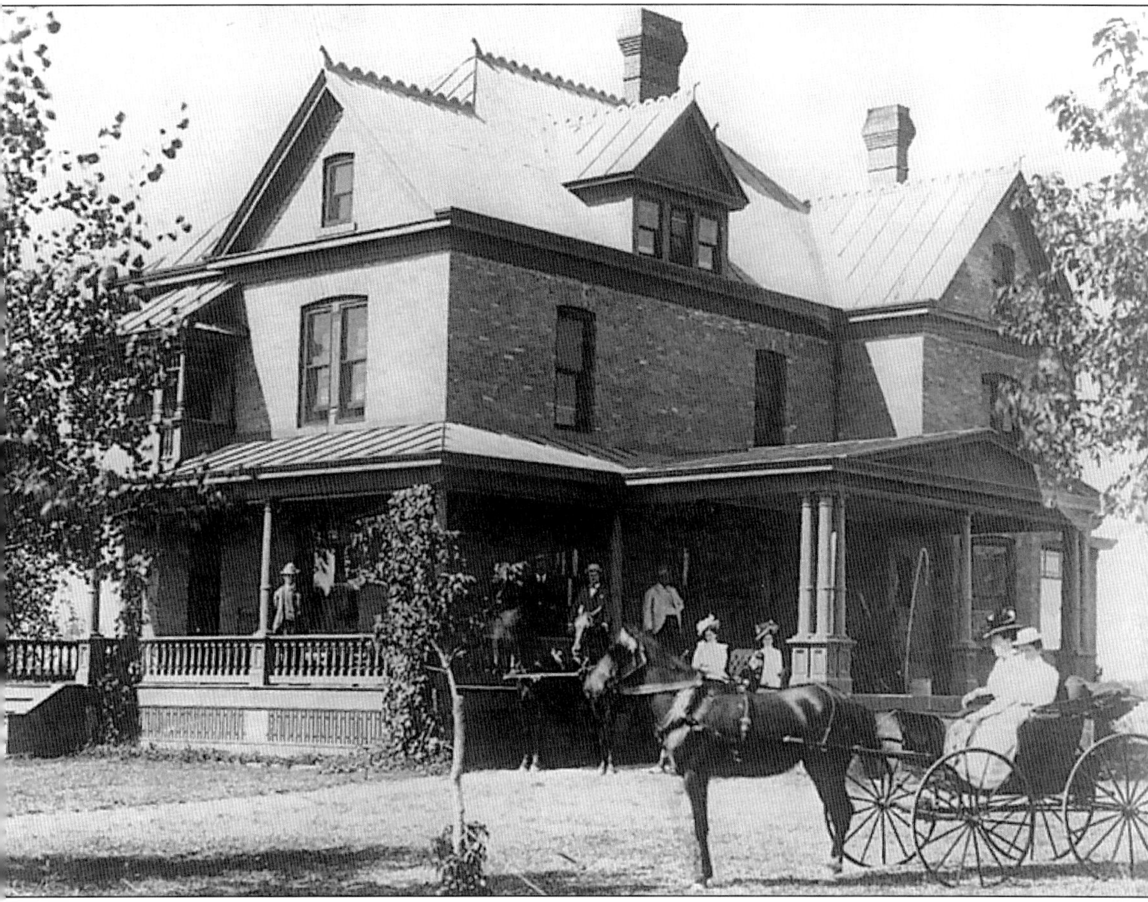

A.L. Plummer built this house in Hillsboro. It is now the Traill County Historical Society Museum.

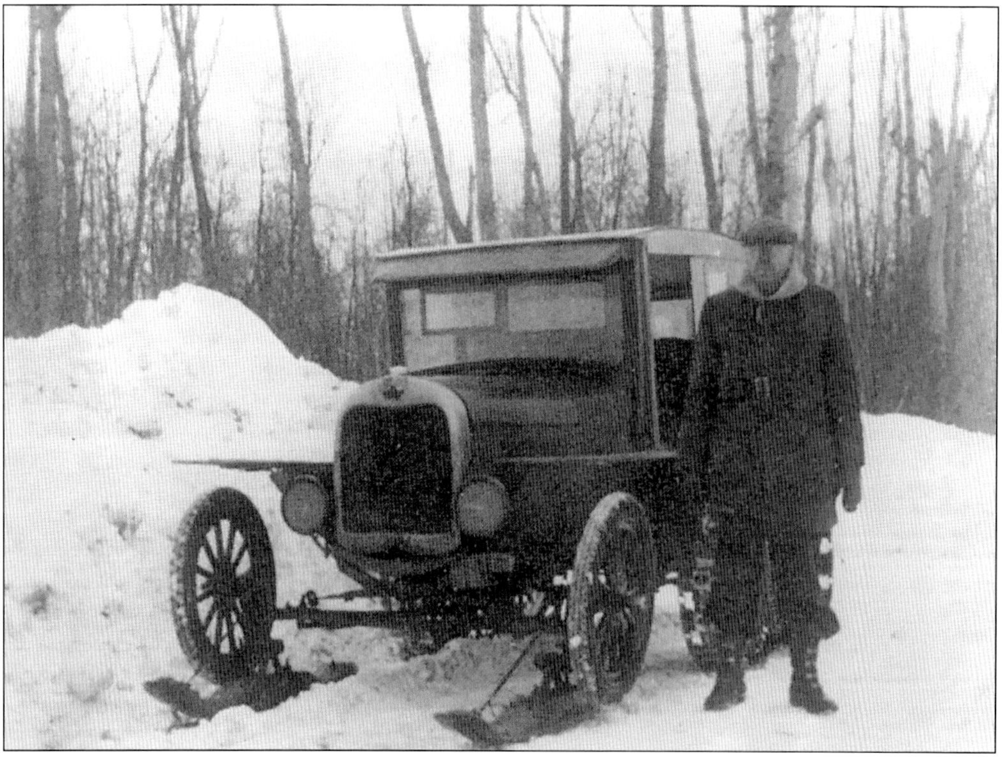

Paul Myron of Hillsboro delivered mail from 1911 to 1943. Like many North Dakota mailmen, he had to put skis on his car during the winter. When he first started on his mail route, he drove horses. North Dakota has many unsung heroes and its mailmen, and women, should be on the list!

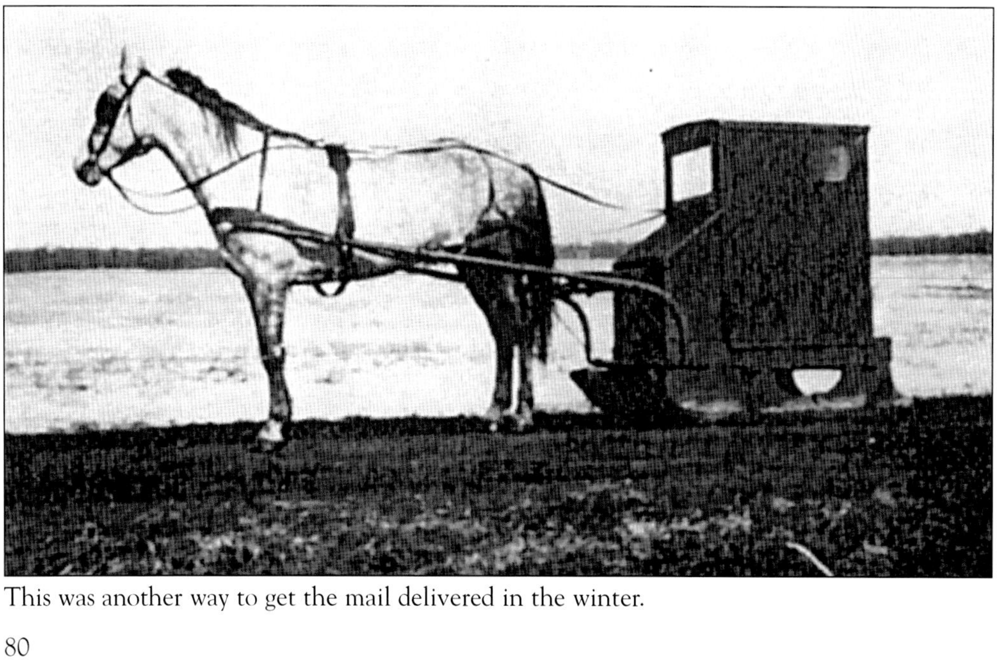

This was another way to get the mail delivered in the winter.

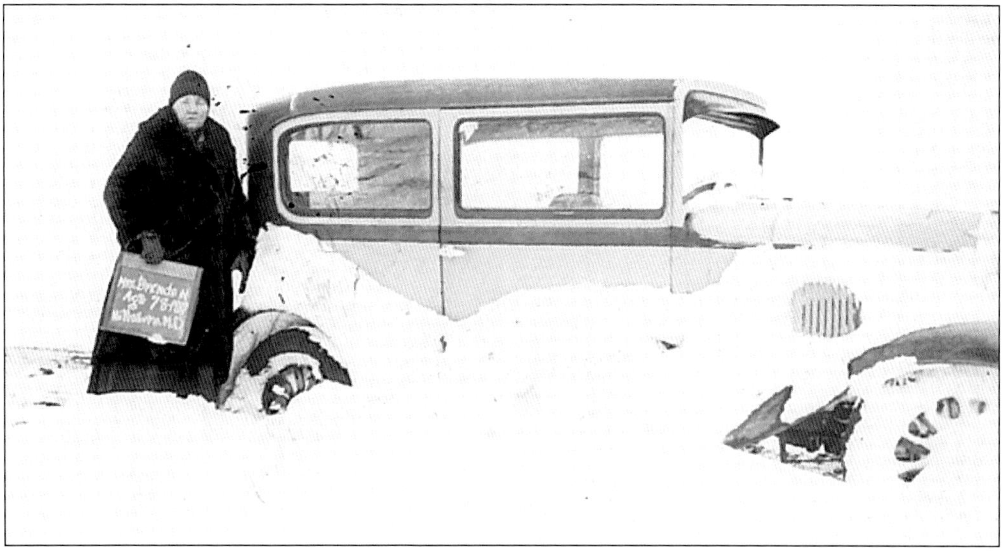

These snow photos indicate the severity of North Dakota winters at this time. It is a fact that winters are getting milder, even in North Dakota. One particular winter day in 2000 was warmer in Grand Forks than it was in Palm Springs, California! It's in the record books!

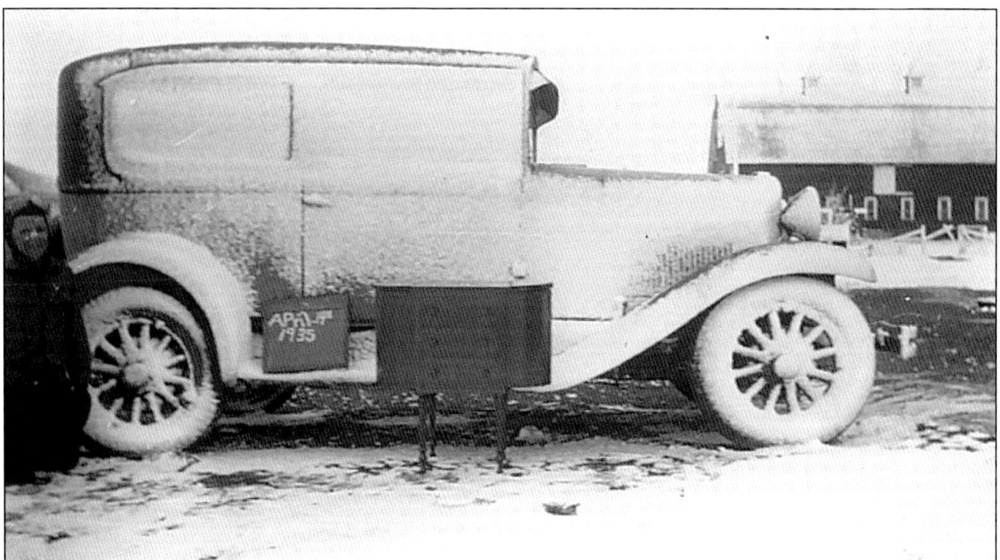

Conversations in North Dakota often turn to discussions about the weather. For example, you will probably hear about 1936—the hottest, driest, and coldest year on record. Wishek had an official reading of 120 degrees that year.

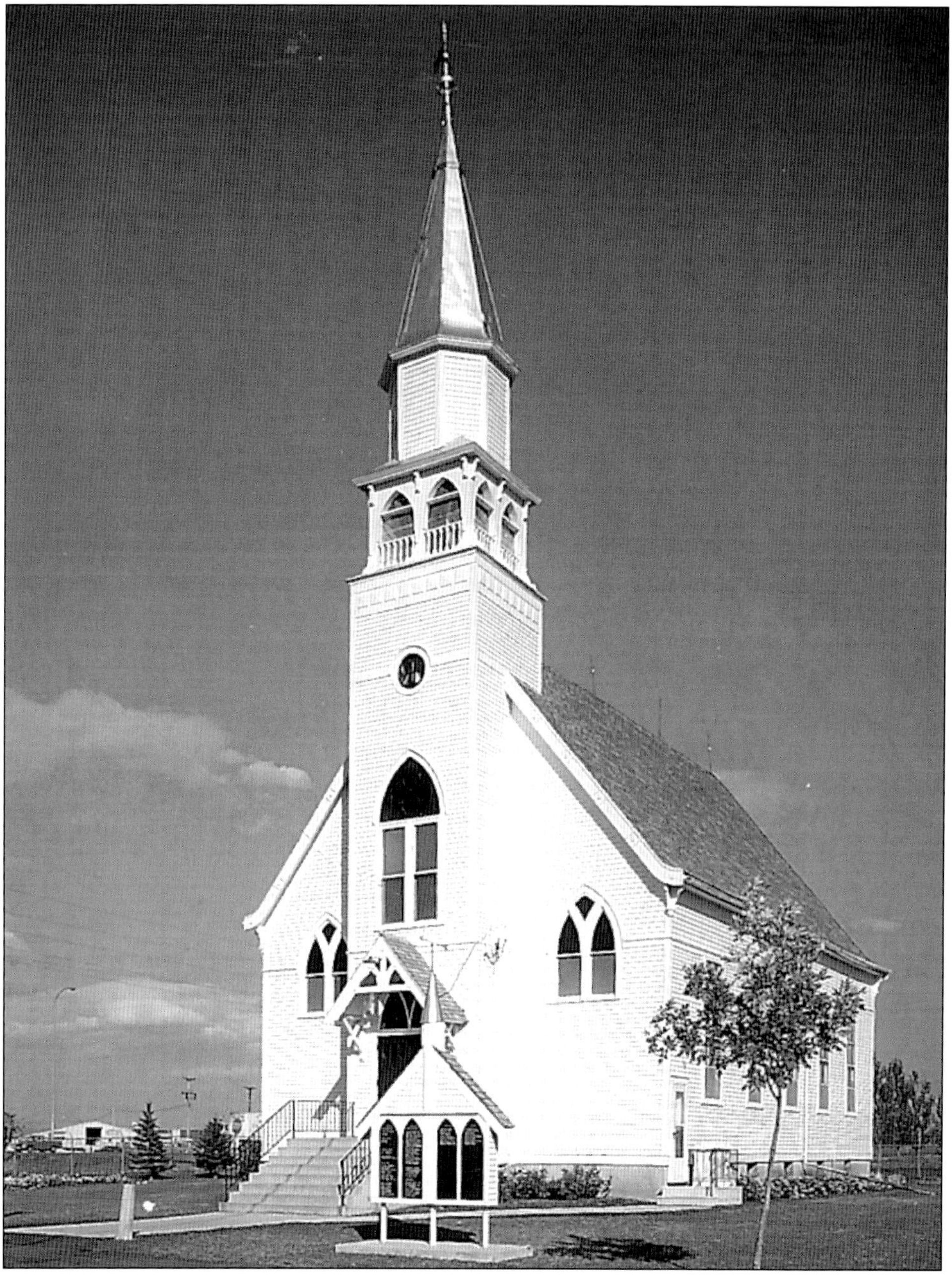

Churches have always played a major role in North Dakota life. In pioneer days, the church was the center of life in the community. Today many of the little country churches have closed down, but the churches in the cities are well-attended and growing. The cemeteries around North Dakota are silent reminders of the men and women who braved brutal winters, blazing dry summers, and crushing economic pressures to start a new life in a flat, cold, and demanding part of the United States. A number of churches have been moved into historic areas, like St. John's Lutheran Church in Bonanzaville, near West Fargo. In several areas of the state, many old churches have been moved or have burned down, leaving only the gravestones as evidence of what was once there.

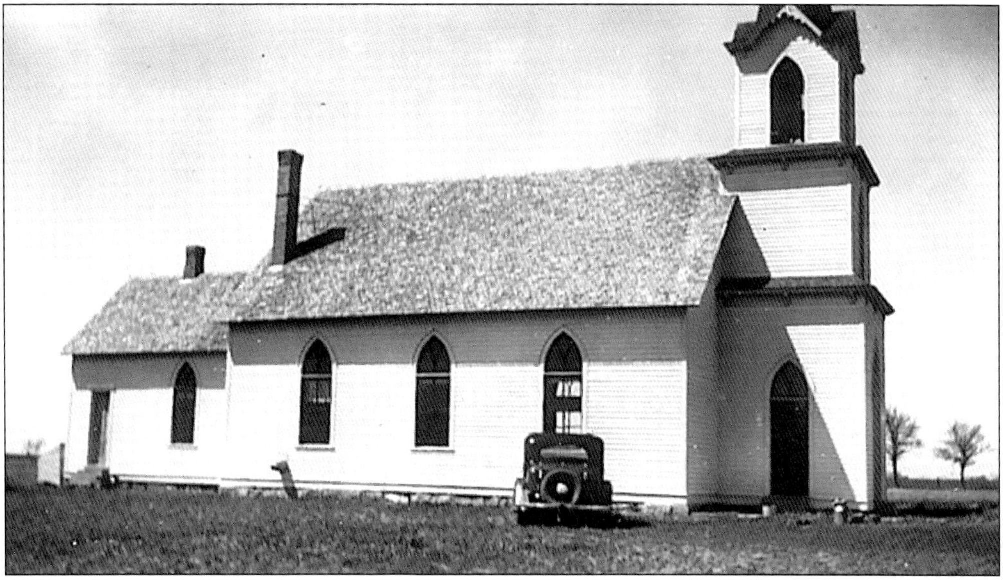

St. Olaf Lutheran Church has suffered the same fate as many small rural churches in North Dakota. It stood near the town of Taft for many years. When membership dwindled to five people, the church was closed. Most of the pews, the altar, and other items were moved to a chapel in Hillsboro, and the church was burned.

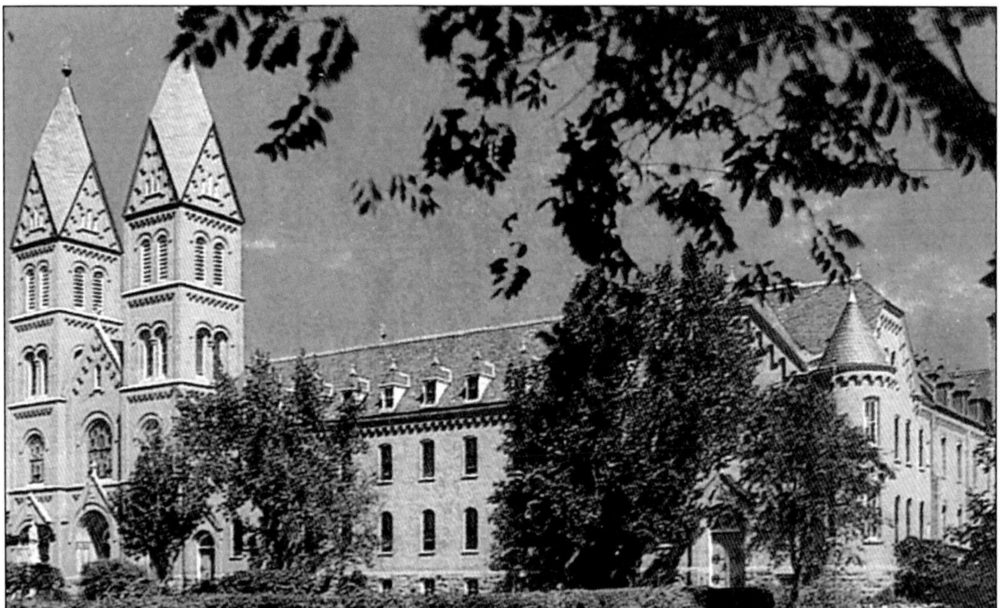

The Assumption Abbey in Richardton, North Dakota, is one of the most famous churches in the state. Other notable churches in the state include Saint Mary's Cathedral in Fargo, which is often visited by baseball fans. That is where the funeral was held for famous baseball player Roger Maris.

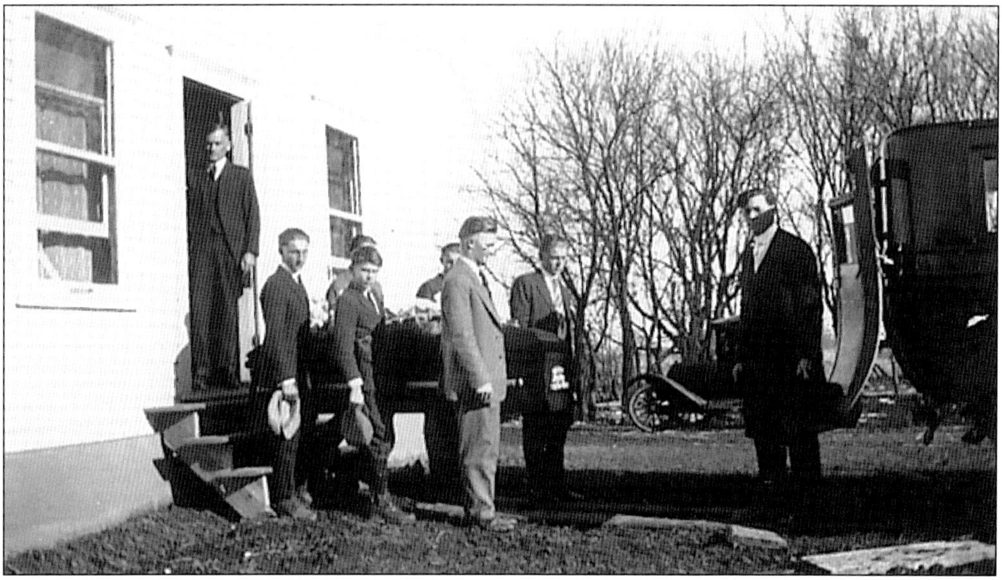

In the early days in North Dakota, it was usually the custom to bring the deceased to his or her home before the final service and burial. Now this custom has been mostly discontinued. In the photograph above, a grandfather leaves his house for the last time, carried by his six grandsons.

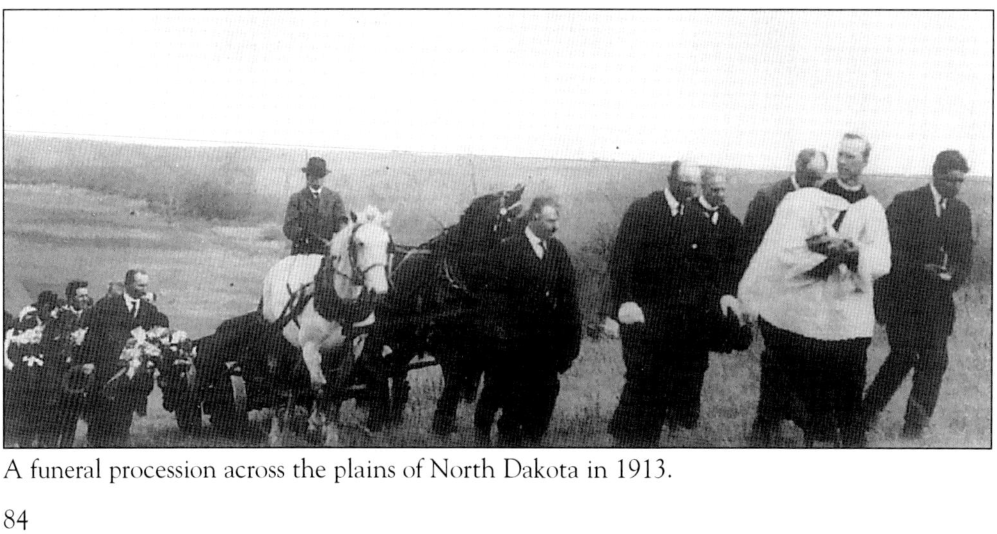

A funeral procession across the plains of North Dakota in 1913.

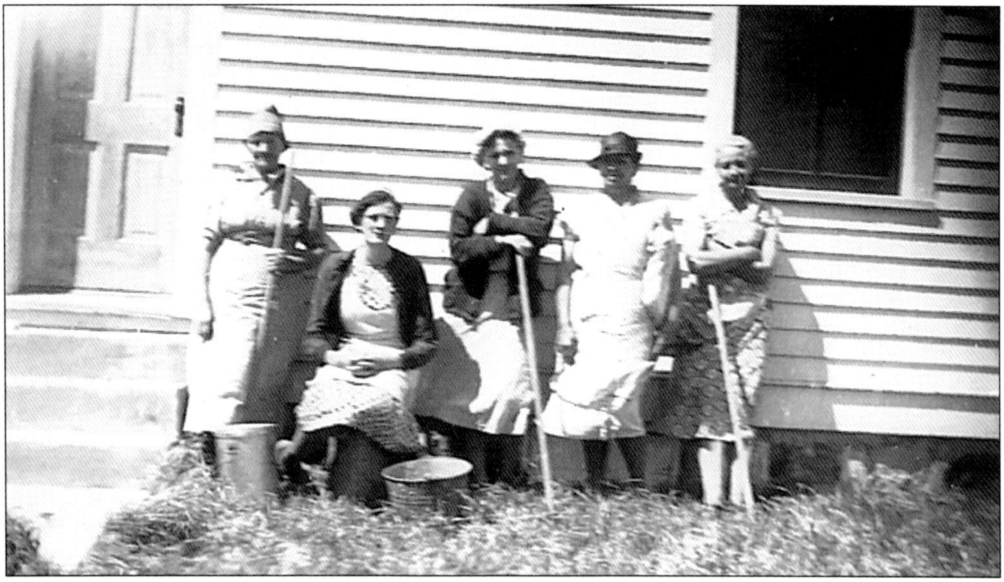

This is a ritual that took place in North Dakota churches every spring, "Clean-Up Day." These women from St. Olaf church near Taft called it "Wash Day." Whatever it was called, it was always spelled W-O-R-K!

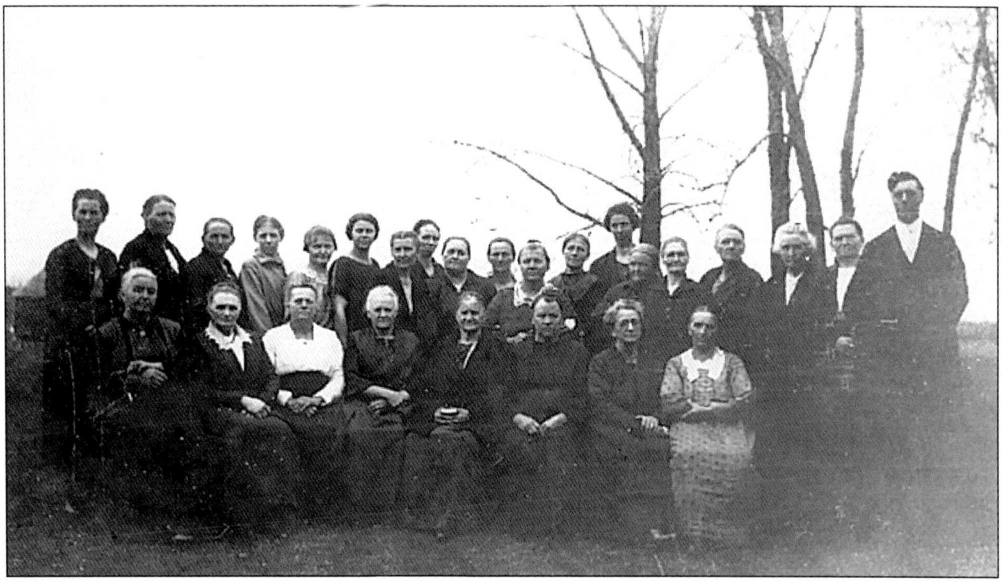

Ladies Aid groups were a popular and powerful unit in many churches. Their church suppers raised a great deal of money that was added to the mission fund to be spent locally and abroad to help people. Pictured above is the Nora Ladies Aid of Noble Township, Cass County, in about 1924. Rev. J.O. Ronsberg, who served as pastor from 1923 to 1930, is standing at the far right of the photo. As the men in the church were busy in the fields most of the time, it would be safe to say that most of the church work, including cleaning the church and putting on church suppers and other events, was left pretty much to the church women.

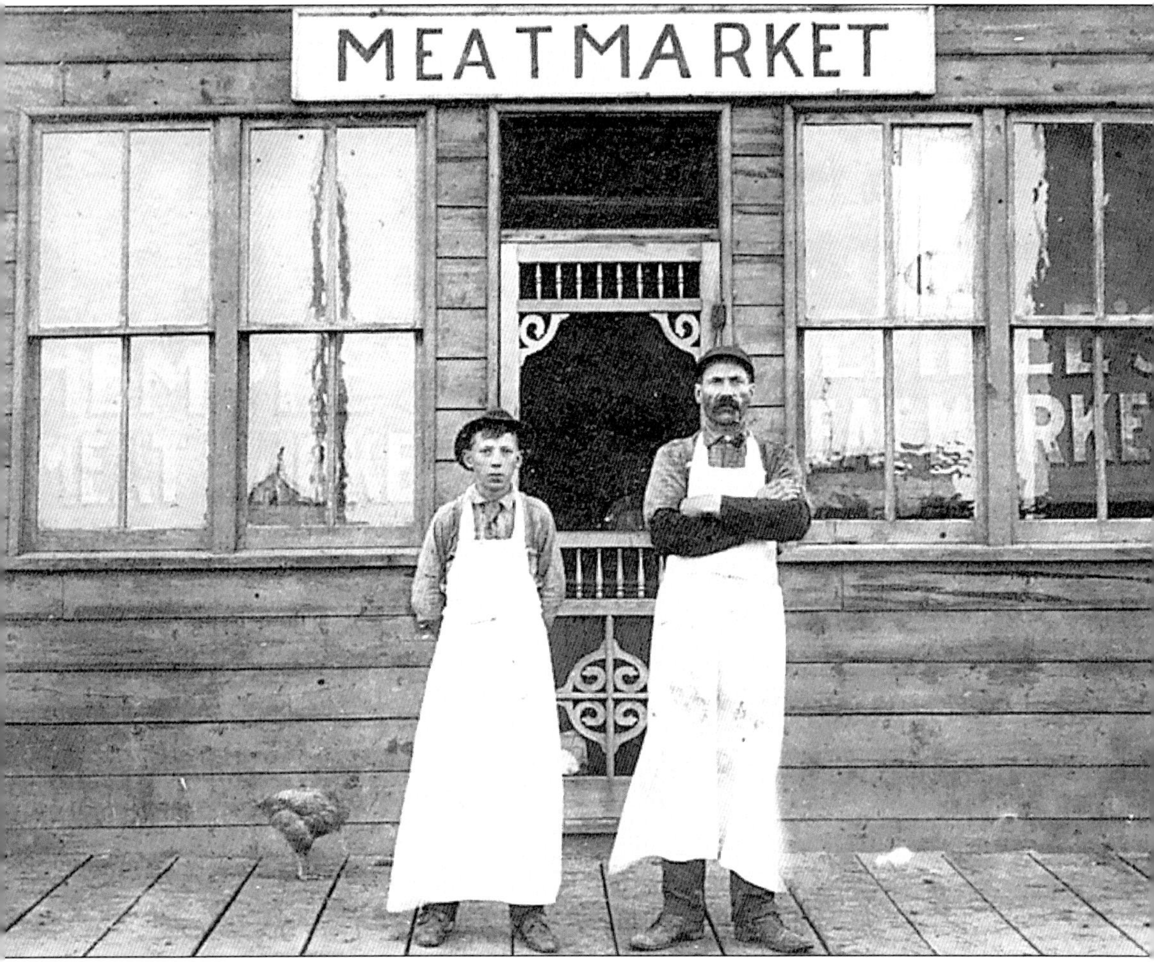

This butcher man and butcher boy stand out in front of their meat market, sometime around 1910. The chicken on the left is in the wrong place!

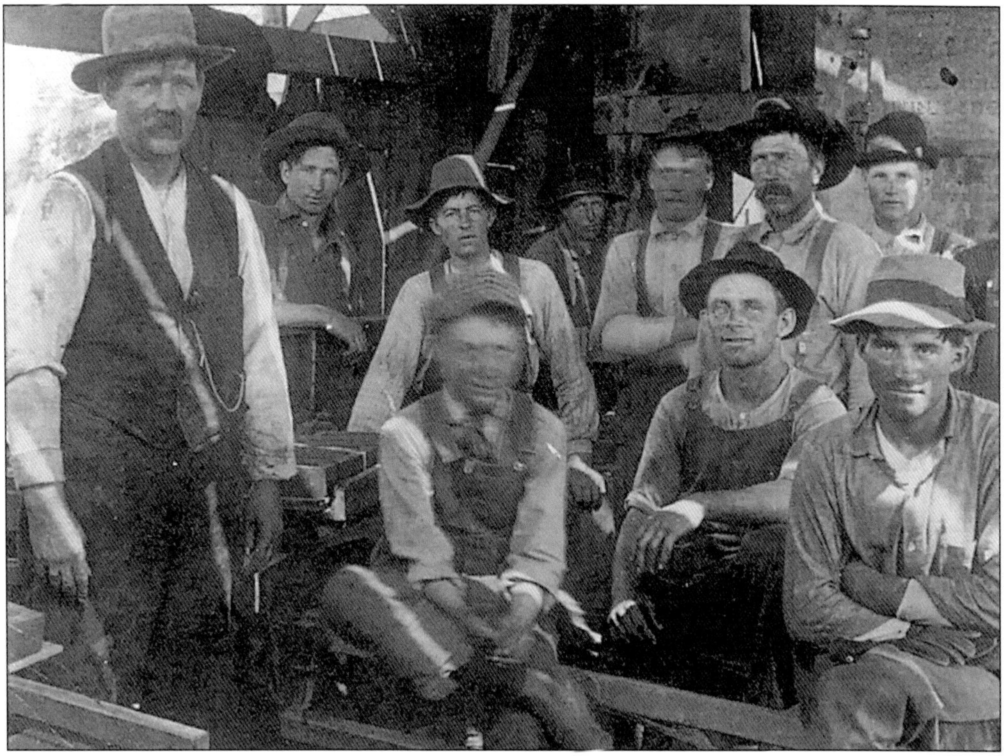

North Dakota once had a number of brick factories. Pictured here are workers at a factory in Hillsboro.

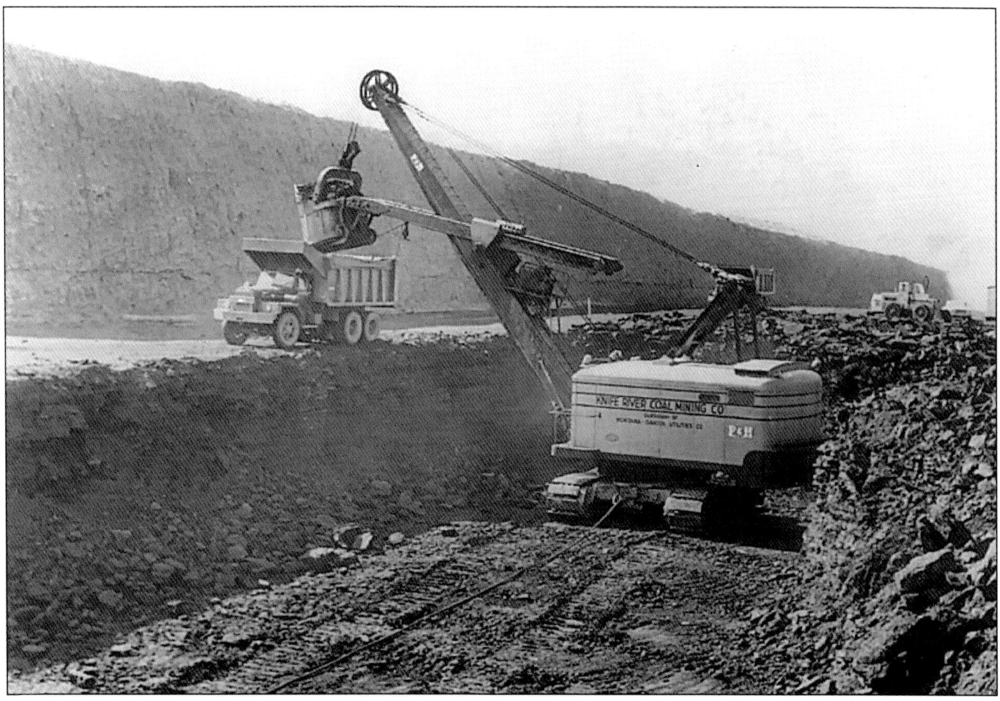

This photo of open-pit mining was taken near Beulah.

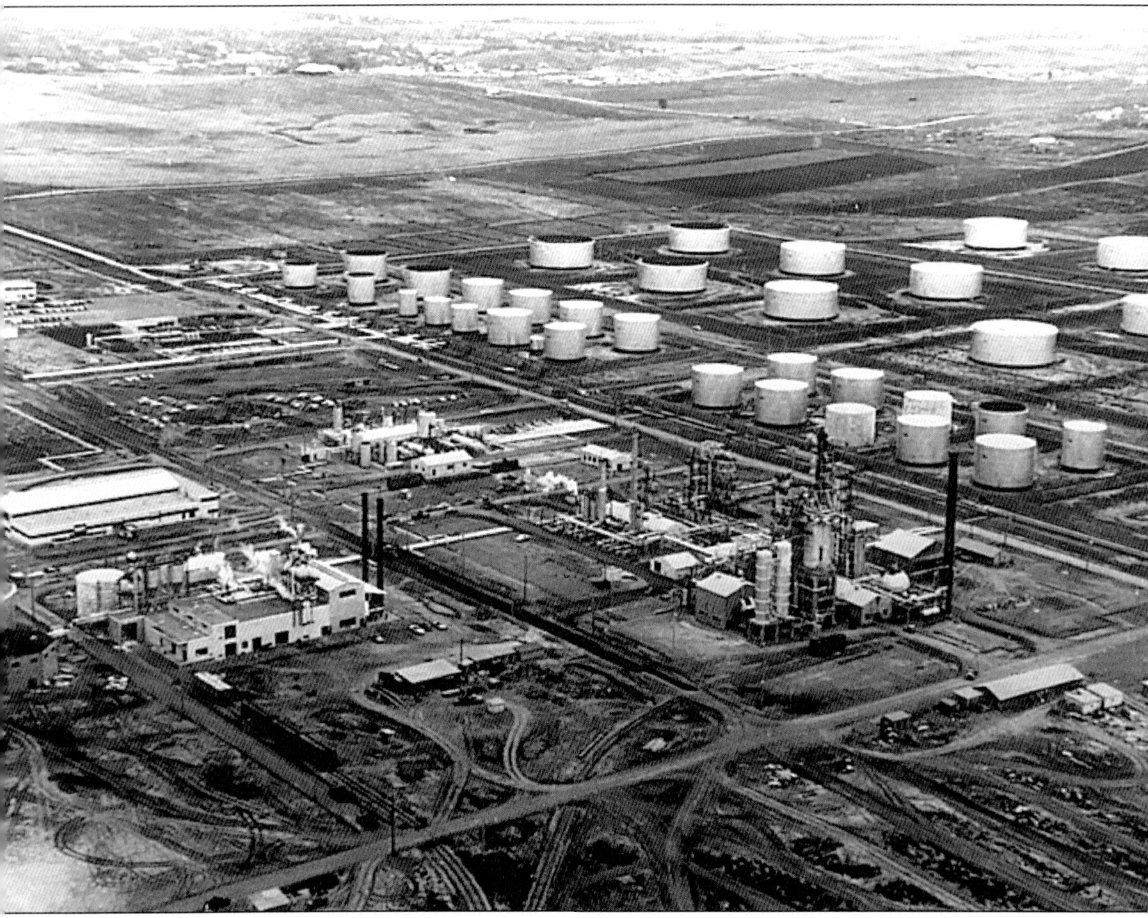

This refinery at Mandan is run by Standard Oil. From 1900 to 1940, there was little industry of any kind in the state.

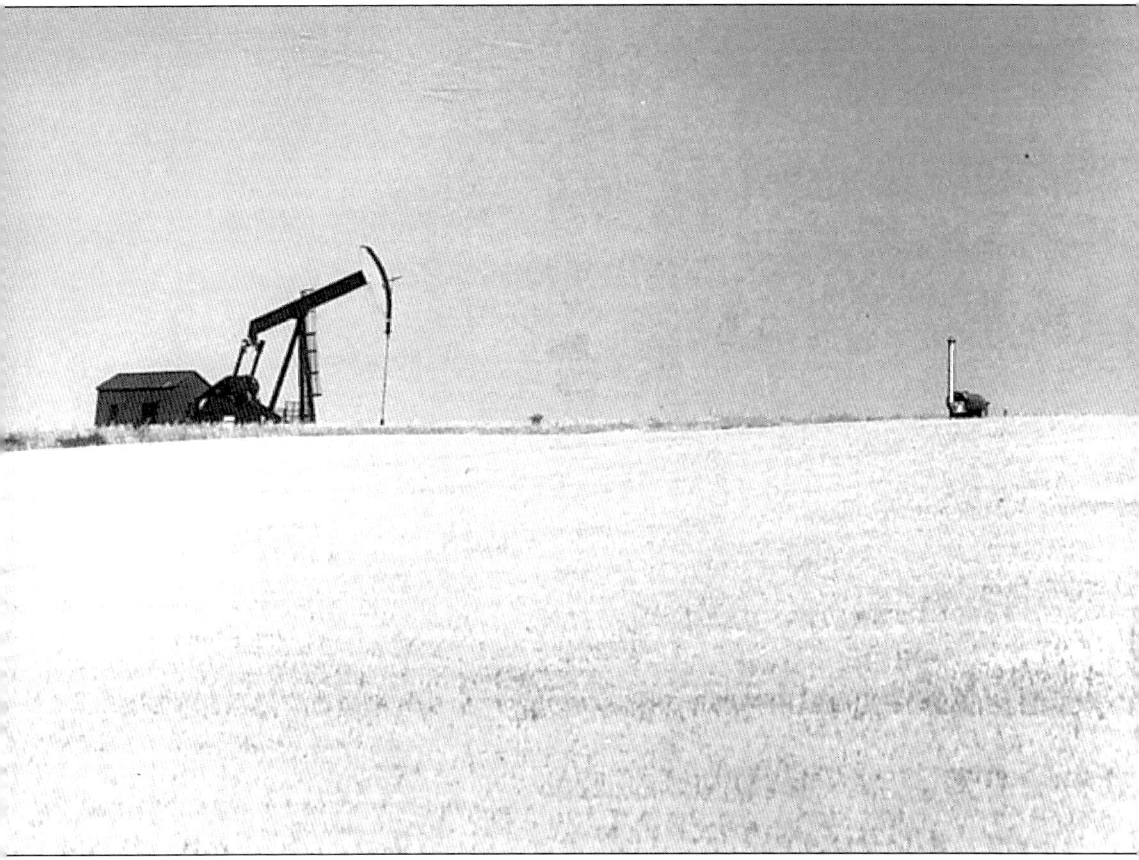

Oil was discovered at Tioga in the early 1940s. In western North Dakota, it is possible to get photographs of cattle and buffalo eating grass around an oil well.

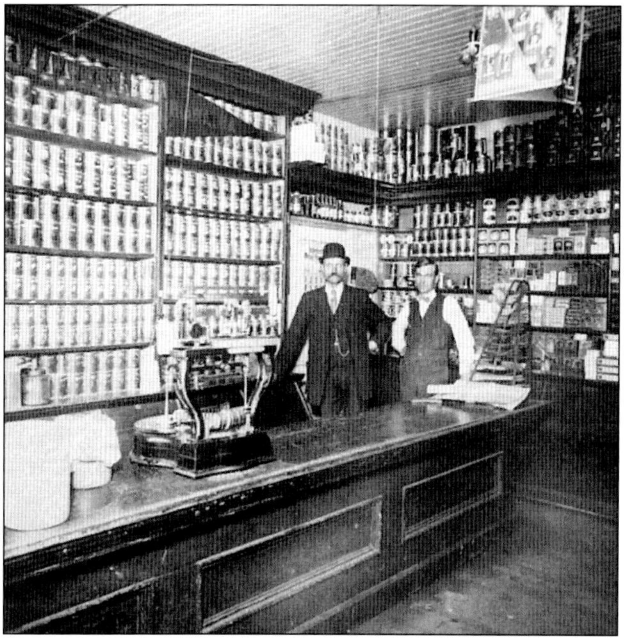

Simon and Carl Anderson ran this store in Hillsboro.

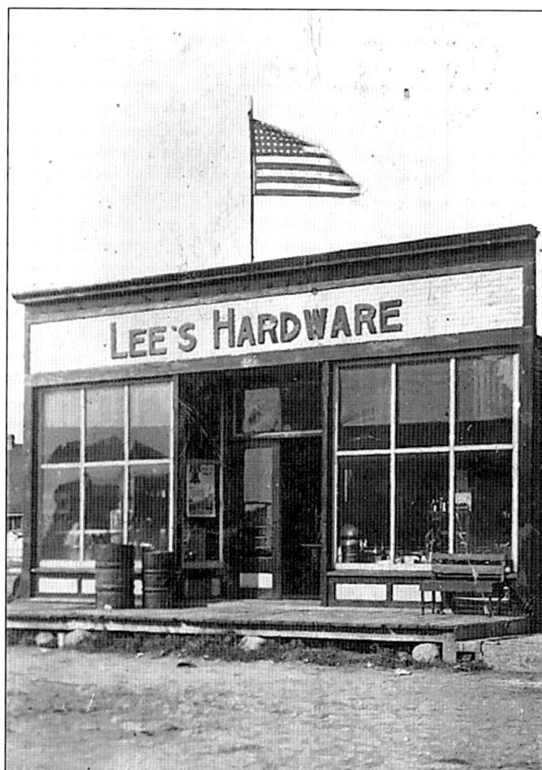

During the first half of the twentieth century, North Dakota had thousands of stores that looked like this one. As roads improved, one could drive to a major shopping center in a matter of minutes. Many of these shopping centers are located on the edges of the cities, and consequently, the downtown stores have lost business.

Pictured here is Roger Maris (1934–1985), North Dakota's most famous baseball player. As a football player at Shanley High School, he once ran back four kickoffs for touchdowns! This photograph was taken when Roger, about 19, played for the Fargo Moorhead Twins. Baseball has always been popular in North Dakota, but the state has not turned out as many stars as the Southern states or the Caribbean. In 1935, the famous Satchel Paige pitched Bismarck to the national semi-pro title.

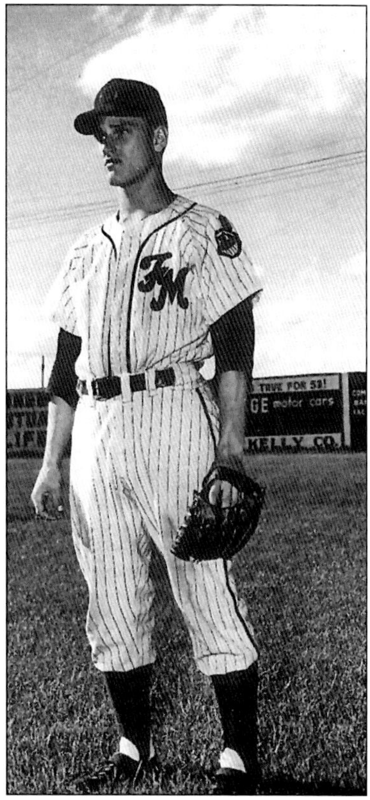

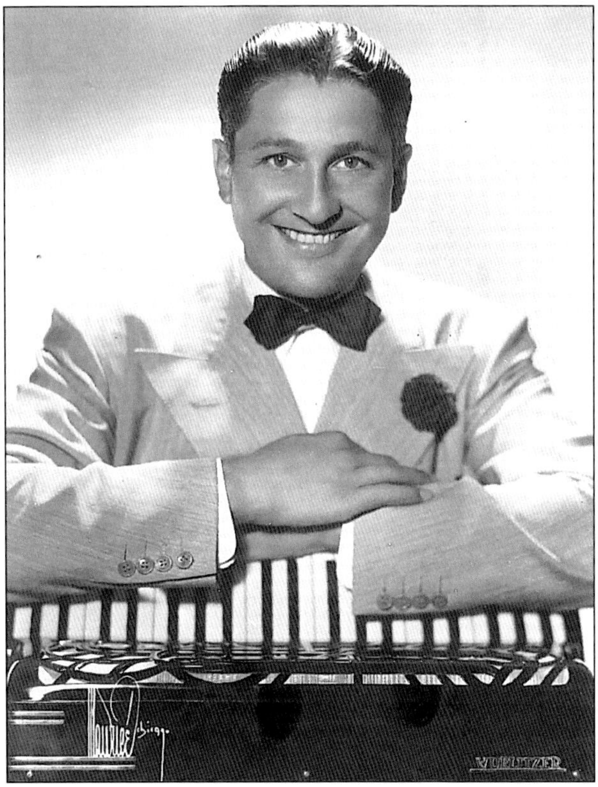

One of North Dakota's most favorite sons must be Lawrence Welk.

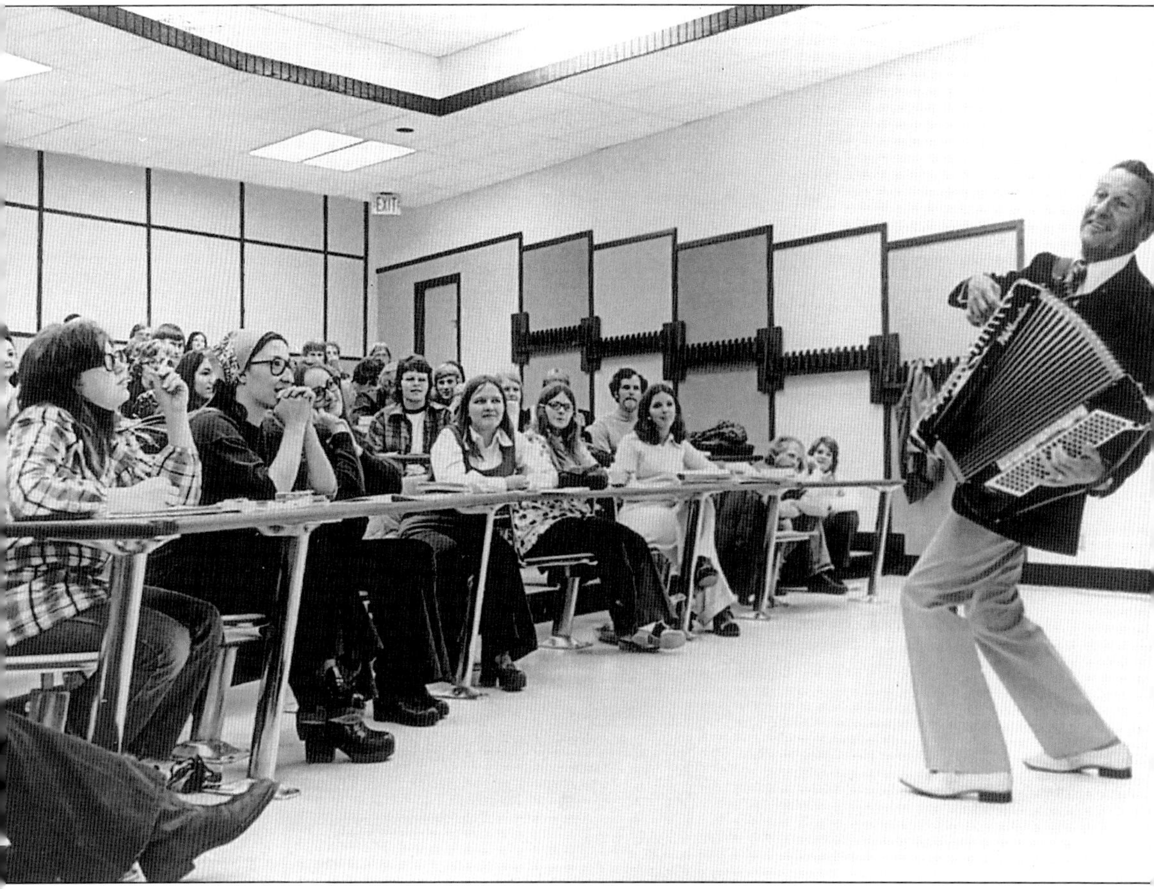

Lawrence Welk was born March 11, 1903, in Strasburg. Before he became nationally famous, his orchestra played at dances all over North Dakota. In his autobiography he describes the icy roads he traveled, and how the lack of money sometimes forced him to pawn his rings to buy gasoline to get to the next town. Here he is pictured playing for a class at the University of North Dakota in 1973.

Eight

North Dakota Snapshots

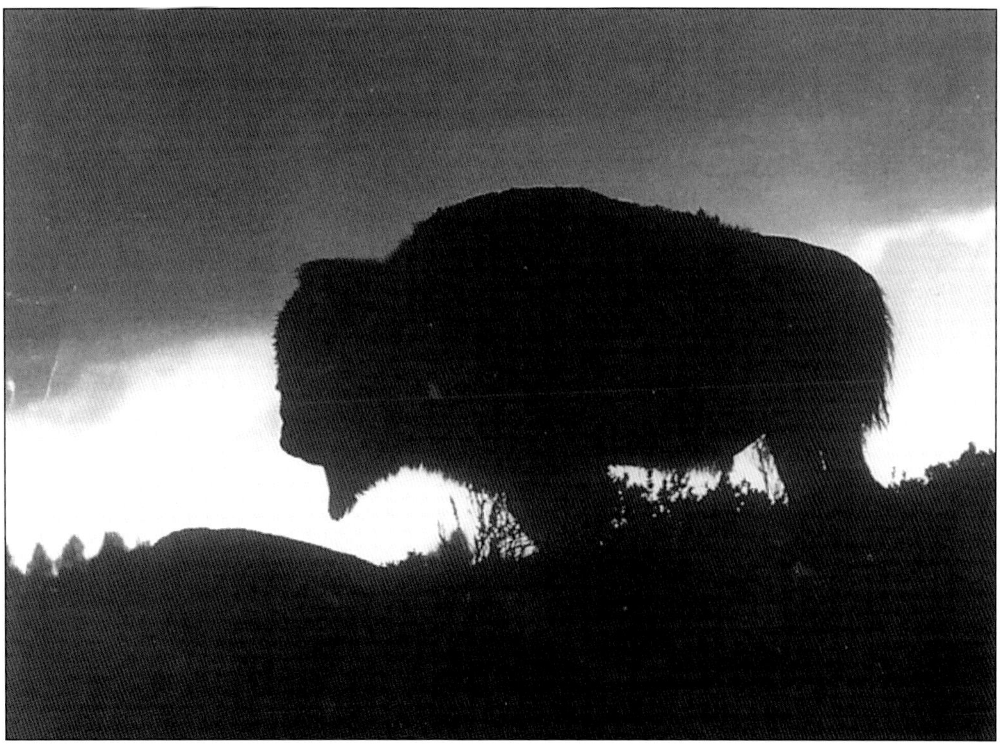

The mighty bison, popularly known as the buffalo, is making a comeback in North Dakota. They are being raised for their hide and meat, and also as a tourist attraction.

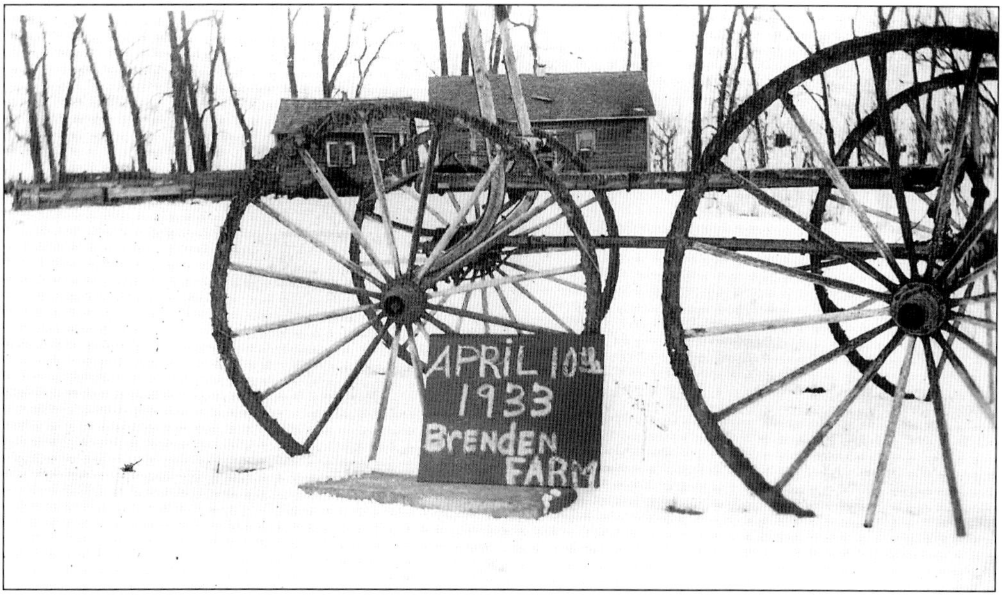

North Dakota weather can play pranks on people. Apparently on April 10, 1933 it snowed in North Dakota. This skeleton of a buggy is still used by the kids.

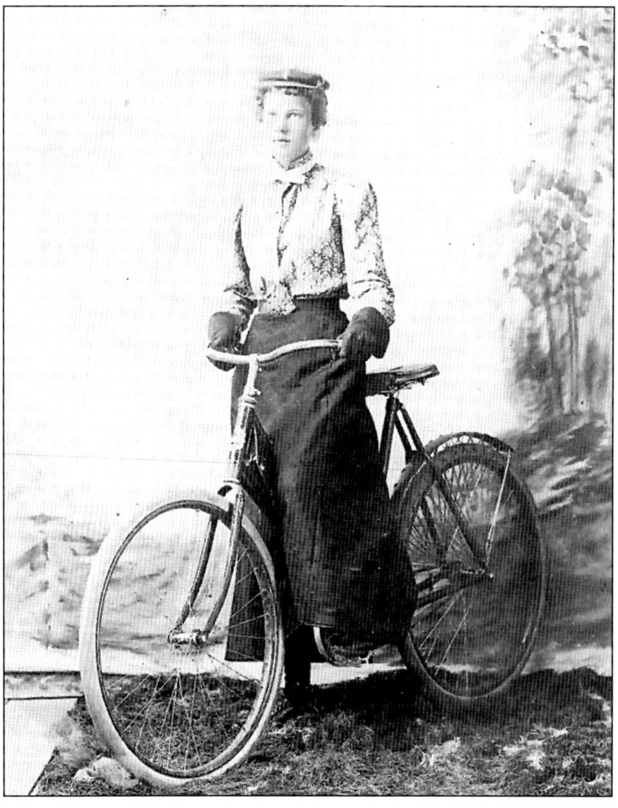

This photograph was taken by M.G. Markell of the Cabinet Portrait Studio in Williston. Williston writer Bill Shemorry wrote "What were the women of the old West like? They might look like this belle of the old West but, more than likely, the real woman of the old West would be gaunt, sad-faced and wearing a ragged sun-bonnet. But with indomitable will she conquered all, nursing her man's hurts and illness, often raising their family without benefits of doctors and medicines, contriving, managing, but most of all surviving, as she built a home in the wilderness."

This fashionably-dressed lady is standing by her touring car in 1928.

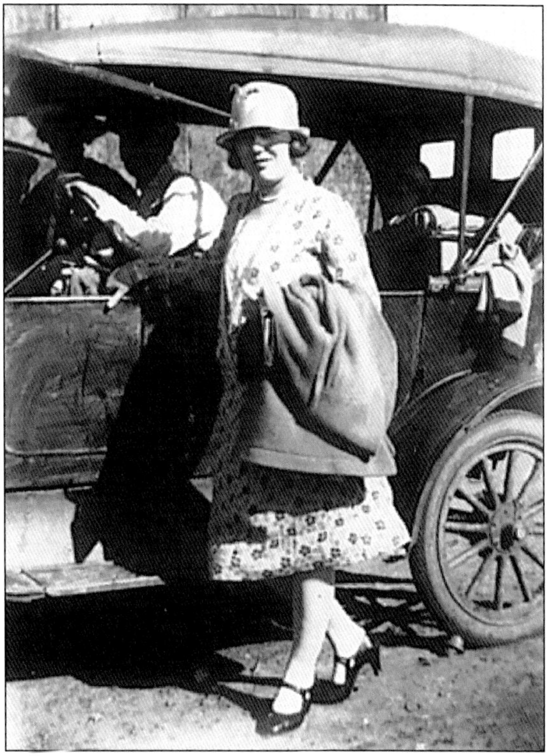

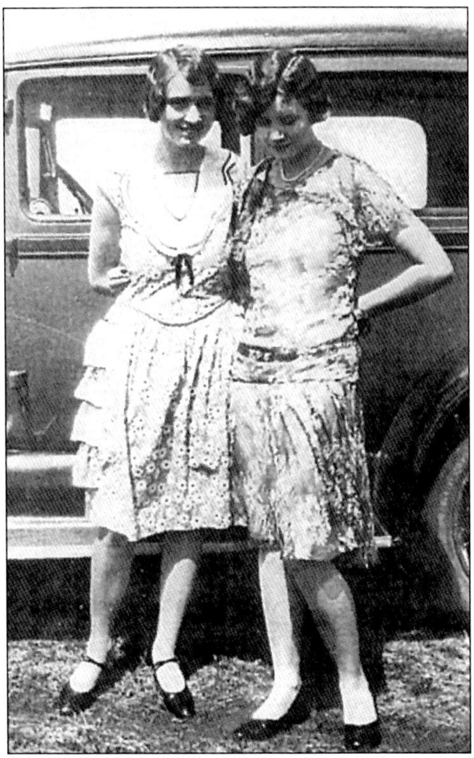

The Pearson Girls, Elsie and Lucille, wore these attractive dresses about 1928. *The Pearson Girls* is a book by Kathy L. Plotkin about a family growing up in Emmons County, North Dakota.

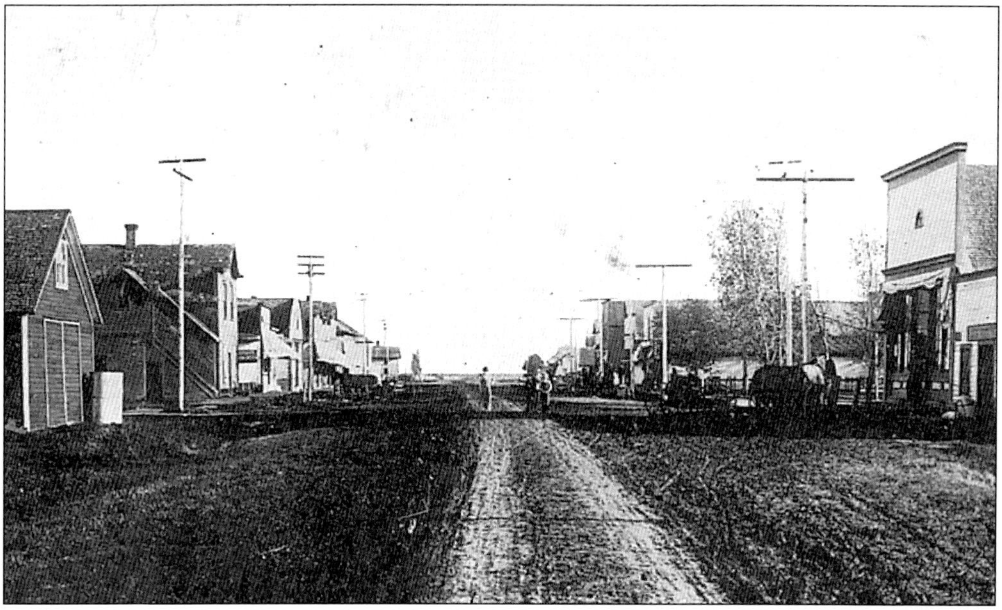

Perley, Minnesota, is just across the Red River and to the north of Fargo, North Dakota. This is a view of Perley around 1909. Many North Dakotans shop in the Minnesota towns across the Red River, including Hendrum, Climax, Halstad, and Ada.

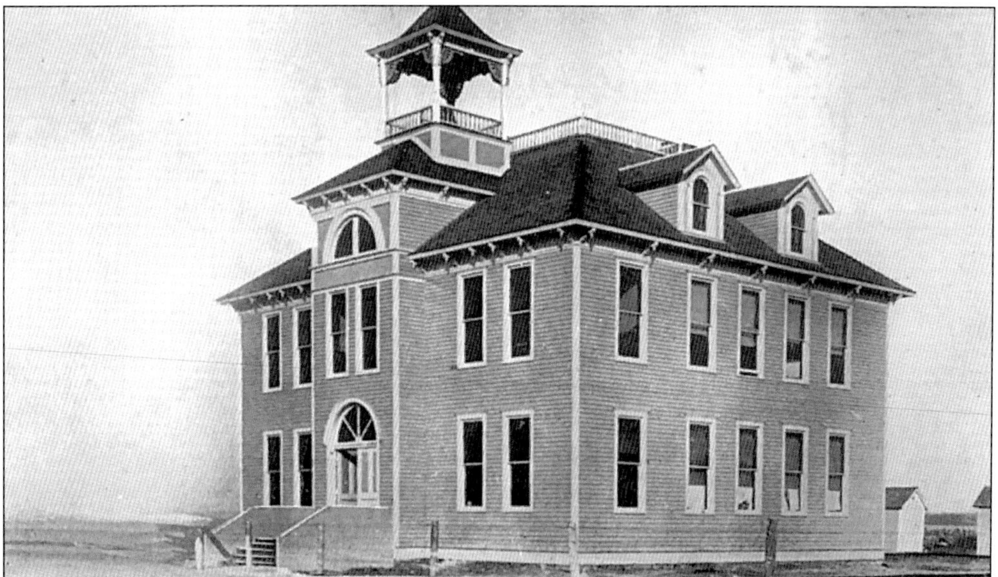

This is a photograph of the Perley school building. In the early 1900s there were no school buses, so getting the kids to school was a challenge. In the winter, one way was a sled full of hay, cowskin robes, and kids with their lunch buckets.

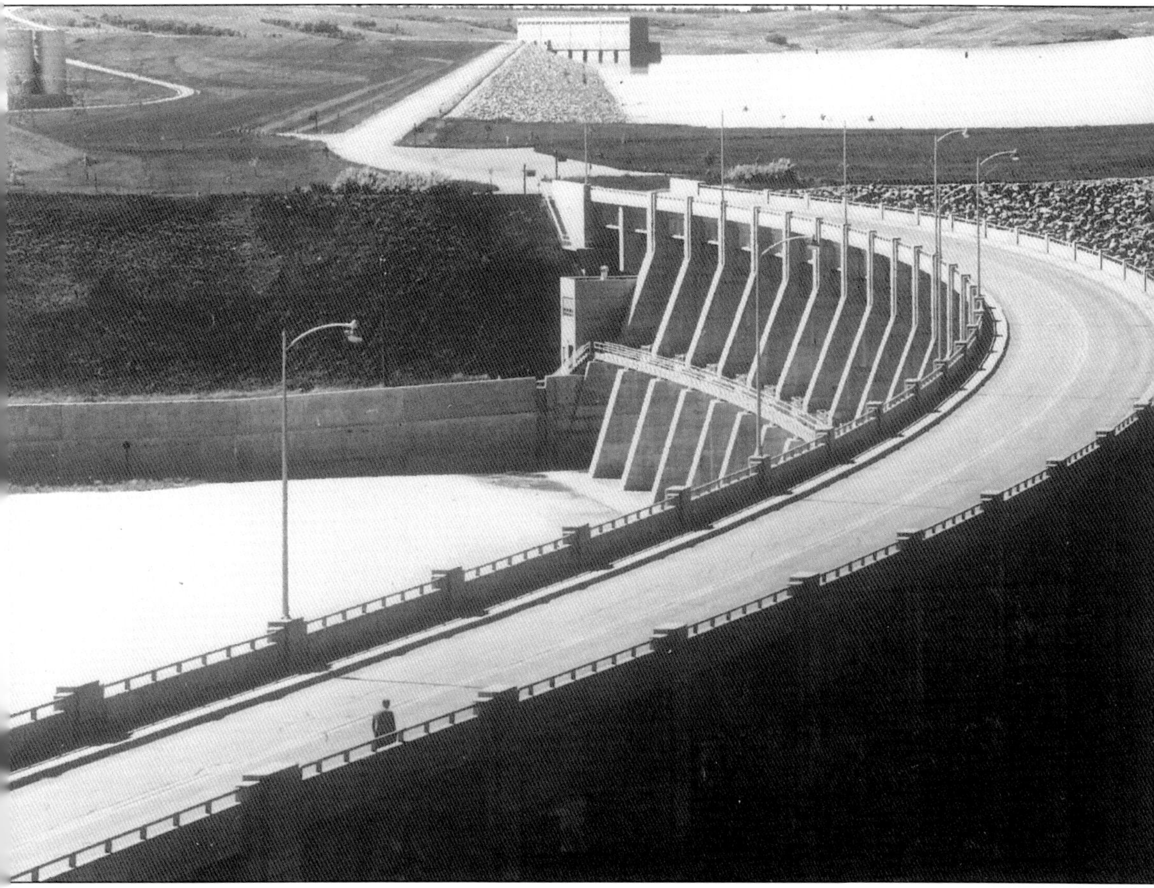

Garrison Dam was authorized by the United States Congress on December 22, 1944, although plans were drawn up many years before that. When it was completed in 1960, it provided flood control, irrigation, and hydroelectric power. This photograph shows the completed dam.

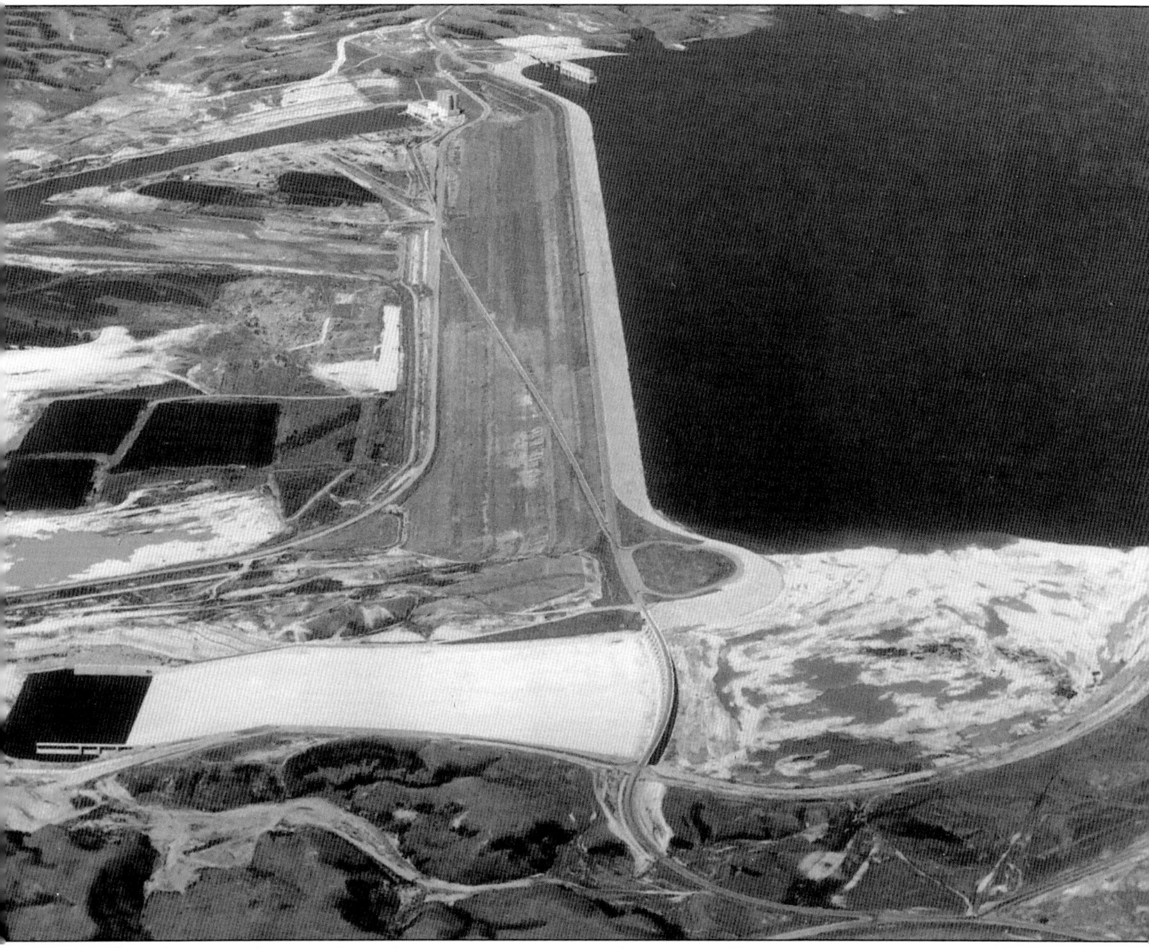

This photograph was taken during construction of Garrison Dam.

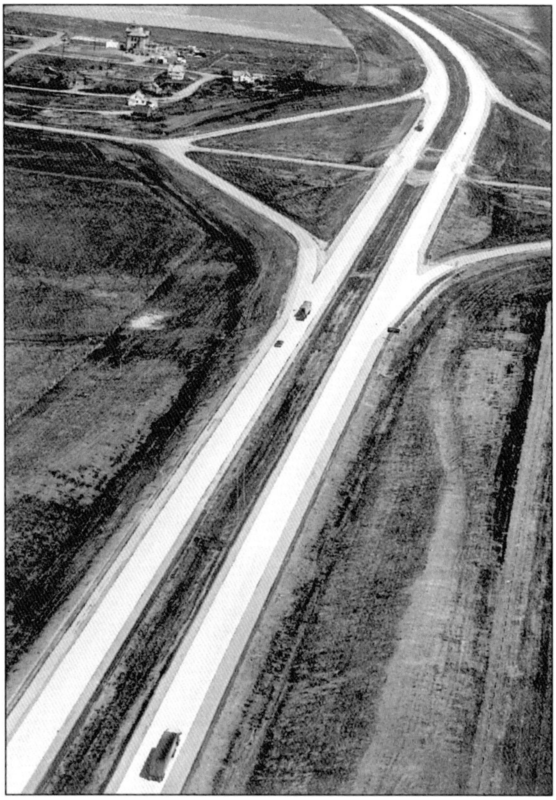

Speeding is always a major problem in North Dakota since the roads are temptingly straight and flat, and traffic is usually light. The author's father died in 1928 when another car ran into his Whippet near Fargo. The author's mother was killed 25 years later in a car accident near Hillsboro.

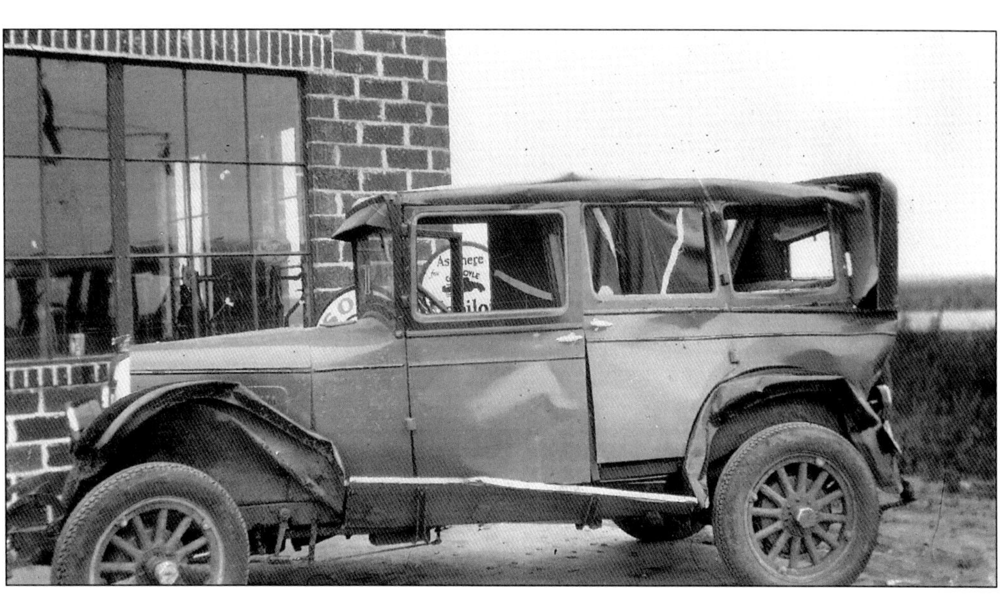

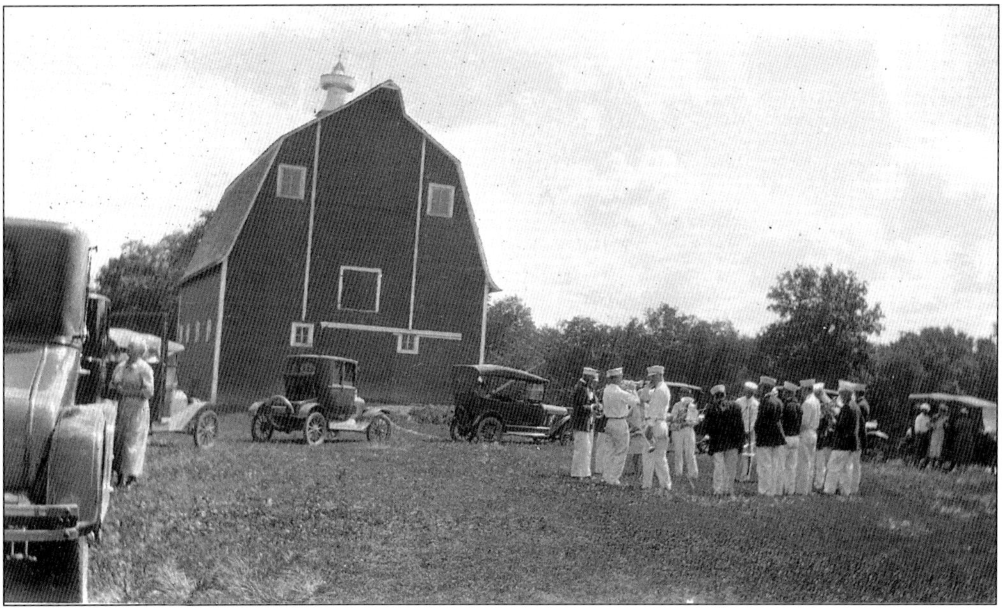

It was a big honor for you and your farm if the community band paid you a surprise visit. The cars in this image indicate the photo was taken with a box camera in about 1918.

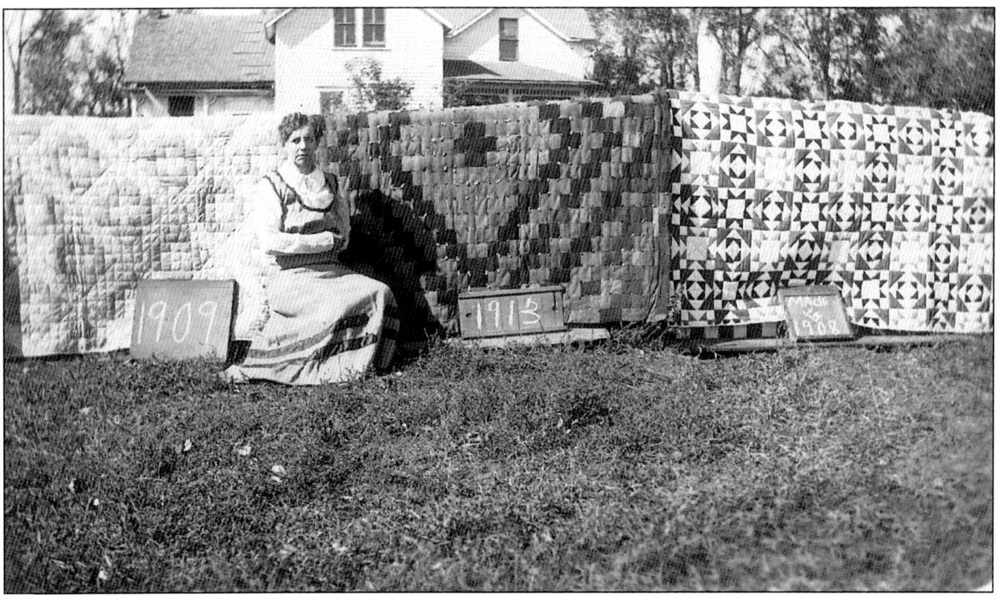

Quilting was a popular occupation for North Dakota women, especially in the wintertime. Each woman came up with her own design, and the quilts were often entered in the county or state fair. A quilt frame would be set up in one room all winter long, allowing for work to be done anytime a spare moment could be found.

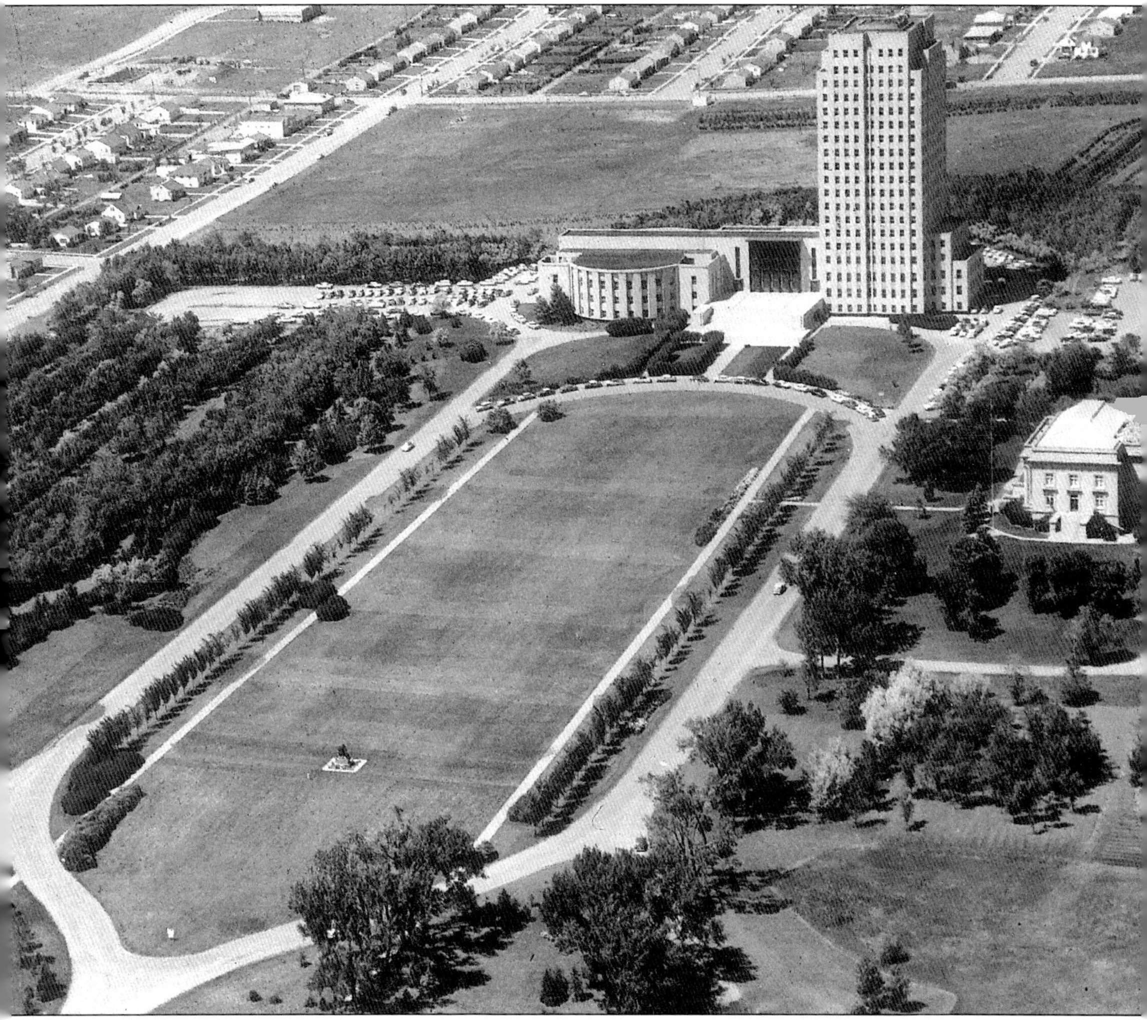

Many people have said that North Dakota has one of the most beautiful capitol buildings in the United States. It is pictured above.

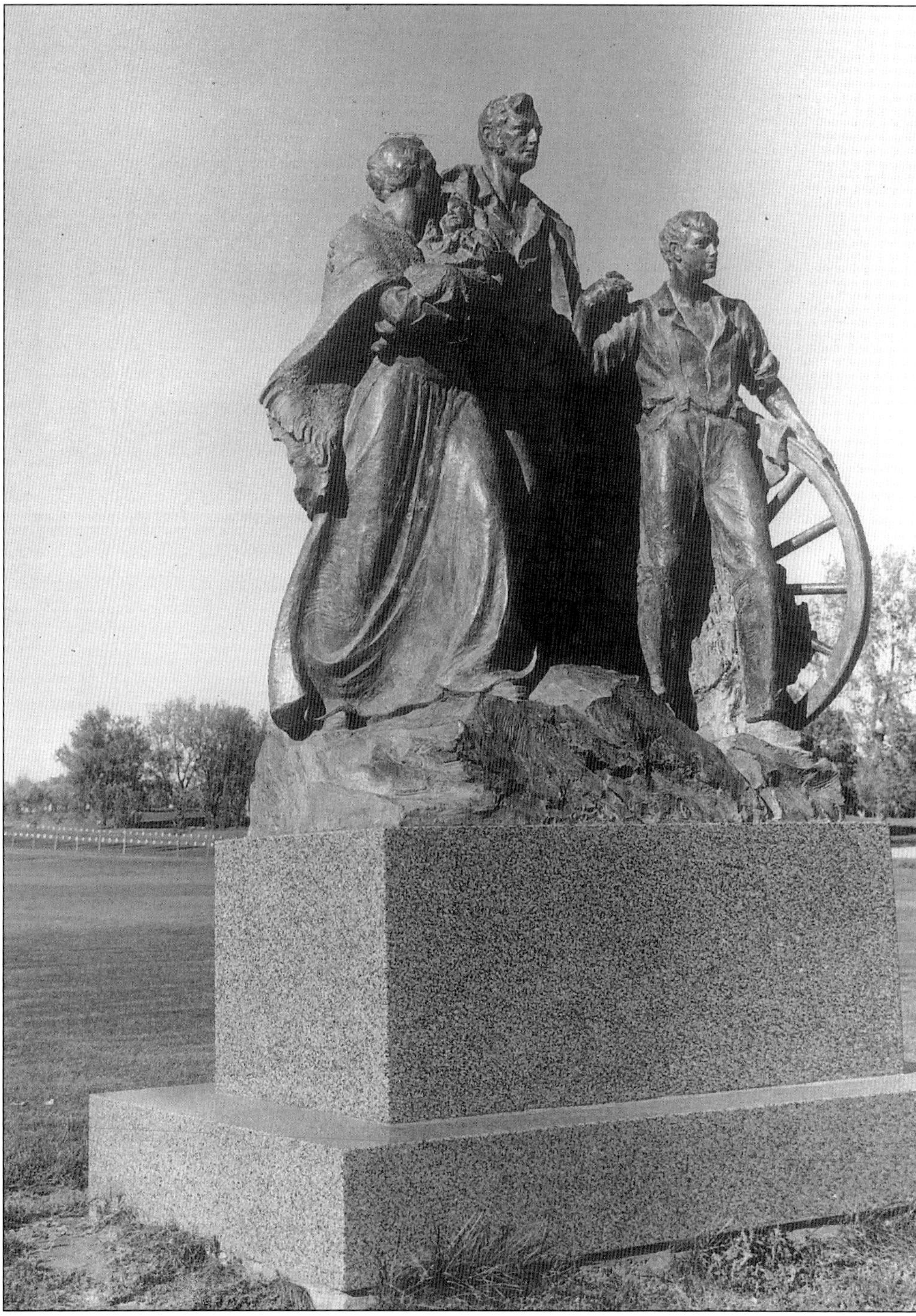

This statue honoring pioneers stands in the middle of the lawn in front of the North Dakota State Capitol in Bismarck.

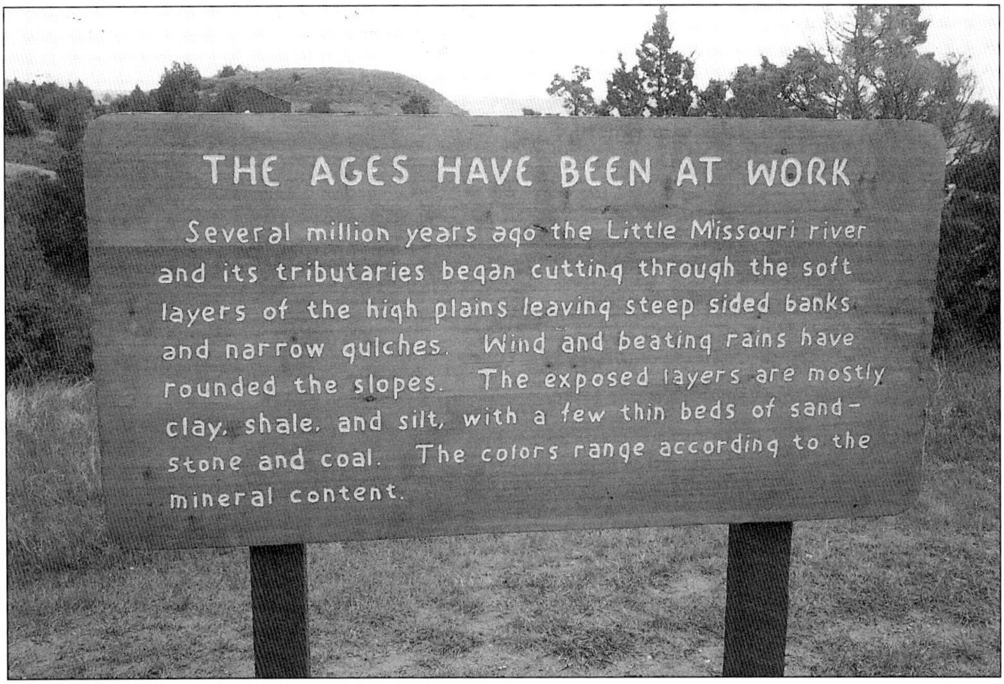

This wooden sign in the North Dakota Badlands tells visitors how these rugged and magnificent badlands were formed through the ages.

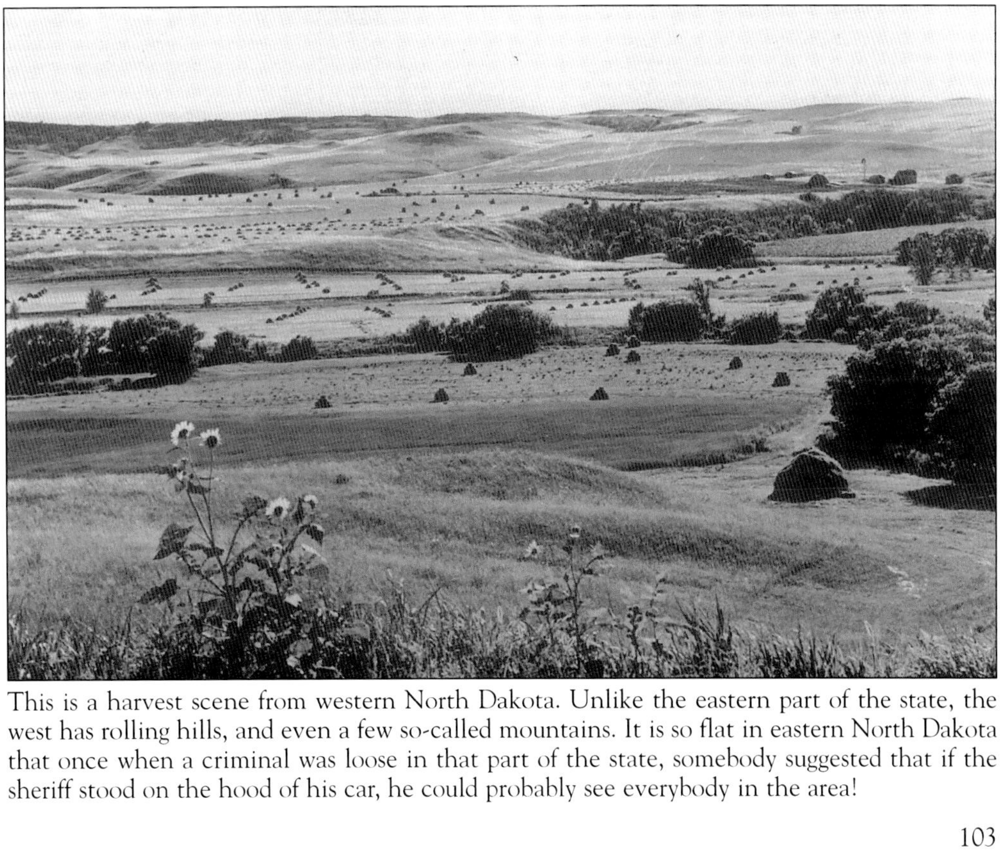

This is a harvest scene from western North Dakota. Unlike the eastern part of the state, the west has rolling hills, and even a few so-called mountains. It is so flat in eastern North Dakota that once when a criminal was loose in that part of the state, somebody suggested that if the sheriff stood on the hood of his car, he could probably see everybody in the area!

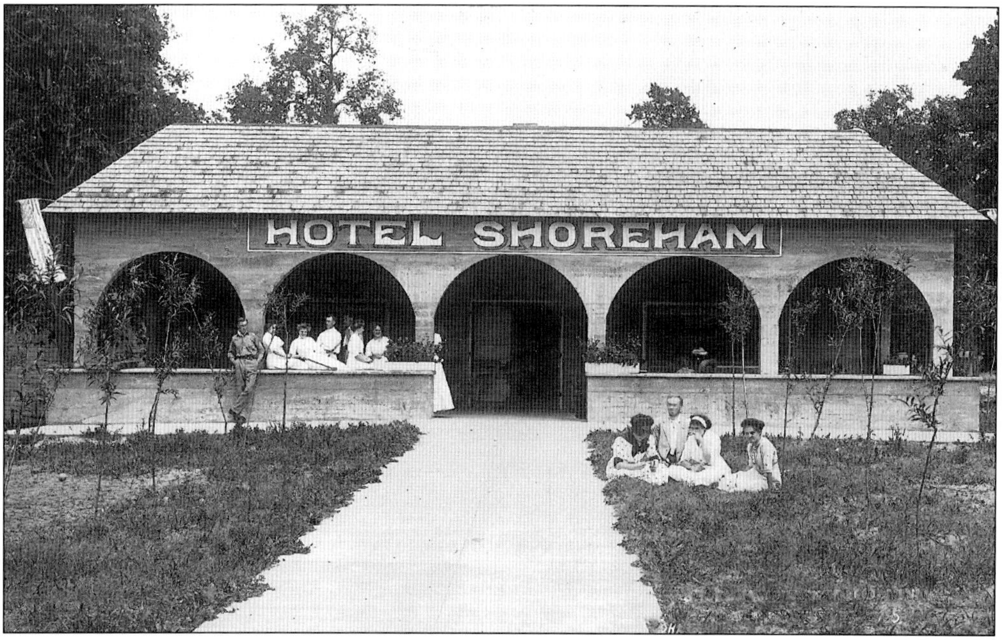

Many eastern North Dakotans drove over to the Minnesota lakes in the early 1900s. That was where the water was! Now North Dakota had built some lakes of its own—a smart investment. The Detroit Lakes area was popular with Fargo people and other eastern North Dakotans. Many people spent their honeymoons at lakes in Minnesota. Postcards were sent back to North Dakota to make the relatives and friends jealous!

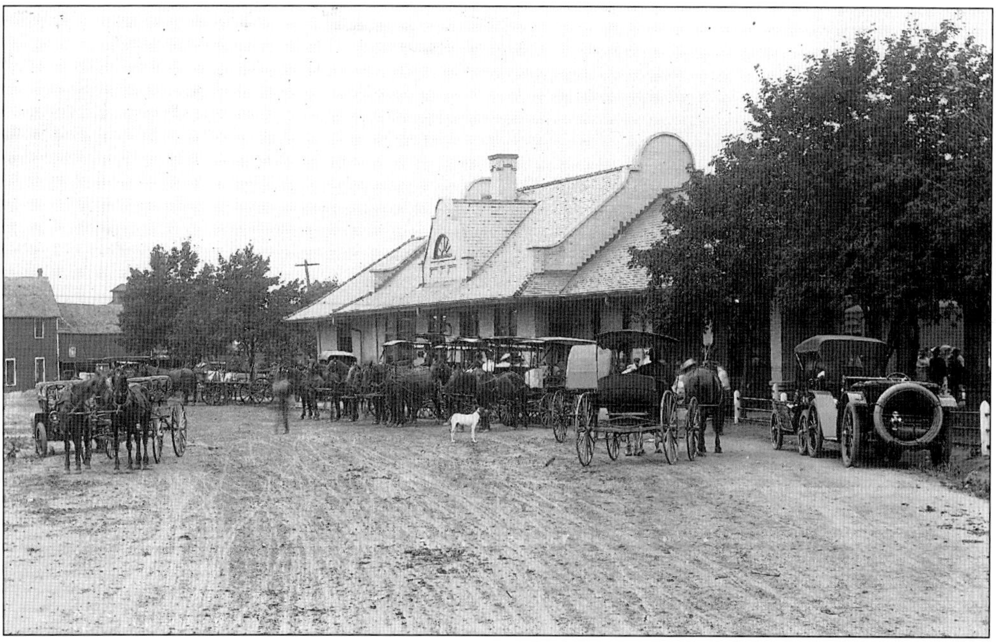

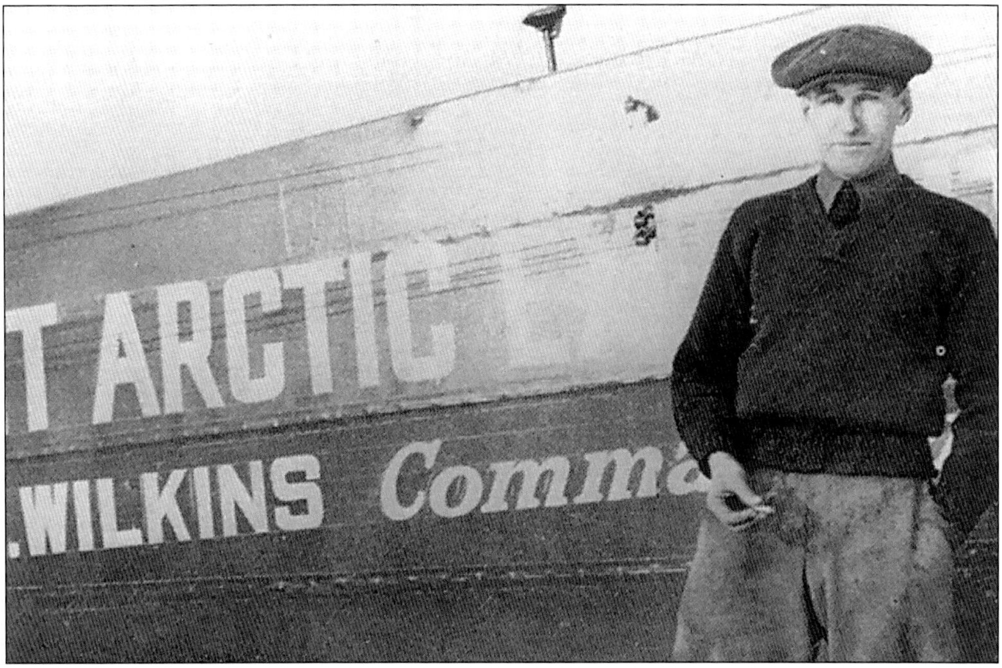

Pioneer Aviator Carl Ben Eielson of Hatton, North Dakota, flew over both the Arctic and the Antarctic in 1920. He was killed in a crash off Siberia during a rescue mission. In 1998, Tom Smith and Bill Signs commemorated the 1928 Polar Flight of Eielson, flying from Barrow, Alaska, to Spitsbergen, Norway. Tom Smith is a graduate of the journalism program at the University of North Dakota, and a native of Grand Forks.

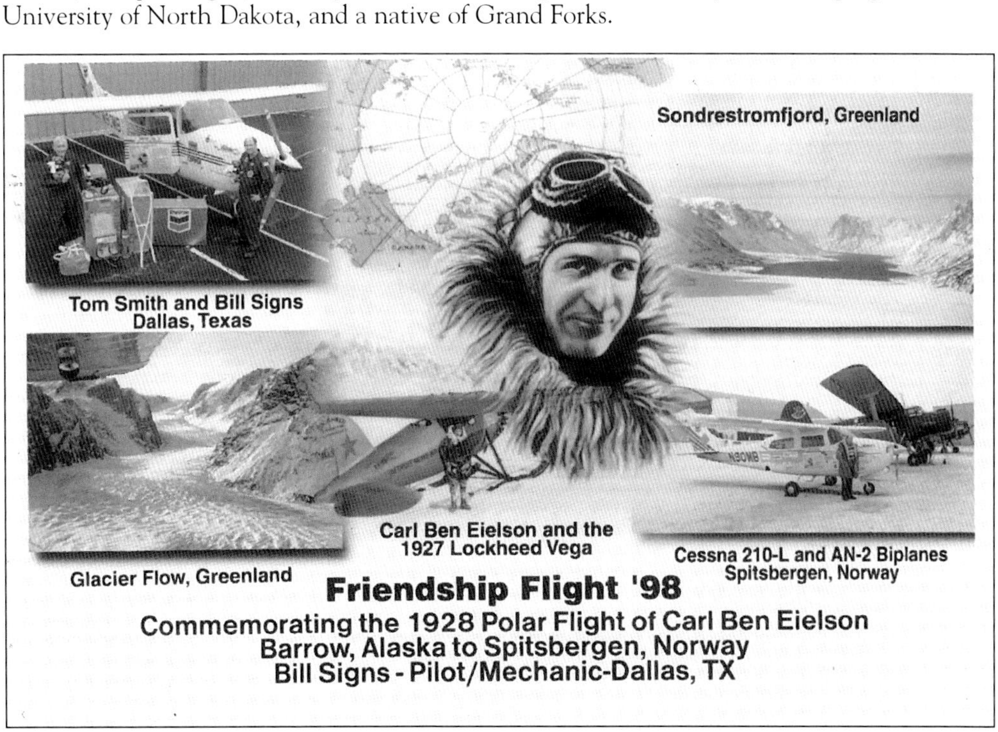

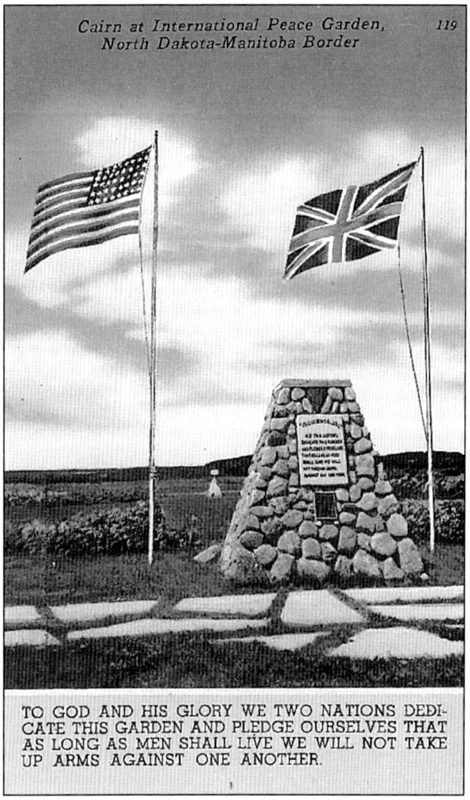

The International Peace Garden on the North Dakota–Manitoba border represents a pledge that the U.S. and Canada will "not take up arms against one another." The pledge has been kept, and the border is one of the most peaceful in the world. North Dakota's official nickname is "The Peace Garden State."

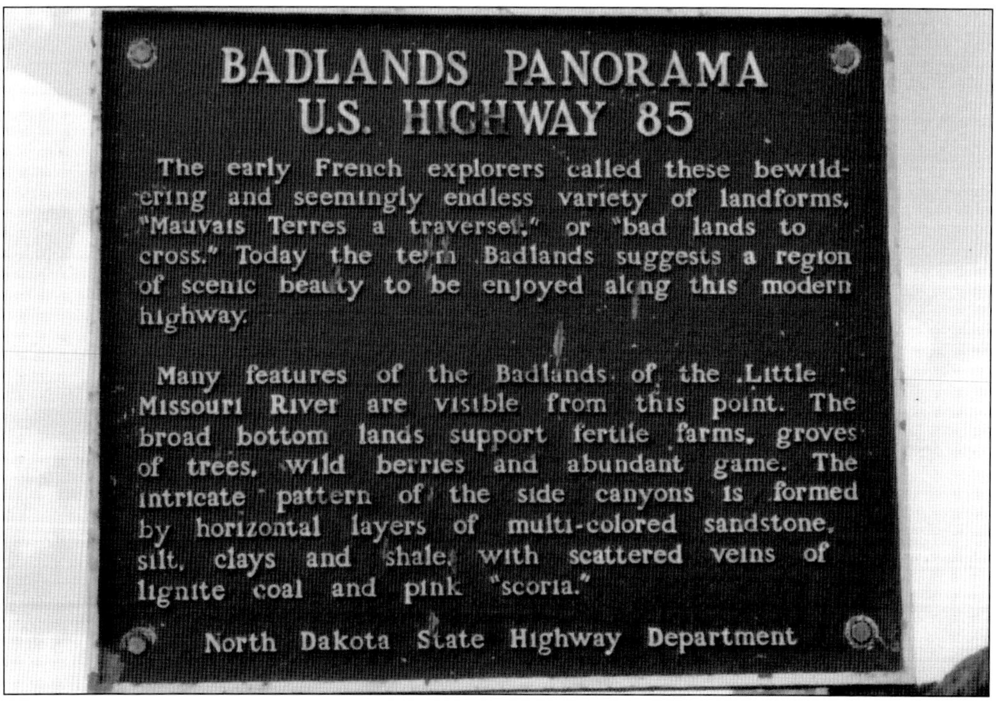

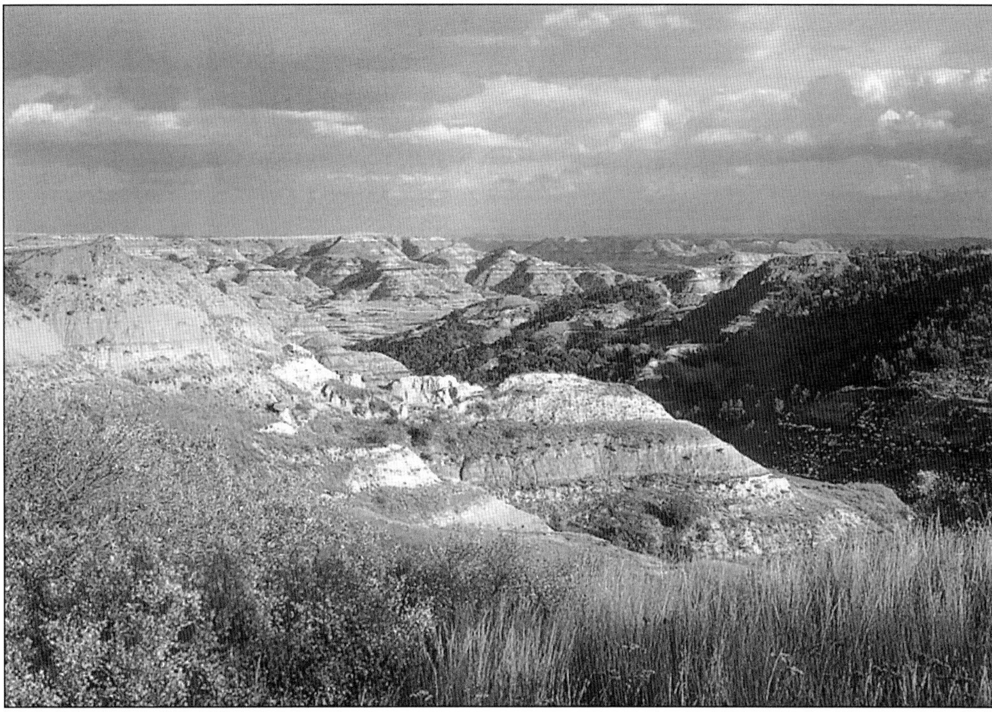

The Badlands of western North Dakota are a great asset for the state. Many people in the United States do not know this, including some from eastern North Dakota.

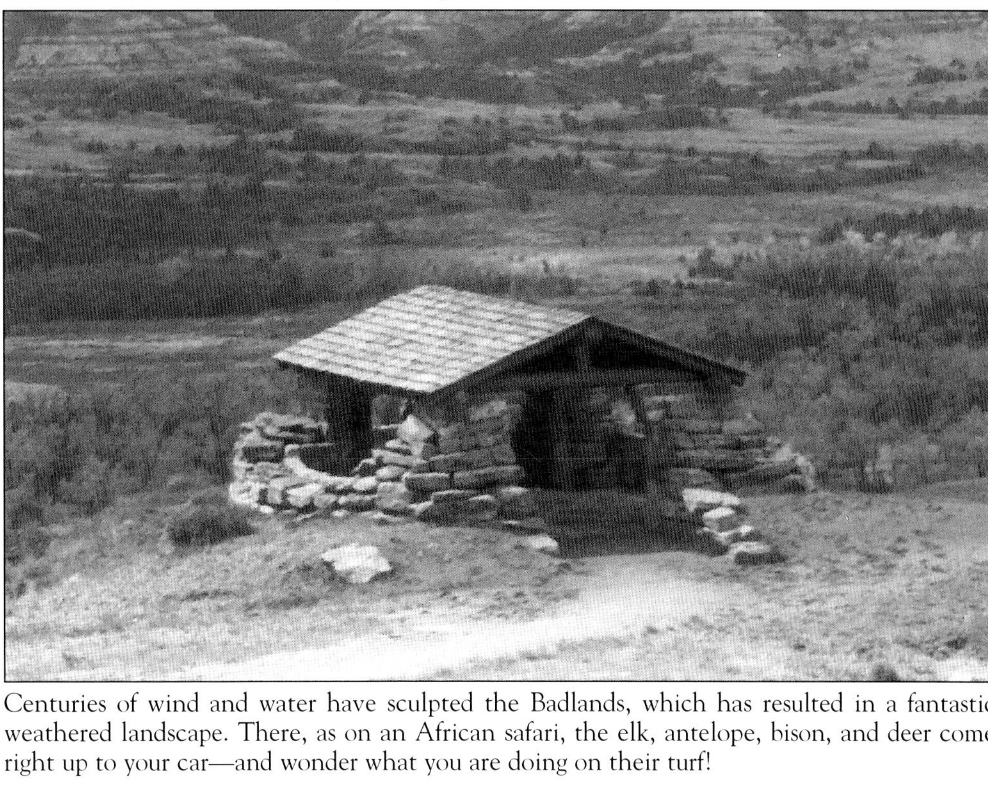

Centuries of wind and water have sculpted the Badlands, which has resulted in a fantastic weathered landscape. There, as on an African safari, the elk, antelope, bison, and deer come right up to your car—and wonder what you are doing on their turf!

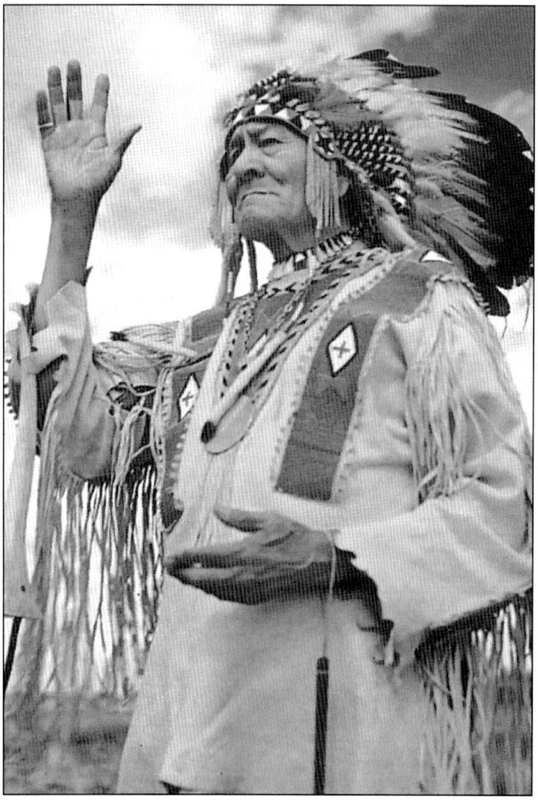

The Sioux have been living in North Dakota for a long time. According to the *Columbia Encyclopedia*, the Sioux are known for their physical and mental abilities.

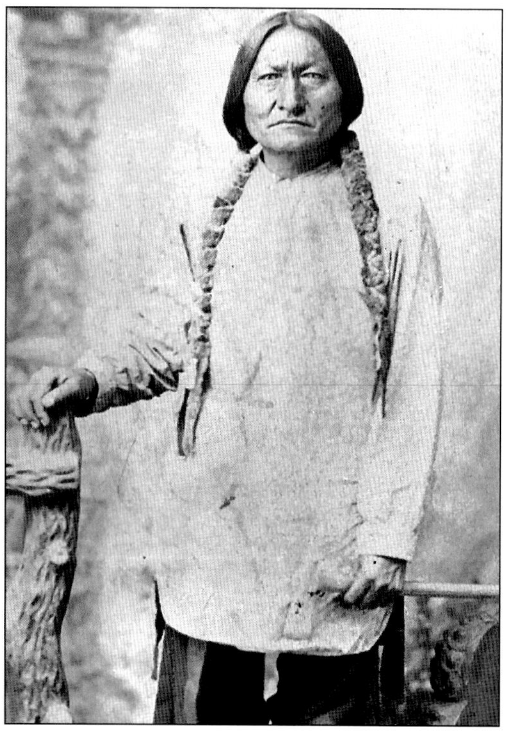

Sitting Bull was probably the most famous Sioux leader. Because it was thought that he had a "demoralizing influence" among the Sioux, he was arrested and later killed by United States officials.

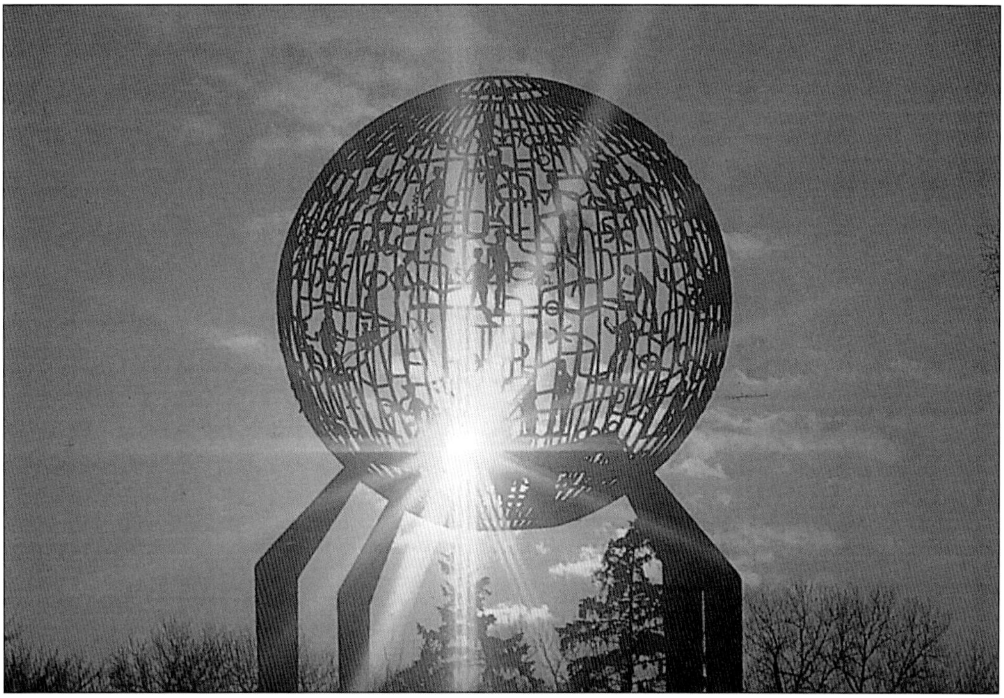

The University of North Dakota at Grand Forks is the oldest university in the state. It was founded in 1883, even before North Dakota became a state. This memorial sphere represents the eternal quest for knowledge.

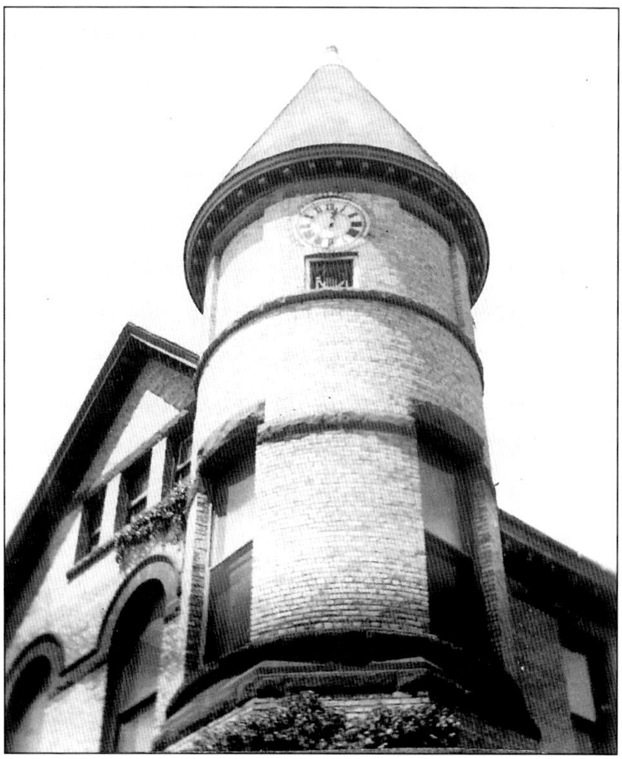

North Dakota State University was founded in 1893. The 267-acre campus is located in the northwest part of Fargo.

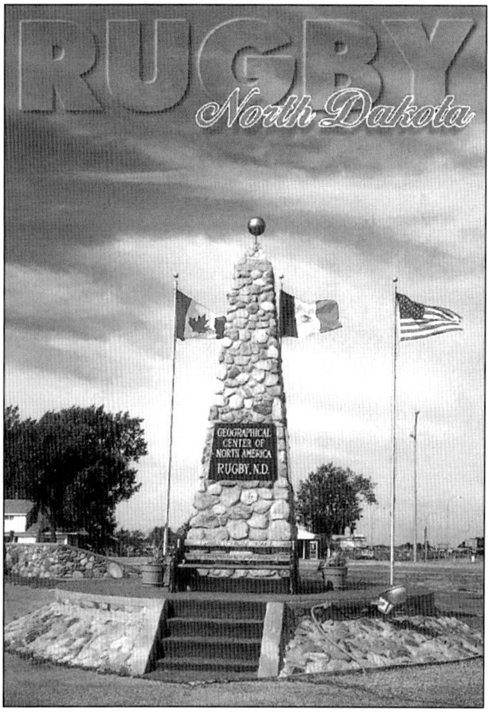

Rugby, North Dakota, is proud of being the "Geographical Center of North America."

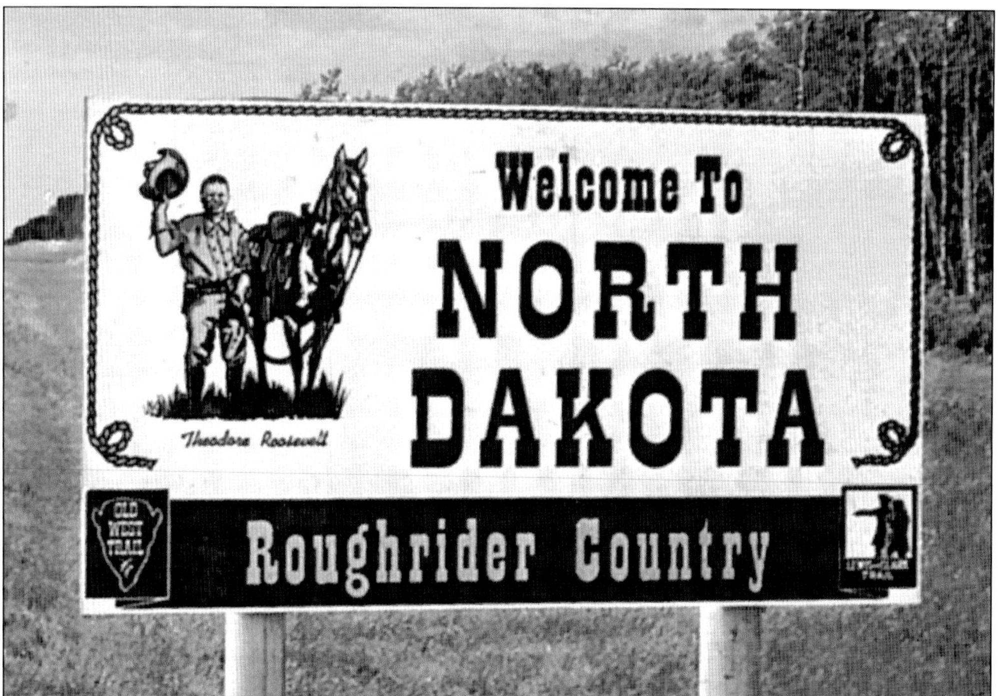

North Dakota has several nicknames, including the "Roughrider State," the "Flickertail State,"and the official nickname, the "Peace Garden State." Other lesser used nicknames include "The Friendly State," "The Golden Grain State," and the "Land of Fresh Horizons."

WDAY in Fargo was the first radio station to start broadcasting in North Dakota. From 1900 to1940, radio played a key role in the life of North Dakotans. Radios offered news, entertainment, weather reports, and commodity prices, among other things. It also helped to fight loneliness and a feeling of isolation on the farm. Later radio, and even television, was available on tractors. These photographs were taken in the WDAY lobby.

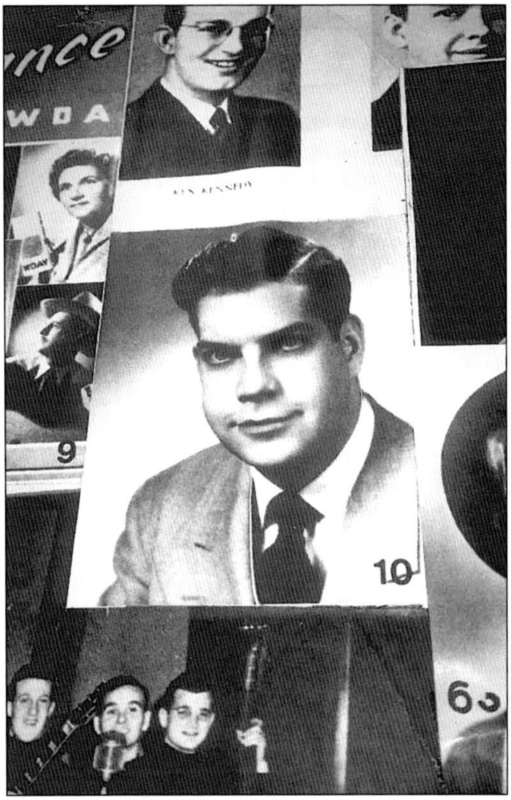

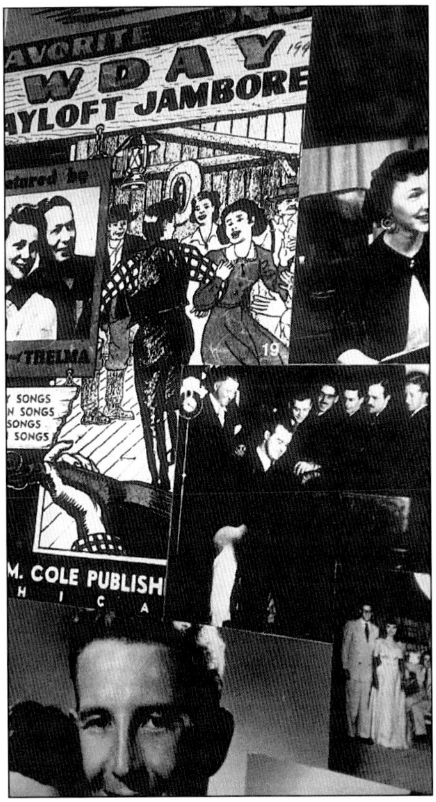

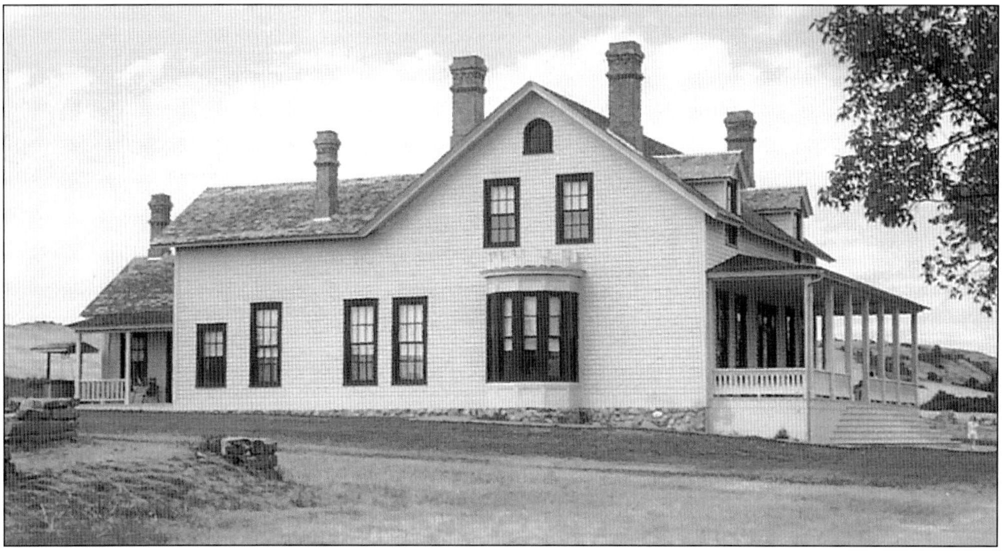

The house that General George Armstrong Custer lived in has been rebuilt and can be visited at Fort Lincoln State Park in Mandan.

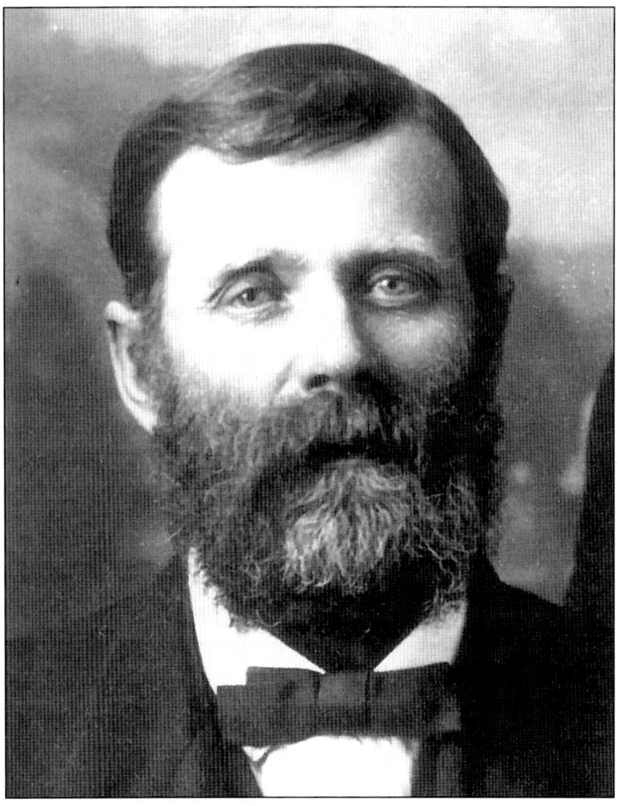

Many men wore beards in the first two decades of the century, like Torger Brenden, pictured at left. Many towns recently celebrating centennials had beard-growing contests as a reminder of the past.

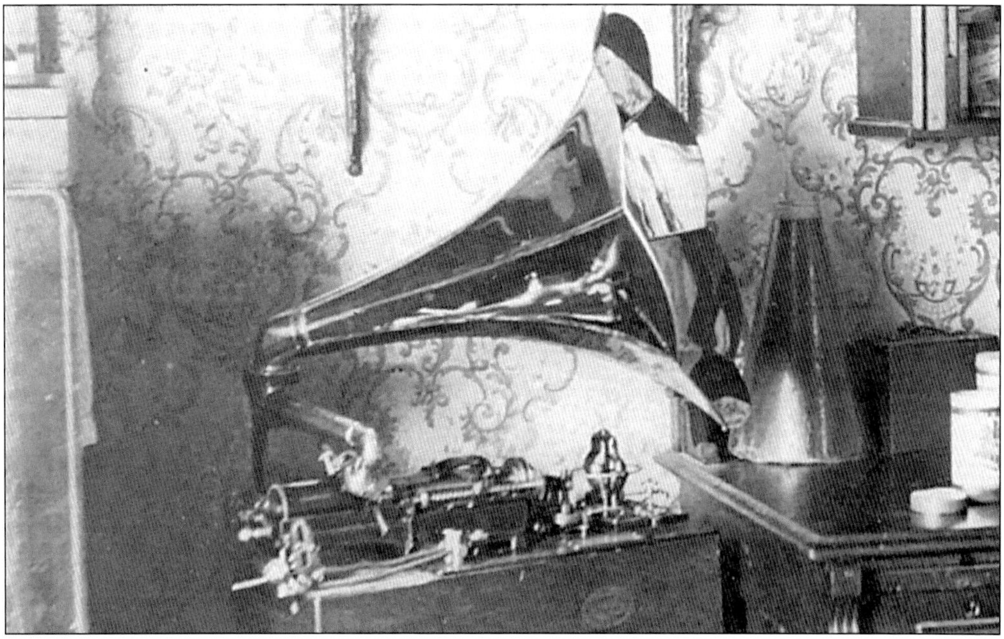

Pictured here is a gramophone, found in many North Dakota homes early in the century. The gramophone played cylinder records.

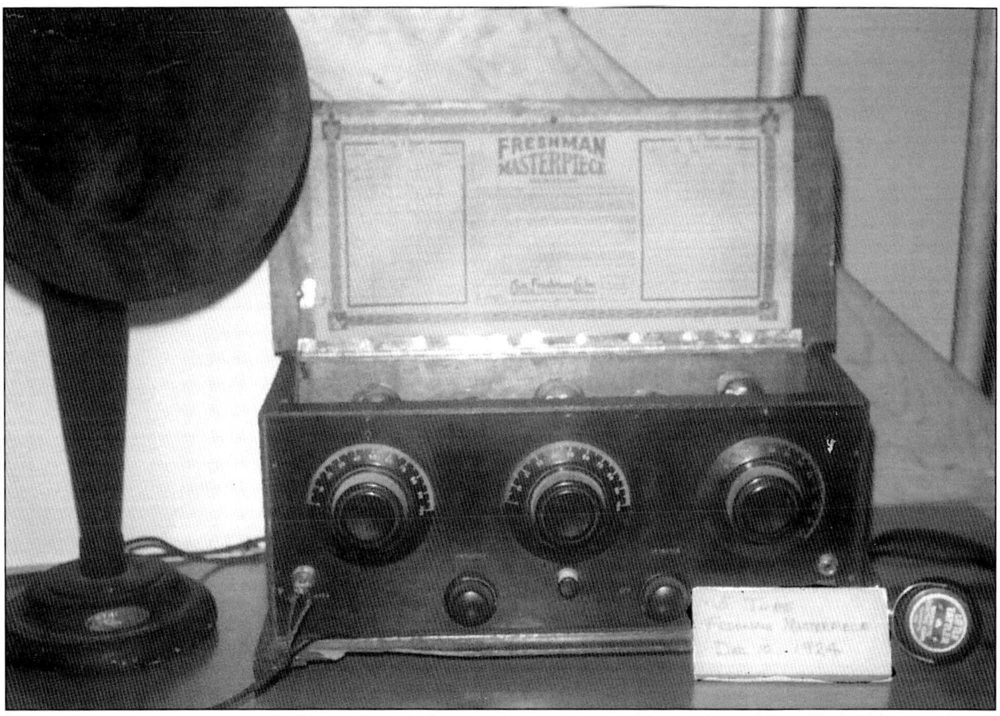

This old battery-operated, five-tube radio was bought on December 10, 1924. The author's father sold one cow for $40 to buy the radio called "Freshman Masterpiece." When Charles Lindbergh was making his historic flight across the Atlantic, the hired men came in from the field every hour to hear news about the flight.

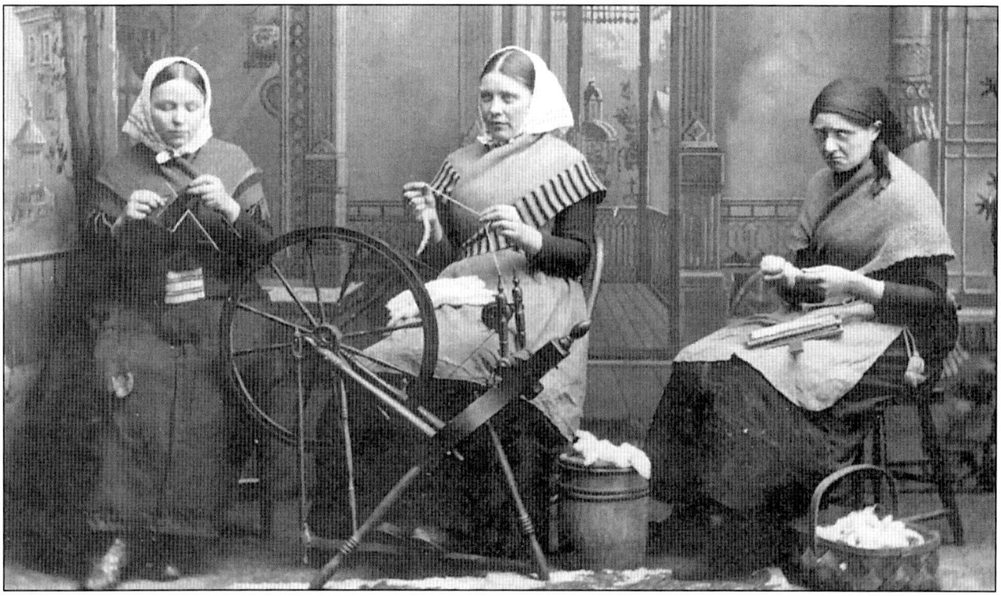

Most of the early North Dakota homes had a spinning wheel like this one, which was often used far into the night. There was never a minute wasted!

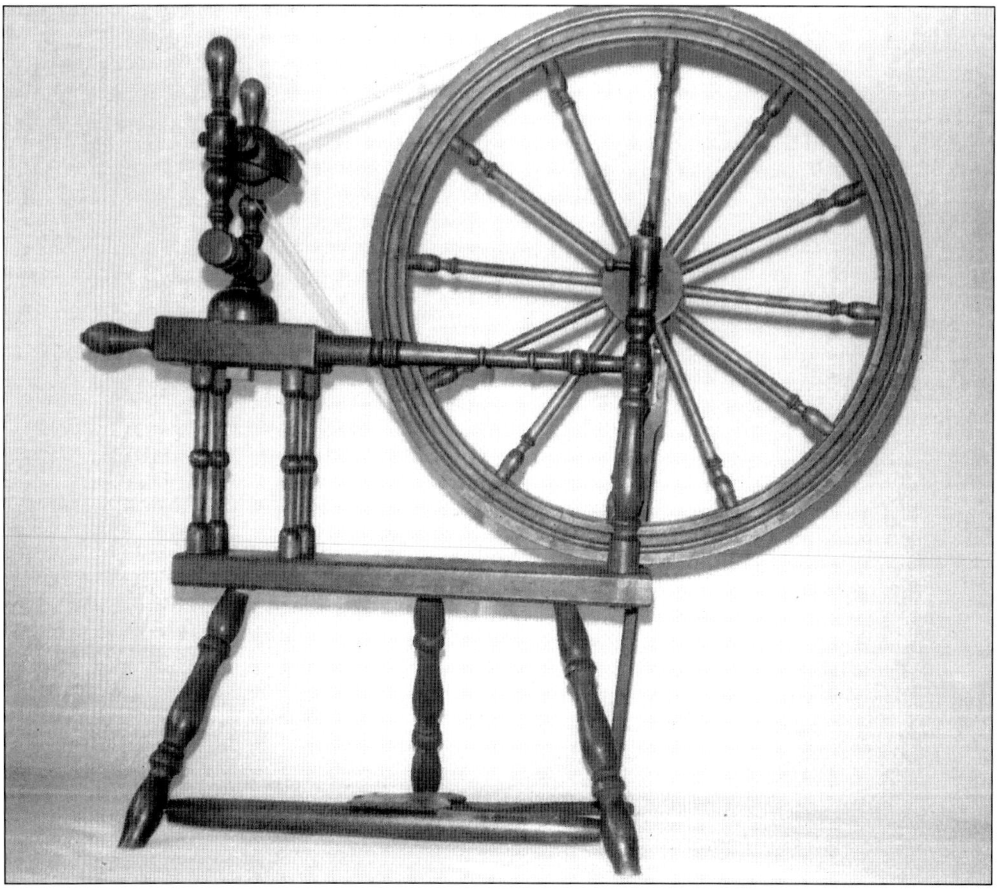

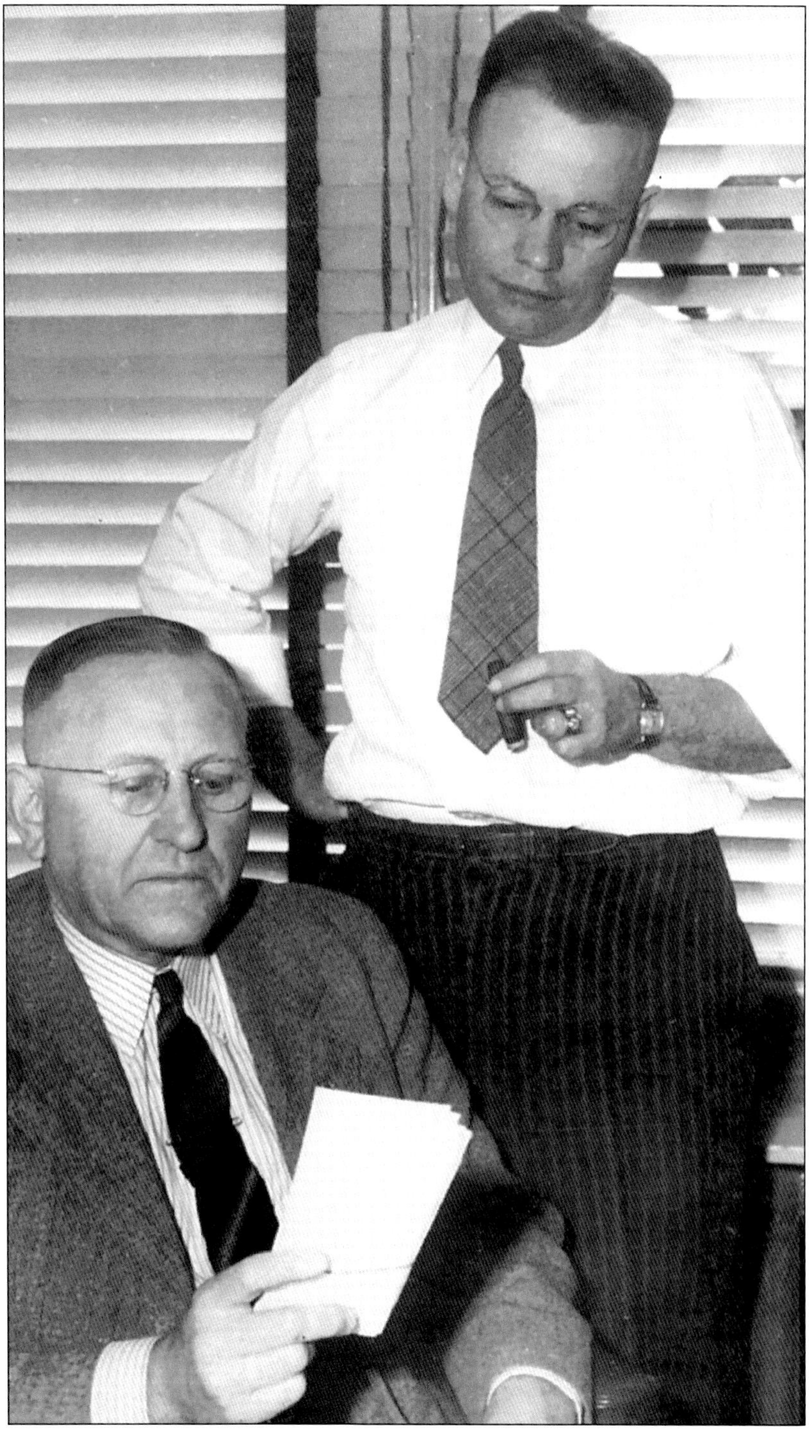

During the Depression of the 1930s, North Dakota bankers had a difficult time. During the years 1923–1933, 573 of the 898 banks in business in 1920 had failed. Besides financial problems, there were also many bank robberies. These two well known Hillsboro bankers, J.I. Hegge and Leonard Beal, struggled through those difficult years.

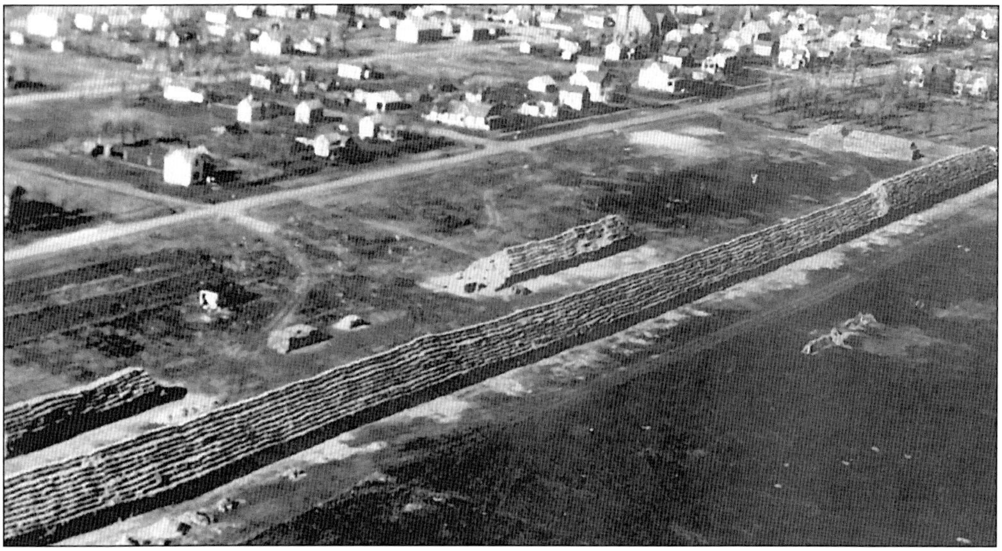

In November of 1934, this pile, made up of countless bales of straw, was trucked out to farmers in western North Dakota who were experiencing a severe drought. It is believed to be the largest pile of straw bales ever assembled in North Dakota.

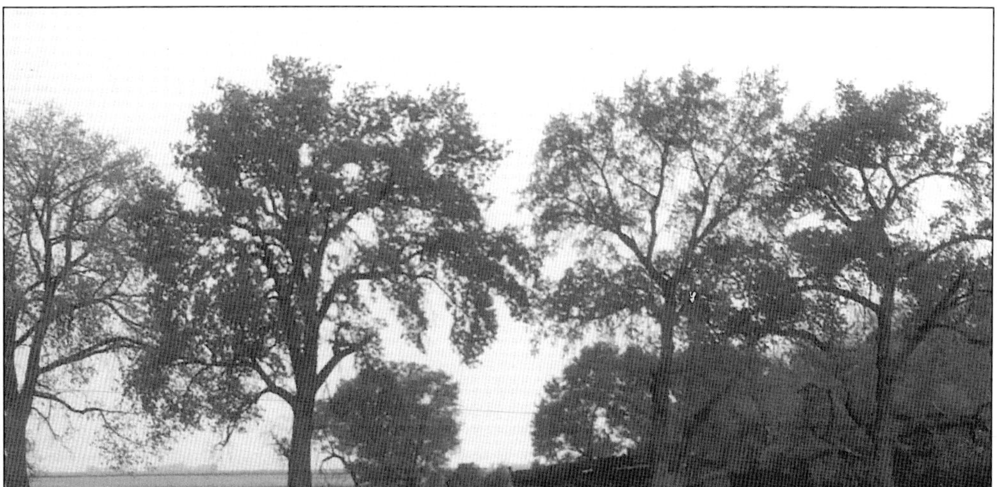

Cottonwood trees are found all over North Dakota, but the state tree is the American elm. As North Dakota poet Thurston Nelson once said: "Can you hear the whisper of the cottonwood leaves?" From 1900 to about 1930 there were very few trees in North Dakota. One western town had one tree, and that was where the town held all its picnics. In the early 1930s, the state shelter belt program was begun. These beautiful shelter belts are now all over the state, reducing erosion, minimizing the impact of the North Dakota wind and snow, providing shelter for birds and wildlife, and adding beauty to flat, open fields.

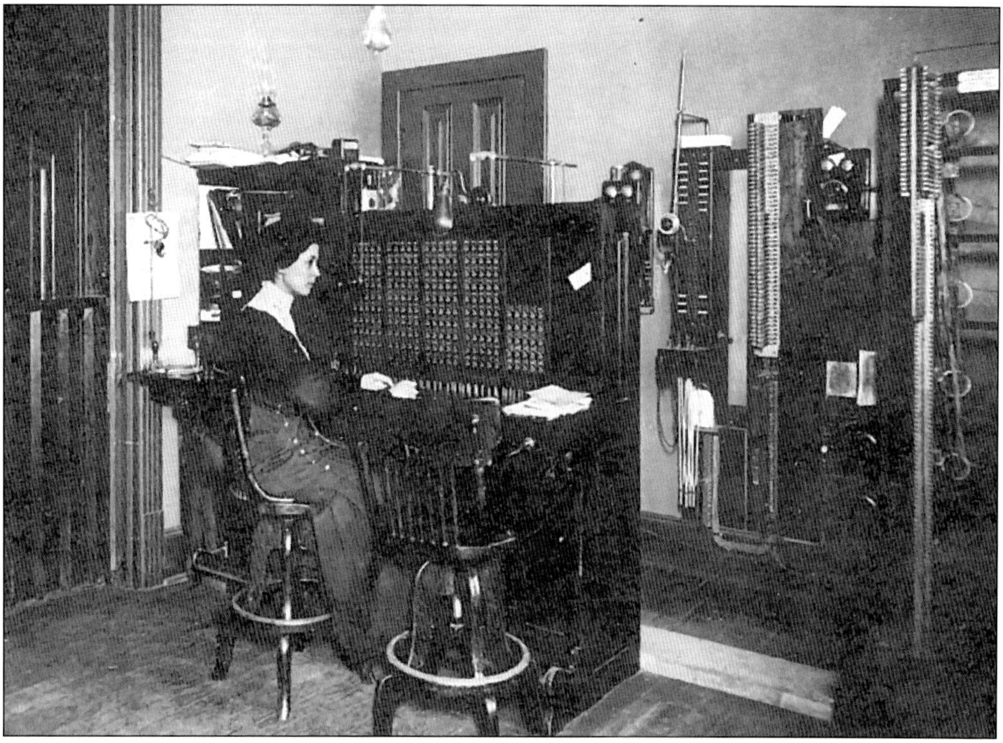

Early telephone systems had the human touch—an operator (like the young lady above) who knew everybody in town and often knew where they were at any given time. With the phones being "party lines," there were no phone numbers. Your "number" might be one short ring, and two long rings. Your neighbors could listen to your calls, but it is doubtful if anybody would be that nosy... Pictured below is a typical switchboard of the time.

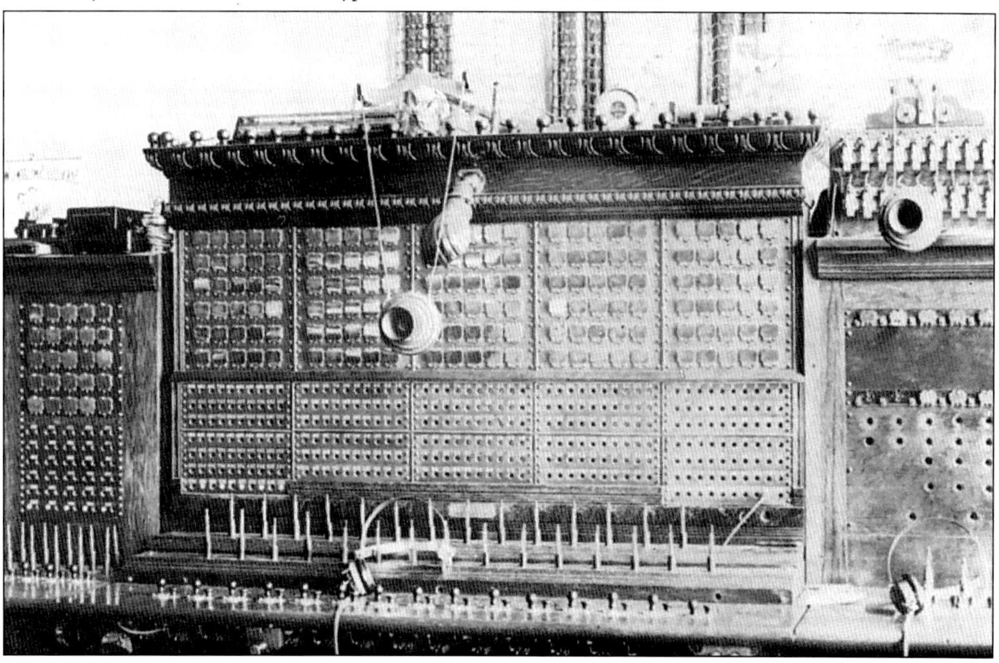

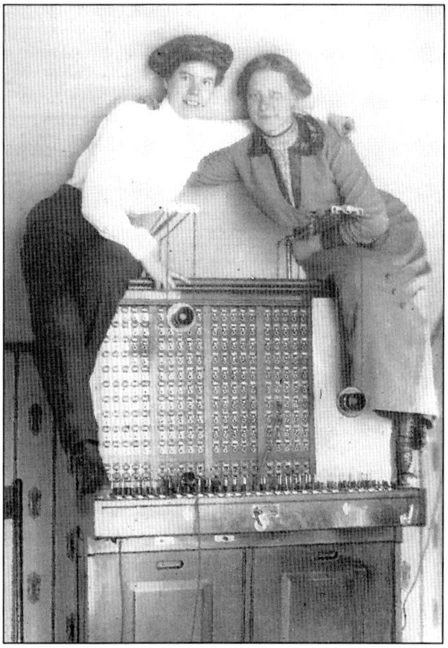

The women who controlled the switchboards also had fun!

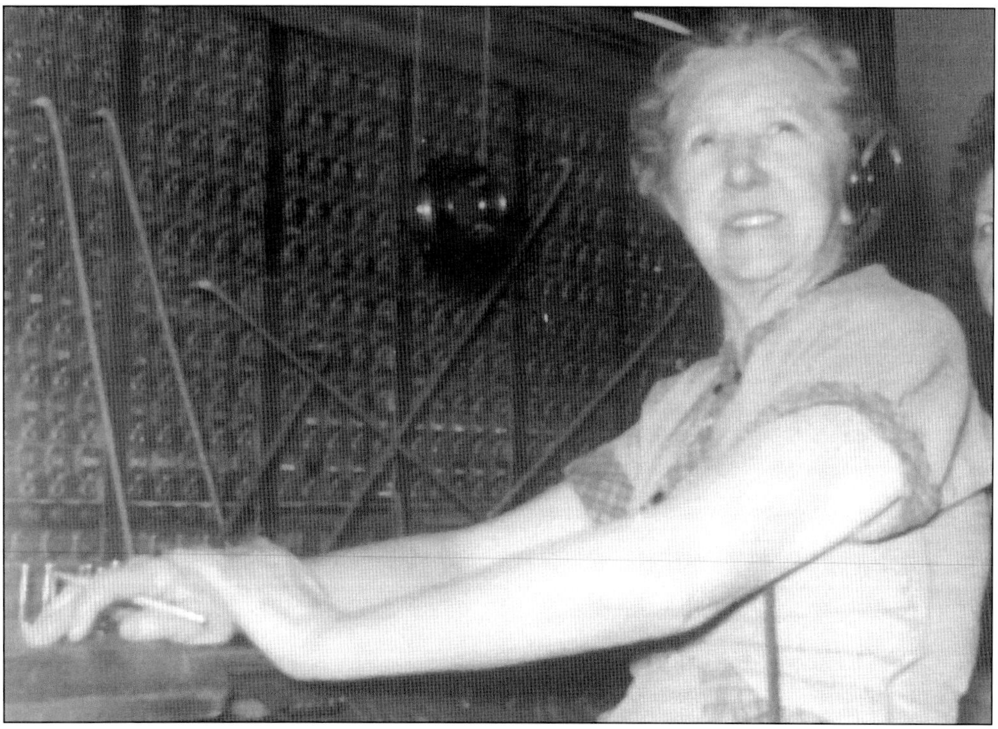

Clara Myren Robinson, who took many of the photographs in this book with a box camera, was the switchboard operator in Hillsboro for many years. Since she could hear the calls, she was privy to many secrets, which she did not spill. For example, North Dakota had a very heated governor's race, and both candidates were attacking and denigrating each other. For some strange political reason, they decided to hold a secret meeting in a law office in Hillsboro. The media and the public never knew about this meeting. But Clara Robinson did, and she never said a word!

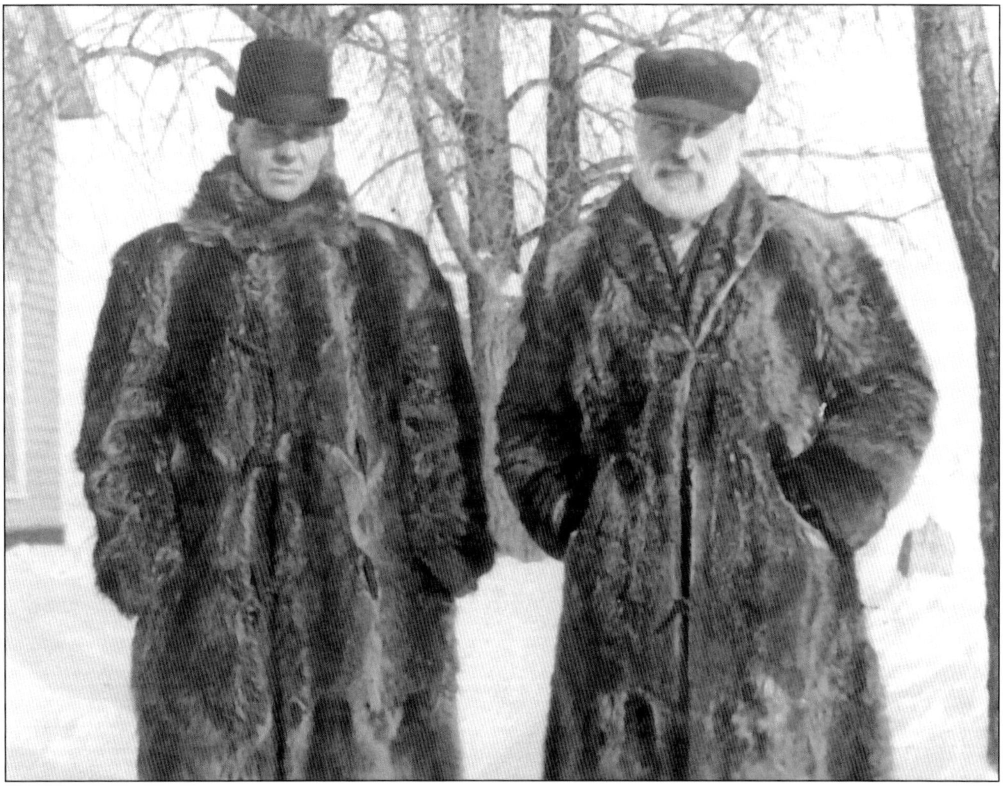

Fashions of the day in 1925 included big fur coats and muffs, worn to keep the hands warm. George Robinson and "Pop" Otto show off their fur coats.

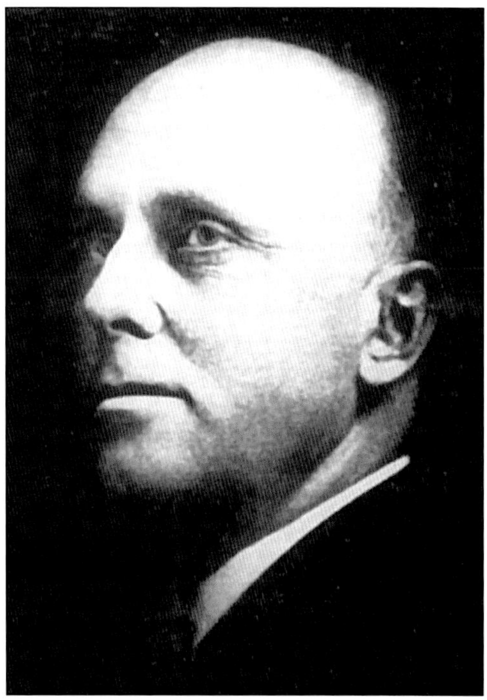

Alfred Arvold was head of speech and drama at North Dakota State University for 45 years. He founded the Little Country Theatre in 1914 and made great contributions to the people of North Dakota, bringing drama and culture to people all over the state.

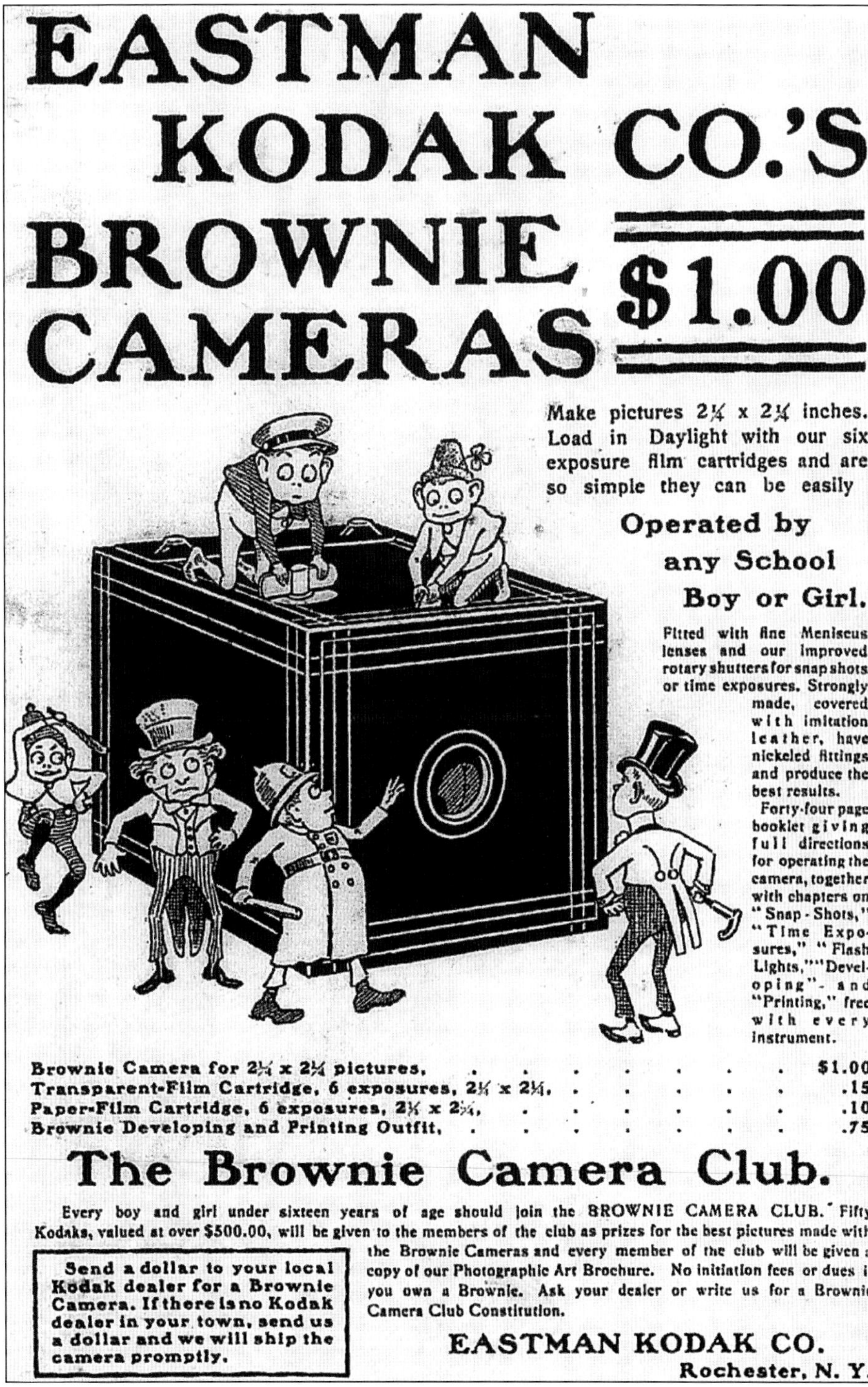

The box camera the author's mother Clara Aasen used to take many of these photos was a number 2A Brownie camera. This camera was sold by Eastman Kodak from 1907 to 1924, and cost $1. Eastman Kodak sold over 2,100,000 2A Brownies before 1921.

Nine

North Dakota Governors 1901–1944

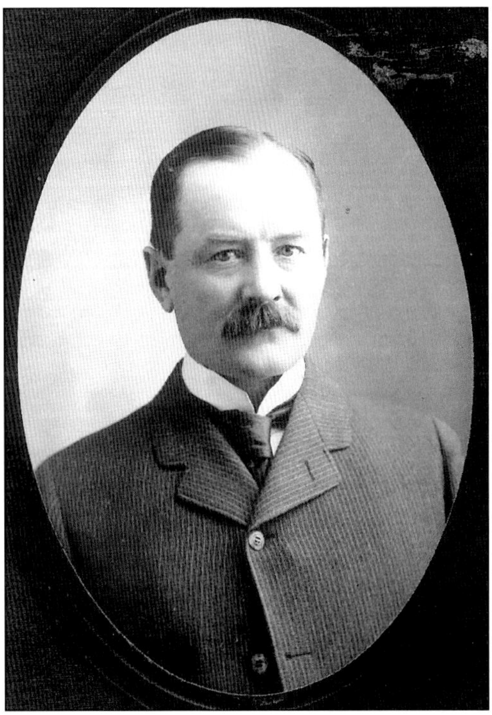

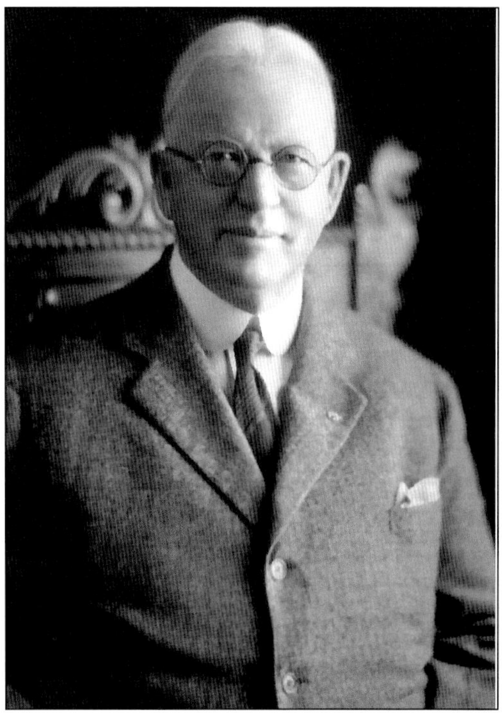

Frank White, pictured at left, was governor of North Dakota 1901–1904. He became the first governor to serve more than one term. Ellmore Y. Sarles, pictured at right, served from 1905–1906. He was a banker from Hillsboro.

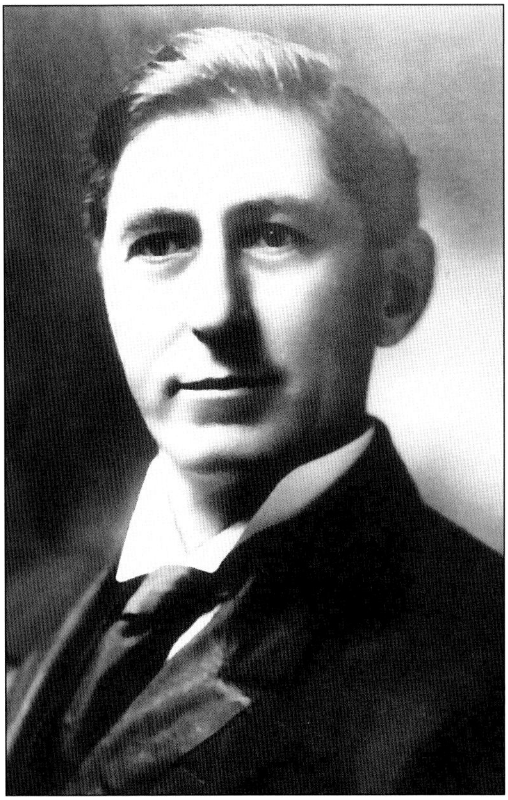

John D. Burke served from 1907–1912, becoming North Dakota's first three-term governor. He later became treasurer of the United States. Woodrow Wilson wanted him as his vice president, but the plan failed.

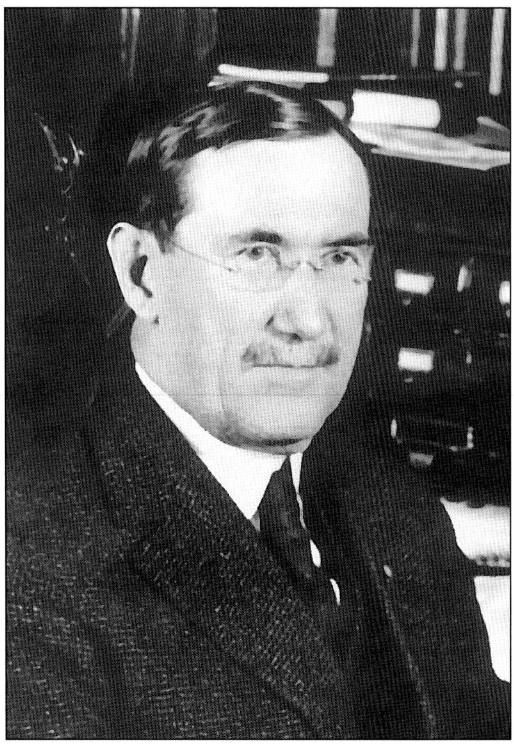

Louis B. Hanna served from 1913–1916. During his term, the legislature passed a law making bootlegging a crime punishable by imprisonment.

Lynn J. Frazier served from 1917–1921. He was recalled on October 28, 1921. However, in 1922, Frazier was elected to the U.S. Senate. Other North Dakota officials who were recalled during this period were William Lemke and John N. Hagan. All of these men belonged to the Nonpartisan League.

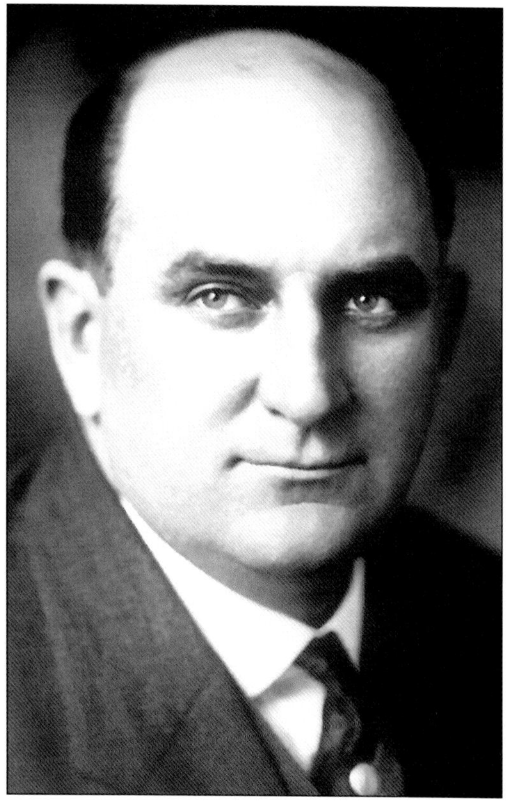

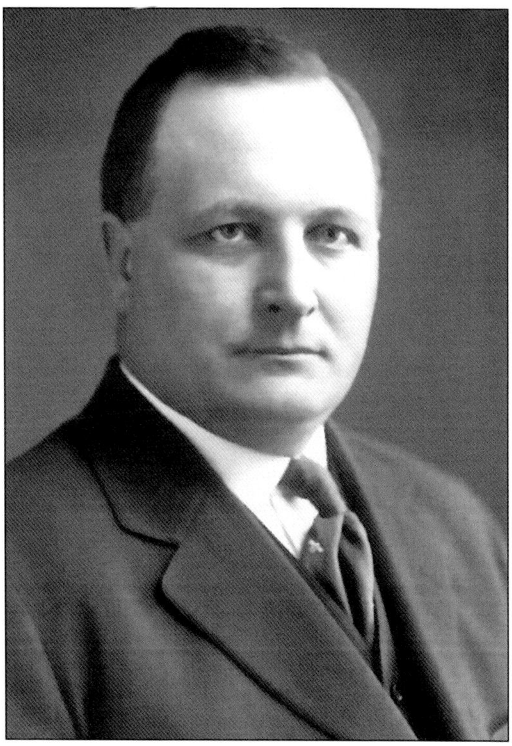

Ragnvold A. Nestos served from 1921–1924. During his term, the first State Mill and Elevator was opened at Grand Forks in 1922.

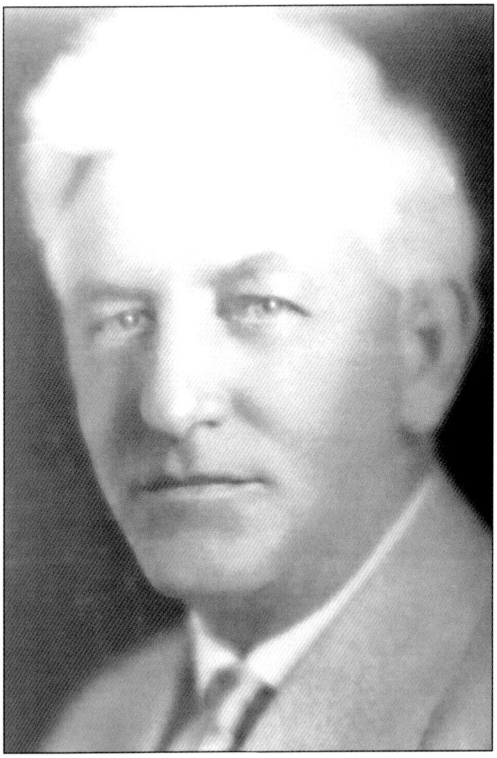

Arthur G. Sorlie served from 1925–1928. He died in office on August 28, 1928.

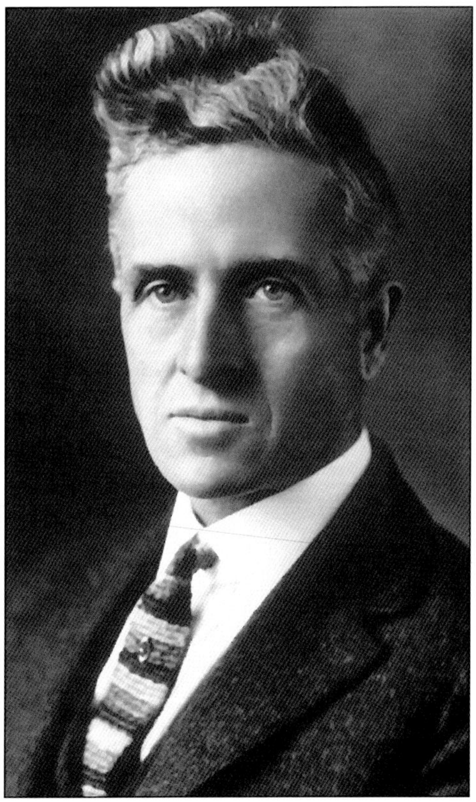

Walter J. Maddock completed Sorlie's term in 1928.

George F. Shafer served from 1929–1932, during the Depression and drought.

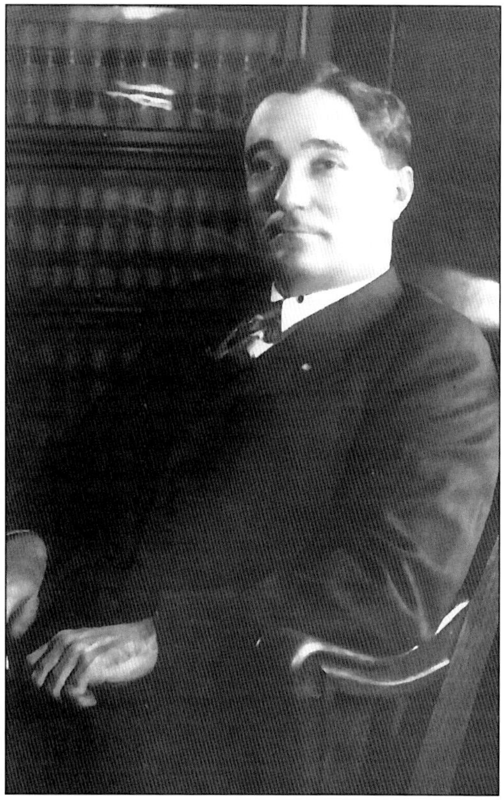

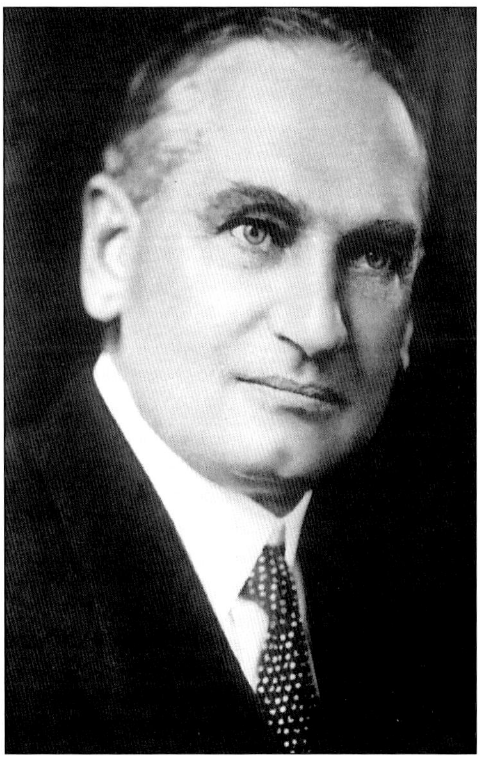

William Langer served from 1933–1934. He was removed from office July 17,1934, as a result of his conviction for campaign law violations. Langer was elected governor a second time, serving 1937–1938.

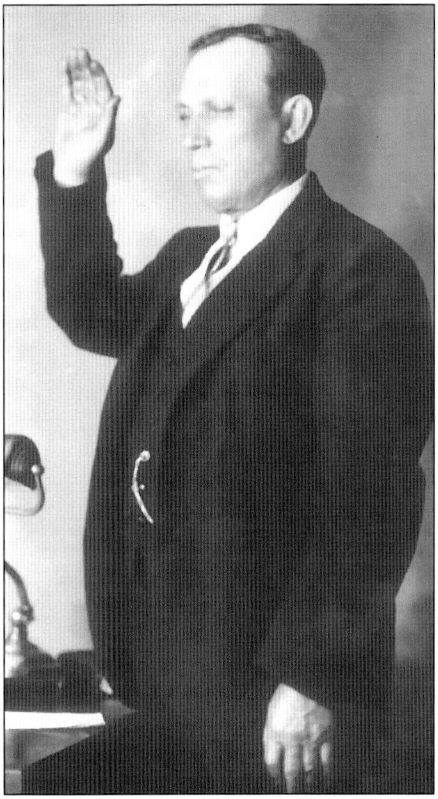

Lieutenant Governor Ole H. Olson completed Langer's term in 1934.

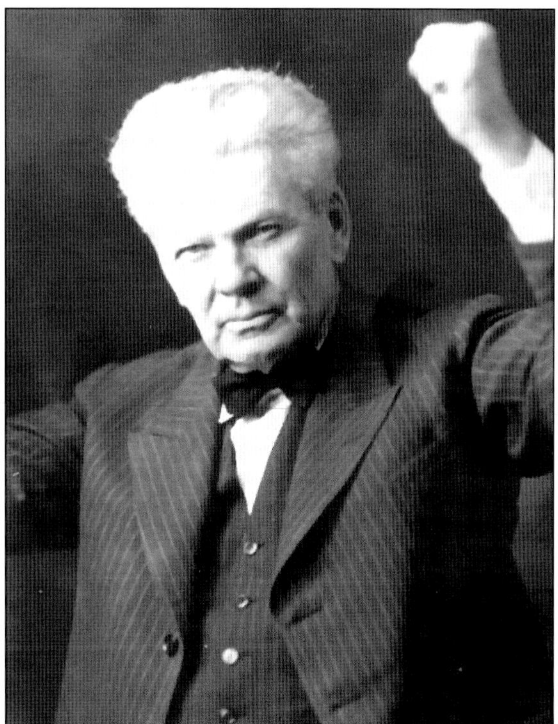

Thomas H. Moodie served as governor for only four days in 1935. William Langer discovered that Moodie had voted in Minnesota. Consequently, the State Supreme Court declared Moodie ineligible to serve as governor of North Dakota.

Walter Welford served 1935–1936. He succeeded Moodie and became the fourth governor to serve in seven months. During his term, the new capitol building was completed (1935).

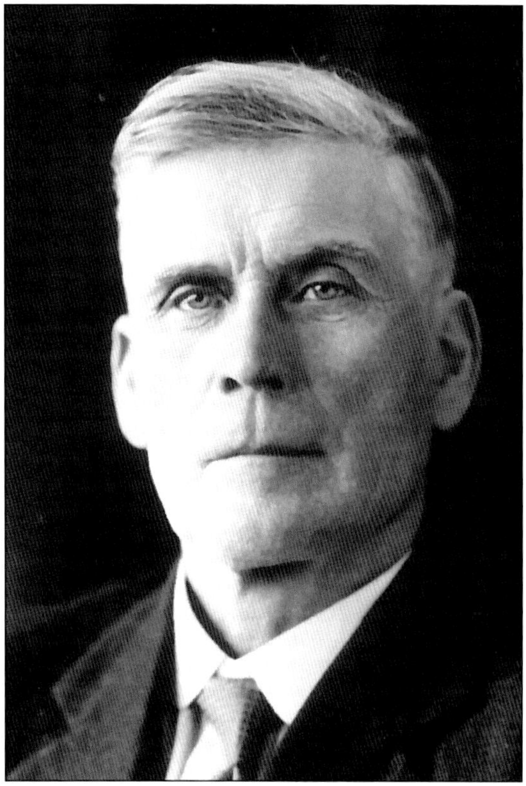

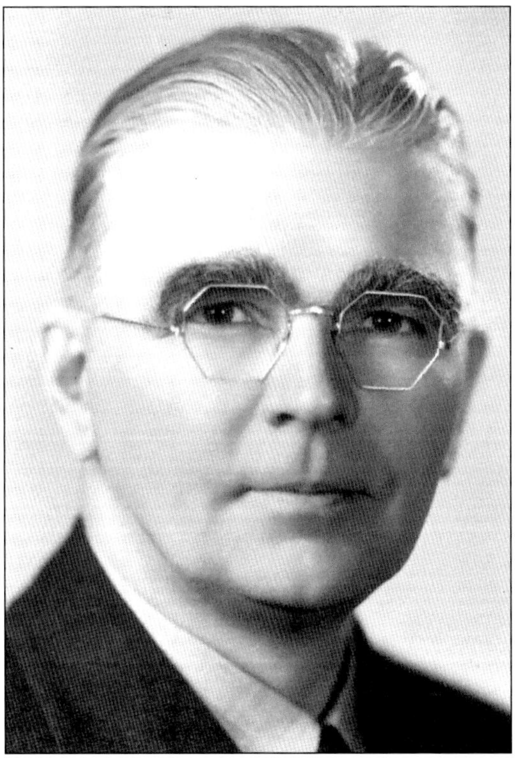

John Moses served from 1939–1944. During his term, the North Dakota 164th Infantry was ordered into federal service. It became the first national guard unit to fight in the Pacific during the battle for Guadalcanal in 1942. North Dakota led the nation in per capita war bond sales.

SUGGESTED READING

Anderson, Clarence and Kaldor, Jean T. Hillsboro, N.D. Centennial, 1981

Berg, Francie M. *North Dakota, Land of Changing Seasons*. Hettinger, ND: Flying Diamond Books, 1977

Bread Basket of the World: Fargo, Grand Forks and the Red River Valley. Dakota Graphic Society, Fargo, 1985

Conrad, Charles and Joyce. *50 Years North Dakota Farmers Union*. 1976

Danbom, David B. *Born in the Country: A History of Rural America*. The Johns Hopkins University Press, Baltimore and London, 1995

Federal Writer's Project. *North Dakota: A Guide to the Northern Prairie State*. Oxford University Press, 1950.

Jaeger, Alvin A. *North Dakota Blue Book*. Bismarck, 1995 and 1997–1999

Lysengen, Janet Daley and Ann M. Rathke. *The Centennial Anthology of North Dakota History*. Journal of the Northern Plains. State Historical Society of North Dakota, 1996

Meier, Ben. *North Dakota Centennial Blue Book*. 1889-1989

Robinson, Elwyn B., *History of North Dakota*. University of Nebraska Press, 1966

Institute for Regional Studies, North Dakota State University.

Shemorry, Bill. *More Lost Tales of Old Dakota*. Williston, N.D: William E. Shemorry, 1988

Sherman, William C. *Prairie Mosaic: An Ethnic Atlas of Rural North Dakota*. North Dakota Institute for Regional Studies, 1983

Traill County History Vol. I. Taylor Publishing Company, Dallas, Texas

Traill County History Vol. II. Taylor Publishing Company, Dallas, Texas